SLOW TRAVEL NEW MEXICO

SOUTHWEST ADVENTURE SERIES

Slow Travel New Mexico

Unforgettable Personal Experiences in the Land of Enchantment

JUDITH FEIN
PHOTOGRAPHS BY PAUL J. ROSS

University of New Mexico Press • Albuquerque

Printed in the United States of America

ISBN 978-0-8263-6584-2 (paper)
ISBN 978-0-8263-6585-9 (ePub)

Library of Congress Cataloging-in-Publication data is on file with the Library of Congress.

Founded in 1889, the University of New Mexico sits on the traditional homelands of the Pueblo of Sandia. The original peoples of New Mexico—Pueblo, Navajo, and Apache—since time immemorial have deep connections to the land and have made significant contributions to the broader community statewide. We honor the land itself and those who remain stewards of this land throughout the generations and also acknowledge our committed relationship to Indigenous peoples. We gratefully recognize our history.

Cover photograph by Paul J. Ross
Designed by Felicia Cedillos
Composed in Minion Pro

It takes a village to write this kind of book.
We invite you, our readers, to the village.

Contents

PART TWO. NORTH CENTRAL

PART THREE. NORTHEAST

PART FOUR. CENTRAL

PART FIVE. SOUTHWEST

Introduction and Author's Note

Dear Amigos,

I'd like to invite you on a slow travel adventure with me.

My husband Paul Ross and I are travel journalists, and he is also a photographer. But during the pandemic our wings were clipped. No more hunting for white truffles in Italy, swimming in a lake with stingless jelly fish in Palau or shopping in the *souks* of Tunisia. We wondered if we would ever again enter a Thracian tomb in Bulgaria, marvel at the Upper Paleolithic cave paintings in the south of France, or bathe in donkey milk like Queen Cleopatra in Egypt.

Over time, we began to venture away from our home in Santa Fe, New Mexico. First it was hiking through a slot canyon by day and desert star gazing at night. Then we progressed to multi-hour hikes around towering white rock formations, half-day visits to ancient sites still inhabited by ancestral spirits, and day outings with gourmet take-out picnics along the banks of the Rio Grande. Pretty soon we were overnighting and spending a week or more at off-season ski resorts, ghost towns redolent of the Wild West, and sacred pilgrimage sites where purported miracles had happened. Everywhere we went, we met people—cowboys, Hispanic weavers and lowriders, Native American medicine people, women baking traditional bread in outdoor *hornos*, storytellers, costumed historical reenactors, chefs, mountain bikers, opera singers, hip hop artists, pecan and chile farmers, and a broad swath of friendly and welcoming folks.

By the end of two years, we had fallen helplessly, hopelessly in love with New Mexico and discovered that our state offered marvels equaling many of those we had found around the world. And, perhaps most importantly, we codified a way of traveling that we had unknowingly been practicing for decades: Slow Travel. It was the secret to how doors opened, people materialized, surprising events unfolded, and each trip—no matter how short or long, close by or in remote settings—became deeper, richer, more personal and memorable. We realized that although we had the epiphany in New Mexico, it could be practiced anywhere in the world.

Slow Travel means that you allow yourself to stop running from site to site and you decelerate so that you can indulge your five senses in the world around you. When you pack your bags, you include imagination and curiosity. You see the people everywhere you go and know that each one carries a special story. You notice details that perhaps no one before you has ever paid attention to. You connect to what you are feeling and what types of learning and exchange enhance your life. You smell the air and can differentiate city from country, mountain from desert floor, forest from beach. You can hear the unspoken nuances when people speak, taste not only the food but the culture of the folks who planted, harvested and prepared it. You are not just going . . . but also growing.

It seems like an oxymoron, but when you slow down, your life becomes more exciting. No matter what you do or where you go, you begin to discover new aspects of yourself and what is possible in your life. Your attention span increases, you become more curious, your imagination is childlike and boundless, and you start to hear the Velcro of your heart ripping open as it becomes free to feel, explore, and embrace the world around you.

This book is an invitation to show up in a place and let it reveal itself to you, *on its own terms*, rather than planning everything out in advance and meeting it with the reports of other visitors.

Slow Travel New Mexico is not about off-the-beaten path. It's about off-the-beaten mental path—learning to look, see, open up, and explore differently. It's a guide to unforgettable experiences.

Once, when I was giving a workshop to international travel industry professionals, I asked them to write, in ten minutes, what their most vivid travel memories were. Almost all of them told tales like their vehicle breaking down and how locals showed up to help them, connecting with someone with whom they didn't even share a language, bonding with children, going to a folk healer, buying art directly from the artist, impulsively swimming while in their clothes on a hot day, discovering new and different foods, falling in love with a stranger, getting caught in a storm, seeming misadventures that morphed into unforgettable stories. Although they had been to the top tourist destinations in the world, their unexpected personal experiences made for their greatest memories and stories to tell. And often, their fondest memories included people they met and connected to along the road.

So, how do you become a slow traveler?

No Expectations

It may surprise you that I do almost no research and generally make no advance plans other than booking accommodations when I travel. I want to be like Marco Polo, Ibn Battuta (often called the Islamic Marco Polo), and Jeanne Baret (disguised as a man, she became the first female to circumnavigate the globe). They had no Internet. They went, they saw, they marveled. Everything was new to them. And when I am on the road, it's new to me too.

You may be more comfortable planning your itinerary in advance, or you may travel with a group. Whichever way you go, leave room for wandering, discovery, meeting people, exploring beyond the main sites, spontaneity. That is where the trip becomes yours alone, unlike what others may experience. The book will tell you how we do it and how you can do it your way.

It is also a great relief to give up expectations of yourself. You don't have to speak the local language. When you meet a Hispanic person who speaks only Spanish, or a Native American who converses in her mother tongue, either someone will show up who speaks English, or you play a travel version of the game charades, where you mime and use hand signs to communicate. You'll probably end up sharing a few laughs. And there's always the backup of a translation program on your cell phone.

You don't need to know in advance the history, topography, or foods of the place you are visiting. When you do Slow Travel, your mind and ears will be open to listening, learning, paying attention, and discovering all the time. It's liberating and fascinating to learn from people who live there and whose ancestors, perhaps, passed down stories, information about the land, and ways of preparing and cooking special foods. In this book you will get a grandmother's recipe for posole, hear the words of a Mescalero Apache medicine man at the end of a moving ceremony, and learn directly from a Crypto Jew about her ancestral connection to the Inquisition. You'll discover the rich, layered history of New Mexico from guides, locals, and amateur experts.

Embrace the Unexpected

Travel will almost never go exactly as planned. When you head for a specific destination, you may get lost, and when you make a few wrong turns, perhaps you will end up in a fascinating place that you didn't know about. Or you'll discover a family restaurant that serves the best enchiladas you have ever tasted.

Perhaps you will see a flyer or hear about a fiesta. Unless I have advance reservations somewhere else, I will usually check it out and either postpone or ditch my prior plans. This is how I learned about the three-day, sacred ceremonies at Tortugas Pueblo you will read about, and how I ended up visiting the place where animal tracks were made tens of millions of years before the dinosaurs.

When you see something unusual, don't just pass it by. Stop and find out what it is. That's how we discovered Whatville in Angel Fire.

There is a risk in telling you about fascinating, educational, mystical, and immersive adventures you can have. When you decide to do some or all of them, the people, places, or experiences may have changed from exactly the way I described them. People may have switched jobs, events are possibly canceled, sites are no longer open, natural disasters may have altered the landscape. For that reason, each story has a takeaway, something specific to incorporate into your travels, and if you can't do it with the people and in the places that I describe, this book will help you develop the skills and tools to search for and find an alternate person, place, or site on your own that is similar. And what you learn can be applied to anywhere you travel, from the town next to you to New Mexico to anywhere in the world.

If you are already familiar with some of the locations in the book, perhaps you weren't expecting what I discovered and recommend. I hope you will be open to experiencing the places in a new way and from a different point of view.

Be Curious

Most of the guides I have met in New Mexico report that people rarely ask them questions.

If I hadn't asked a guide about the women at Fort Union, I would never have learned about a freed African American named Cathay Williams who changed her name and enlisted as a man or about the requirements for a soldier's wife before she could come to live with him.

Unless I asked a Navajo artist how to create layers when making a painting, I would never have learned the liberating way he does abstract art.

A friend of mine always says, "If you don't ask, you don't get." Perhaps you will meet someone on the road, and you are dying to ask them questions. Why hold back? Ask politely, and you will likely find out something fascinating. If you are concerned that you may be tiptoeing across someone else's boundaries, request the person's permission to ask a question. I've never known anyone who refused.

Few people know the important second part of this well-known aphorism: "Curiosity killed the cat. But satisfaction brought it back."

It can be immensely satisfying to have a deeper exchange with someone. I find mundane discourse to be boring and superficial chitchat maddening. I have rarely been on a guided tour when I had no questions. Learning takes place when we are active and participatory, not passive and removed.

Curiosity about other people and places is a way to expand not only your travels, but also your life.

Be Open

When you say "no," a door closes. When you say "yes," it swings open. All of us have likes and dislikes—things we love to do, and those that seem to be of no interest. But what if the latter turn out not to be true? I was not particularly intrigued by going to a ghost town . . . until I saw what I believe was a ghost or an apparition. Opera? I urge you look at it differently, and you may be drawn into that multisensory, psychologically, theatrically rich world. Hiking in an arid riverbed? It may surprise you to get a radically different point of view of the river and the shore.

Slow Travel New Mexico is an invitation to try new things, adventures you have a negative idea about, destinations that don't appear on the surface to match your idea of romantic, luxurious, or worthy of a visit. Discovery is about finding things you didn't know about before.

In my travels, and in my life, I always try to say "yes," unless there is a solid reason not to.

Be Connected

Mike, a young transplant from the Midwest to Mora County, made an indelible impression when he said, "I never met someone who wasn't my friend." I think he meant that he approaches people he meets with a friendly, welcoming mind and heart. This is the perfect way to travel.

You will know, of course, if someone, someplace, or something seems potentially unsavory or dangerous. Absent that, life is a smorgasbord waiting to be enjoyed. And people are longing to be seen, heard, acknowledged, connected.

Mitákuye Oyás'iŋ (We Are All Related) is a prayer in the Lakota language. We are all connected, all related, in a web that science calls quantum entanglement. We are all one—two leggeds and four leggeds, those that fly or crawl on the ground, mountains and valleys, trees, plants, and all of life.

It's a beautiful sentiment I share wholeheartedly.

When you travel, most folks you meet will be happy to tell you about their lives, culture, foods, art, and customs with you if they think you are really interested.

And your world will expand because of it. If you are shy, start by asking them where they bought their embroidered boots or how they prepare a traditional dish. Inquire if they can help direct you to a restaurant they like, or a local market. You may discover that meeting you is an adventure for them too. They may love your accent or ask you about where you come from. You talk, exchange ideas, and a former stranger can easily become a friend.

How to Use This Book

The immersive experiences in the book are listed in six geographical locations: Northwest, North Central, Northeast, Central, Southwest, and Southeast. I specifically organized the book in this unexpected way because it's an unhappy truism that most people live in and travel to Santa Fe, Albuquerque, and Taos—all of which are in the North Central and Central regions. I would love people to discover other areas in New Mexico. The hotspots are great, and naturally I write about them, but most visitors and New Mexicans will be surprised and delighted by lesser known and unknown places, people, and experiences that are equally exciting and appealing.

I am also trying to defy other expectations. You may notice, for example, that there are several recommended forts. If you are like I am, you probably never visited one of them because they evoke Indigenous oppression. But they have gone through several iterations and have been repurposed. One has a desert botanical garden and offers hands-on experiences with adobe brick-making and replica potsherds. It pays tribute to the Jornada Mogollon Indigenous people who once lived there. Another was a cutting-edge tuberculosis sanitorium and then an internment camp for German sailors during World War II; astoundingly, their beloved ship captain was given almost full control of the camp.

I am trying to change perceptions and beliefs that some of you may have held for a long time. I trust they will evaporate during adventures that lead to revelations, eye-opening realizations, and surprises.

I hope you discover, above all, that Slow Travel is highly personal. No one else will have the same adventures as you, even if they go to the identical places. It's your life and you get to do it your way. You and I are different, and even when you meet the people and go to the places I write about, your experiences will be yours and yours alone. You will find what I missed and see things in your own way.

Sometimes in this book I invite you to come along into experiences where peoples' customs, traditions, beliefs, and ways of life are quite different from mine or yours and what we each know and are used to. When I write about them, I try to be as aware as possible about their sensitivities and norms. For this reason, I sent people what I wrote about my experiences with them and their culture and asked them to correct anything that was potentially inappropriate, inaccurate, or offensive. I also made sure that the experiences would be available to you, too.

Slow Travel New Mexico is not an exhaustive guide to sites and places. It is, however, curated. It's quite simply about the most memorable experiences we have had over the last two years. The adventures include culture, history, hikes, food, nature, spirituality, ceremonies, wildlife, humor, archeology, paleontology, art, ecology, photography, architecture, music, and beyond.

And for each geographic region, you'll get to hear from the folks who live there in their own words, and I'll tell you how and where we met them to give you some ideas about how and where you, too, can meet folks on your travels.

At the conclusion of each section are Paul's Photo Tips—which are more about your involvement with a place and its people than they are about mechanical techniques. They invite you to become a visual storyteller, where you are part of the story. The suggestions offered are meant to help focus you, the photographer, as much as your image capture device. They are applicable to dedicated cameras (digital and film) and to increasingly sophisticated, capable, and affordable phones.

For Whom Did I Write This Book?

Whether you live here or are planning to explore and learn about New Mexico or choose to travel with me in your armchair, I wrote the book for you.

In each place, I invite you into a story because I believe that people remember stories more than they retain facts.

I invite you into the complex reality of a land that belonged sequentially to the Native Americans, Spain, Mexico, and then, the United States. In our travels, we entered and became part of the story of the land, leaving our footprints with all those who walked before us. And you will add your own footprints to ours.

Welcome to a world of timelessness where everything is possible, and you can experience wonder and joy. This book is about slow travel on the road. . . . And in life.

It was hard to end this book, because almost every day there is something new that I want to include.

Wishing you great adventures,
Judith Fein

P.S. Please remember to check time, days, and other details for every place before you go. They can change and you'll be disappointed if you miss a longed-for experience. Also be sure to read recommendations about heat, cold, the need for water, hats and protective clothing, sturdy shoes, personal safety, locking your car, etc. You don't want anything to detract from your adventures.

I

Diné (Navajo) hogan, Navajo Nation Museum, Window Rock.

Introduction

From the minute we arrived in Gallup, surprises started unfolding. Because we were there in summer, we attended the free, outdoor, Native American dances that are offered three evenings a week at the Cultural Center as part of the Indigenous Dance Program. Each night, a different tribe is featured, and dancers in brightly colored regalia generously share part of their culture with visitors. As we watched an eagle dancer from Zuni flap and spread his feathered wings and soar on wind currents, an excited child who was seated behind me exclaimed, "He's flying, he's flying!"

Before the deer dance, the Native American announcer explained to the audience, "When a deer is killed, it's dressed in traditional Zuni clothes and brought back to Zuni where prayers are said over it to thank it." Only a heart of stone wouldn't be touched by that.

Gallup bills itself as the "Indian Capital of the World." It's within easy driving distance of the Navajo Nation and Zuni Pueblo and was the perfect place for us to be based as we fanned out and explored Indian Country.

We also had an opportunity to hang with wolves, paint with a Navajo (Diné) artist, discover WPA art, meet locals, eat at their favorite restaurants, attend special events, enjoy the murals, discover Zuni Pueblo, eat in a Zuni home, learn about Diné history, art, and culture, hike on top of a mesa, and realize how fortunate we are to have such rich, enduring cultures in New Mexico that offer interested visitors personal experiences they will always treasure. Reading about cultures can be enjoyable and informative. Interacting with and learning from people of different cultures, and getting their perspectives in their own words, is unforgettable.

We're likely to return for the annual Gallup Intertribal Ceremonial, which takes place every August at Red Rock Park and features parades, performances, singing, dancing, art, pageants, and a chance to meet and interact with Native Americans from different tribes.

WPA art at the McKinley Country Courthouse in Gallup.

A Private Tour of WPA Art

Takeaway: Art that is created by and about Indigenous people can be a springboard for learning and discussion.

"Why are you going to Gallup?" an artist friend in Santa Fe asked me.

"Because it's the Indian capital of the world."

"Do you know about the WPA art collection there?"

Before I had finished telling her that I didn't, she was exuberantly insisting that I had to see it. "Truthfully, we weren't expecting it to be part of the trip," I said.

"It's in the courthouse. It's got an Indigenous connection. Just go."

And so, we went. With no expectations.

In the lobby of the historic McKinley County Courthouse in Gallup, executive director of gallupARTS Rose Eason introduced herself us. In her thirties, with shoulder-length curly brown hair and big brown eyes, Eason was instantly likeable with her refreshingly frank, informed, and unvarnished way of talking about the artists. "Lloyd Moylan was a highly accomplished artist who did WPA murals all over New Mexico and collaborated with Mary Wheelright [she founded the Wheelright Museum of the American Indian in Santa Fe], who fired him after twelve years because he had an alcohol problem."

She went on tell us that Moylan did the most easel painting in Gallup's important and impressive New Deal art collection that includes paintings, sculpture, drawing, prints, decorative arts, furniture, tinwork lights, and murals. The WPA (Work Progress Administration) Federal Arts Project launched a golden age for about 10,000 unemployed artists and artisans during the Great Depression. It was a visionary program that makes many struggling artists today drool. Not only were that era's artists paid for their work, but the program provided them access to viewers. Franklin D. Roosevelt's government commissioned them to create art for municipal buildings and public spaces. The courthouse itself was built as part of the WPA program, so we knew we were walking in art history.

Lloyd Moylan was at the pinnacle of his career when he was hired to create the ten-foot-high mural which extends over the four walls surrounding the second story courtroom. The subject was Southwest history that happened at Gallup's doorstep, from prehistoric times to the twentieth century. It was a lot for a white artist from Minnesota to undertake, and he creatively incorporated some of the architectural features like crossbeams and a door into the design. The scope of the mural is from dinosaurs to humans breastfeeding their young to intertribal warfare, conquistadors, cowboys, and the coming of the railroad. "For the time," Eason said, "his depiction of the 1680 Pueblo Revolt (when the Indigenous Pueblo people drove the Spanish colonizers out of New Mexico) and the Long Walk of the Navajo to Bosque Redondo (p. 17) were progressive." Moylan painted the mural in classical style, where large figures assume almost heroic and mythic importance. Eason said that "Moylan was trying to show the resilience of Native culture. But there are also historical inaccuracies and cringe worthy stereotypes like scalping. I've had informal conversations with people who take offense to the mural (which is thoroughly justified) and think it should be destroyed. I believe we can have a larger discussion around how history has been told and by who, how Native peoples have been (mis)represented in visual culture, and how we can do better."

WPA art lined the hallways of the building, and Eason pointed out that generally the paintings of Taos were more traditional and realistic and others from Santa Fe were more abstract. Farther on, she stopped in front of two striking sand-painting-like wall paintings. I was surprised to see them in a public building because they are used in sacred Navajo ceremonies. Eason explained that they were "turned into artwork by an uncredited Navajo artist. He manipulated the sand painting images a bit so they no longer had sacred ceremonial meaning. Sand paintings call in the holy people, so artists using sand painting designs feared that if they used them in a secular context and put borders around the paintings, they would trap the holy beings. So, there was a transition from sacred to decorative in terms of symbology."

Seeing so much quality art made us wonder what Gallup art is like today. According to Eason who, by the way, is married to a Navajo man, at least 25 percent of McKinley County residents make at least part of their living through the arts. She said that a lot of the Native arts that are sold in Santa Fe are made by artists from the Gallup area.

One of Eason's favorite local events is Gallup ArtsCrawl, a family-friendly and very popular chance to meet, mingle, listen to live music and see the work of artists in galleries that line the street. It's also a great venue for talking about art with artists and art-lovers. It takes place the second Saturday of every month from March to December from 7–9 p.m. at Coal Avenue and Second Street.

"Even though I didn't know what to expect, I loved the WPA collection and your perspective on it," I told Eason.

She smiled modestly.

"And where do you think is the best place to buy Native American art?" I asked her before we left. Her reply concurred with my own feelings and brings us to the next story.

To arrange a free private tour with Rose Eason: executivedirector@galluparts.org; 505-488-2136.

Gallup Flea Market vendor Kirby Spencer displays his hand-painted leather ties.

Gallup Flea Market

Great Deals, Authentic Native American Meals, and Close Cultural Encounters

Takeaway: When you shop at a local flea market, the bonus is meeting and talking to the vendors.

No matter what plans visitors have for Saturday morning in Gallup, culturally curious ones scrap them and head for the bustling flea market. It looks a little rustic, but beyond the tires, farm equipment, and ponies for kids to ride, there are designer treasures, Native American artists, and shoppers never know who they will meet.

I stopped to talk to a Navajo couple who were selling their elegant inlaid silver jewelry that was displayed in tabletop glass cases. The husband wore a turquoise and silver bolo tie and said he had just finished it two months ago. His wife corrected him, saying it was at least four or five months earlier. "Two," he insisted. The woman glanced at our wedding rings, grinned, and said, "You are married. You'll understand this. Our daughter says that we make her crazy because we are always arguing about something or other. She says that when we get dementia, we'll drive her crazier because we'll have the same fight over and over."

We said goodbye and strolled over to the stand where Ted (who uses the name Kirby Spencer for his sewing art) sells the high-end, multicolored, custom leather ties and bags. The ties are beautifully designed, and Ted told Paul that if he purchased one, he might ditch his silk ones forever.

We visited a booth where, for $10 each, a Navajo woman sold white cornmeal for morning prayers and yellow cornmeal for evening prayers. When she saw that I was intrigued and indicated that it might be a saner way to start my day than donning fuzzy slippers and shuffling over to my computer, she told me about the prayers and the offerings—"You get up in the morning when the sun is rising and tell Creator what you want, or that you want good blessings. In the evening you thank Creator for all the blessings of the day and then ask to have good rest. I walk in the morning. I used to run, starting when I was seventeen years old, and I still use the cornmeal every day."

As we walked up and down the aisles of the flea market, Paul mused that it was a perfect place to buy unusual gifts. He thought that a graduate would appreciate the Levi's with dollar bills embedded in the design. "What about newlyweds?" I asked. "Don't you think they'd love a Pendleton blanket and some custom-made throw pillows in their new home?" We had now embarked on verbal repartee about who would like the arts and crafts on either side of us. "I think the hand-beaded cellphone cases are great for women with designer handbags," Paul said. "And check out those boho skirts," I added. "Half the women in Santa Fe would want one." We continued speculating as we walked past a dizzying array of jewelry to adorn almost every body part. And everything was sold directly by the artists.

The flea market is the perfect place for visitors to try Indian fry bread, mutton stew, or tacos. A group of women from Arizona sat in the shade of a tent to eat, and I smiled as I watched them excitedly showing each other some of their finds—art, housewares, earrings, pottery, belts, hats, shoes, designer clothes, cakes, and breads. The last time I was at the market, about five years ago, I bought a multicolored outdoor mobile cleverly made from beer cans. It still brings us pleasure as it whirls on our patio when the wind blows. This time I curbed my desire to shop at a time when I feel overwhelmed by possessions and want to get rid of everything we own and live in a Mongolian yurt. But how could I resist the gently used saddle blanket bags? I was proud of myself that I bought only one, instead of two.

Before we left, we recognized a Navajo woman named Raina Marianito who we had met when we went to Red Rock Park for a hike; she and her sisters were there for the same reason. She is an award-winning Navajo chef, and we talked for a while about food. As we were about to leave, she asked us, "Would you like to go to a one-stop shop for us Navajos?" We followed her to T&R Market on Highway 491, a short distance from Gallup, and were greeted by a pen of live sheep. When we inquired about why they were at the market she replied, "We like food to be fresh."

Inside the sprawling market, she introduced us to Navajo Pride brand loose beans that are grown on the reservation, and lamb backbone chops and "Navajo whole white corn that is ground and roasted to make Kiinaalda cake. It's too much work to grind it ourselves, but we still do that for ceremony."

We strolled through the market's pawnshop with high-caliber jewelry and blankets, and, elsewhere, saw farm implements for growing food and raising livestock.

We passed fresh and preserved food and endless varieties of processed, sugar-loaded candy and confection and remarked that there didn't seem to be any organic produce. "We bought organic tamales in town [Gallup] and liked them and have been eating them ever since," Marianito offered. "Our farmers had their own traditional way of protecting their crops from insects and bugs; they planted corn. I don't know exactly how that worked, but they grew the three sisters—corn, beans, and squash. They were called sisters because they helped each other grow and thrive."

She stopped in front of a shelf that was lined with small plastic bags filled with kernels of dried, steamed, brown and yellow sweet corn. As she picked one up, we noticed the price: $19.99 per pound. "It's very labor intensive to make, and that's why it's so expensive," she said. Paul and I exchanged looks as we remembered that we had once bought fresh corn from a Navajo farmer who was selling it out of the back of her truck. We excitedly told Marianito how the woman explained to us the process of steaming corn. She said it was cooked in a Navajo oven—a "bread house"—that she taught her kids to make from mud and stone. A hardwood fire was lit inside, and when it burned to ashes more wood was added and the process was repeated four times. The oven was sealed with mud, then covered with a blanket and tarp, and the corn steamed for twelve hours. Marianito smiled and nodded. And Paul—who, thanks to the marriage gods, does all the cooking—selected a $25 bag to bring home.

"Not a bad way to spend a Saturday morning," Paul commented as we left the market.

"It was perfect," I concurred with a grin, pleased that I had scored a woven bag at the flea market and Paul was the proud owner of a precious small bag of dried corn. And best of all, we'd met and connected to local people who are still as vivid as I write about them as when I met them. Especially the artists. So what if we visited them where they worked and inquired if we could have hands-on experiences with them?

For more information: Gallup Flea Market is at 120 State Road 608, Gallup; https://gallup9th.com; 505-399-2166.

Jerry Brown, Diné abstract painter.

An Abstract Native American Painter with a Concrete Way to Inspire You

Takeaway: When you make art with an artist, you take home more than a painting.

On Saturday afternoon, inspired by the explosion of creative talent we had seen at the Gallup Flea Market and the T&R Market pawnshop, Paul and I decided that it would be fascinating to make art with a Native American artist. I called Rose Eason and asked who she would recommend. Without hesitation she said, "Jerry Brown. He's a painter." She gave me his number, and I asked no further questions. Excited, I called Jerry. He was a bit laconic, but he gave me specific driving instructions to come to his house.

Two days later, we were on our way.

Jerry lives on the Navajo Nation, a magnificent half an hour drive from Gallup, past red rocks and tent rocks, and then for twelve miles on a blacktop road that extends beyond sparse houses and traditional one-room Navajo houses and ceremonial spaces called hogans. When we arrived, Jerry was standing outside on his land, waiting for us. He has long black hair, a white goatee, and open, penetrating eyes that are framed by blue glasses. He lives in a white hogan next to his studio, where he is surrounded by seventeen feral horses, thirty cats, abandoned dogs he has adopted, a few sheep, and Deputy, a dog with arthritis. "Deputy is a great dog that adopted us," Brown explained. "He found us in Gallup and eventually moved to the Rez with us."

At first, I thought he was quiet, and perhaps a bit shy, but as soon as I asked him about his animals, he became lively and animated as he spoke. "A horse can choose a person, and I guess they chose me or they chose this house, so I feed them. They give birth. They trust me. My grandfather said pay attention to the animals, and my grandma told me to listen to them. I talk to them like I'm talking to you. They teach me how to be in life. In 2019 one of them almost kicked me. I know what their limits are. If you listen to them, they will teach you about yourself. Every two weeks it costs me $250 to feed them." To me, he seemed like a Diné Saint Francis, and he's as authentic as the hogan where he set up blank stretched canvas on easels for me and Paul to paint. Visiting him provided a much-appreciated opportunity to learn more about his culture and his life.

Brown is a Navajo (Diné in their language) artist who has always known what his calling is: abstract art. It's not easy to be a Native American who, in his words, "resists iconic, stereotypical Native American subject matter." But Brown is a man who knows who he is and what sings to his soul as a human and an artist. He says that his is not the easiest path, but it's the most satisfying and nourishing for him.

As we sat together and sipped the water that's obligatory in our arid climate, Brown told us how he got started as an artist and what his childhood was like. "My dad's mother Naali gave me a Big Chief tablet and a coloring book. It looked like crap, and I just colored the whole thing black or red. I was already abstract," he said, laughing. "I went to Crownpoint Boarding School where I had to mop floors and clean toilets and clean urinals with a toothbrush. They gave us buzz cuts. We were clueless. The kids were all Indians, the teachers were mixed and mostly white. The dorm aids were Navajo. It was a kind of military discipline. I was baptized across the board—every kind of Christian service on Sunday because they all gave out cookies and punch afterwards."

A few white clouds floated across an otherwise blue sky as he paused before resuming telling us about his upbringing. "In 7th and 8th grades I got smarter, and I got KP (kitchen duty). They sent me back to the dorm with ice cream, apples, bananas, sweets from the cafeteria, chocolate milk, and Graham crackers. A grandma and grandpa came and taught us to sew, do woodworking, make pillows and stuffed animals, and fix our pants. We had sponsors and with those grants we got up to $250, and then they took us to Grants and let us shop for our own clothes."

Paul and I were fascinated by the details of his life and the path he followed to become a painter. "My mom didn't go to an Indian school," he continued. "She was held back. She did weaving, spoke Navajo, and learned traditional ways. She 'took her journey' in 2019. My great grandfather was a Tahi Bitsui—a medicine man. I went to the Institute of American Indian Arts with great teachers who encouraged me."

We were anxious to begin our painting experience with Brown, but we wouldn't have missed a moment of what he shared with us. "The land here is a ninety-nine-year-lease from the tribe, and it gets passed on in a family, and the lease gets extended. The octagonal hogan you see is female. The male one is all logs. I learned our ways—like we offer corn pollen to the first plant we take and say 'thank you.' Then we take from the second plant."

Brown explained to us that he paints abstractly with layers, and hummingbirds are often featured because of a visionary dream he had. Sometimes it can be difficult to sell paintings at art shows, but Brown shares his point of view about why every show is worthwhile, "I paint while I'm sitting in my booth. So, if people don't buy, I still gain because I have a new painting."

And with that, he was ready for us to paint on our canvases. He provided us with a wide selection of acrylic paints, colored papers, and random materials and told us to just follow our creative whims and paint layers. Paul immediately began to paint an esthetically pleasing nature scene with mountains that reached up to a sky made of thick horizontal bands of orange, yellow, and blue. I, on the other hand, stood motionless. "I understand the word 'layer,'" I told him, "but I'm a novice, and I don't understand what that means in terms of painting on the canvas."

Brown hesitated for a moment, and I could tell that he was uncomfortable with my asking for more direction. He walked over to where I was standing and didn't quite know what to do.

Neither did I. "Jerry, I'd like you to teach me how to paint layers," I said. He tentatively gave me a few suggestions, asked me what I wanted, talked to me about color, and suggested I add another layer of paint over the amoeba-like shape I was painting. "Are you sure?" I asked. "Why would I paint something and then obliterate it?"

Brown smiled approvingly as he watched me change the nature of my painting with every layer; at first, they seemed to hide what was underneath and then magically the underpainting was revealed. I became really inspired and asked him if I could add a small, open tube of dripping paint? He helped me attach it to the canvas with a special layering material. As I worked under his tutelage, he became more animated. By the end of our visit, he had become my creative partner. He also confessed that he was a laissez faire kind of guy and hadn't taught in such a direct way before. He paused for a moment and said he quite enjoyed it and would like to do more of it. I said I was happy I had been his guinea pig, and he was a natural teacher.

When we left, Paul and I both had painted canvases to take home. And equally satisfying, we had vivid memories of Brown, the hogan, the animals, and the great expanse of the Navajo Nation. I watched an artist transform into a teacher, and I think that because I was open about not understanding how to paint layers, he became open to giving me instruction. He taught me something I had never considered before and because I was vulnerable and asked an honest question, he opened his heart and gifted me with a highly personal and authentic experience.

And of course, I wanted to know more about the Navajo, their history and their culture.

To paint with Jerry Brown: jerrybrownart@gmail.com; 505-862-1663.

A sculpture of Spiderwoman weaving the world into existence, Navajo Nation Museum.

A Must-See Navajo Museum and Zoo

Takeaway: Seize every opportunity to broaden your perspective by learning how other cultures see the world we share.

Does the date June 1, 1868, ring a bell? If people are Diné (Navajo), it's a central date in their cultural identity. From 1863 to 1868, in a horribly misguided policy, the US government marched more than 11,000 Diné people from their traditional homeland to a remote outpost in Bosque Redondo. Many perished on what is called the Long Walk and during their subsequent internment. But in 1868, the Navajo became the only nation to use a treaty to end their forced removal and return them to their ancestral home. The Navajo Nation Museum about thirty-five minutes from Gallup in Window Rock, Arizona (it's not technically in New Mexico but is essential to understanding the Navajo people and culture in our state), tells the story of this proud nation and celebrates their survival.

It begins with their origination story, which is magnificently and accessibly told in a series of contemporary sculptures in clay and wood. We met First Man and First Woman, saw their disgruntled and troubled relationship, and learned, from signage, how they separated and then came back together. We encountered Spider Woman, who taught the spirit people how to weave, and we realized that a sculpture is worth a thousand words. We saw how the Twins slayed a monster and saved the Navajo people.

When it comes to the Treaty of 1868, visitors are invited to go behind the scenes and learn how Diné women were left out and how the men served as runners between the male negotiators and the women so they were included in the process. When we looked at the painting that depicts the Long Walk we felt viscerally the enormous courage and intelligence it took to turn the situation into a sustainable future for the people.

A separate room is devoted to the display of treaty itself, which the Navajo men signed with Xs. And near it is a room with a large map where visitors place pins to indicate where their ancestors lived before and after the Long Walk and the Bosque Redondo years. They can also post the names of those ancestors so they are not forgotten.

The museum includes galleries of high-quality contemporary paintings and crafts—squash blossom necklaces, dolls, sculpture, ceramics—as well as a photo gallery that includes portraits of veterans of Iwo Jima and Guam, code talkers, and other Navajo warriors who are honored by their people. The photographer, Kenji Kawano, helped gain national and international recognition for the code talkers who used their language to transmit secret Allied messages in the Pacific theater in World War II.

The theme of the museum is "We are still here," and it echoes through each of the exhibits and galleries.

It is a short distance to the Navajo Nation Zoological and Botanical Park in Window Rock. It has the distinction of being the only zoo in the country with a Native American perspective. Like the museum, it's in the lap of huge, majestic, sculptural, red and beige sandstone rock formations that stand like guardians of the culture.

I am not a big fan of zoos, but this one is exceptional. All the animals housed there are honored for their place in mythology, history, and daily life. Each has symbolic and spiritual significance for the Navajo. We saw, admired, and learned from excellent signage about red-tailed hawks, turkey vultures that live with sandhill cranes, grey and red foxes, great horned owls that are fed mice, as well as porcupines, black bear, bighorn sheep, and golden eagles.

The elk, for example, are greatly respected. In Navajo tradition, a ceremony was held before going out to hunt them, and prayers were said before eating their meat. Their hides could only be used after traditional hunters had tanned them. The owl is believed to be a messenger who warns others of dangers or neglect. Porcupines are thought to have mystical healing powers. The racoon plays a significant part in two ceremonies and developed one of them—the mountaintop ceremony. Frogs are considered to symbolize water and fertility, and when people see them, they can gently pour water on them and politely ask for rain.

It is always fascinating to learn about cultures on their land, in their own words, and see how they describe themselves, their worlds, and their beliefs. It can broaden and expand our own worlds and awareness. Our experiences on the Navajo Nation made us thirsty to visit and interact with people from another nearby tribe: the Zuni.

For more information: Navajo Nation Museum is at Hwy. 264 & Postal Loop Rd., Window Rock, Arizona. navajonationmuseum.org. 928-871-7941.

Navajo Nation Zoological and Botanical Park: Hwy. 264, Bldg. 34, Window Rock, Arizona. www.navajozoo.org. 928-871-6574.

Kenny Bowekaty, guide to Zuni land and history.

A Cultural Adventure with a Zuni Guide

Takeaway: Diversity is not a concept. It is about the joy of learning and exchanging ideas with people from different cultural backgrounds.

I think that most of us live in a cultural bubble. We naturally gravitate to people, places, and perspectives that are familiar. But one of the greatest joys of travel is that it's an opportunity to burst the bubble and embrace the great diversity of people, beliefs, cultures, landscapes, and experiences that are different from ours. It is one thing to read about them and another to know the excitement of expanding and learning and being surprised by what we discover.

When Paul and I teach travel journalism and photography, the first lesson always includes: Go to the source. Don't listen to what others say about any group. Go directly to the group itself and find out for yourself. It will always be different from what others say about them.

Take Zuni Pueblo for example. We drove forty minutes to get there, with no advance research or planning and no expectations, since we had no idea what we would find. We drove down the main street and stopped at The Zuni Visitor & Arts Center. We asked the woman at the front desk if there were Zuni guides who could tell us about and take us to sites of cultural and historical significance. "You are describing Kenny Bowekaty, our lead tour guide," she said. "No one is ever disappointed in Kenny. Let me try to call him, and in the meantime, I think you will enjoy our little museum."

She was right on both counts. The mini museum is a wonderful, accessible invitation to learn more about the deep, ancient culture and traditions, enhanced by videos, artifacts, pottery, jewelry, weavings, and the world-famous Zuni fetishes. "The only thing missing is a connection to a Zuni fetish carver," I said to her. "We painted with a Navajo artist, and I'd give you my special writer's pen if you could find a carver for us to learn from."

"I wouldn't take your prized pen from you," she said, laughing, "but let's see what I can do. Kenny Bowekaty is on his way over here and come back after your time with him."

The moment she spoke his name, Bowekaty appeared wearing jeans, a gray T-shirt, a baseball cap, and sunglasses. A bundle of energy, intelligence, and confidence, he's a trained archeologist as well as a guide. His style is unique: he relates Indigenous origination stories—that may not be linear—and peppers them with archeological information about geological periods and stratigraphic systems.

"Zuni is the largest pueblo," he began, as we stood in front of a map in the museum. "Its origins are in the Grand Canyon; Hardscrabble Wash was the place of evolution, created by North Star and Morning Star. They were sent into Mother Earth through the Grand Canyon." He told us about Father Sun, and how Venus and Earth were his daughters. He described how children were made of mud and clay, and they had webbed hands and feet and tails, with a heart made from mud and grass. They were prophesized to bring a beating heart to a special place—this was during the late Jurassic Period. "That was almost 150 million years ago," Paul whispered to me. If I haven't explained this before, Paul's is a like a walking Wikipedia. Bowekaty went on to tell us what happened to the beating heart, the lizard-like children, and how Zuni and other tribes were formed, and where their migrations took place. Then, after making sure we were wearing good walking shoes, he beckoned us to go outside with him to his car.

We drove to his own ancestral turf, a vast, rocky, shrub-studded desert landscape with trees in the distance, and it seemed as though he knew each stone and every inch of the arid soil. "Welcome to my home," he said. We walked up a hill as he explained that it was on a trade route that was said to go all the way to the Pacific. The sixteenth-century Spanish conquistador and explorer Francisco Vázquez de Coronado took this route looking for gold. And then, before our eyes, Bowekaty gestured, pointed, and related in such mesmerizing detail that we actually felt we were present at the scene when Coronado first arrived. The Zuni people threw rocks or whatever else they had down on him. There was fierce fighting. Then a conch horn was blown, and the fighting ended. The Zuni were intimidated by the thunder of musket fire and the force of the musket balls, and they all fled. The Spanish soldiers were in bad shape—their skin burned by their armor in the hot sun, exhausted, famished. The Spanish stayed there for four months, and then the Zuni from all over the region came back; maybe four to five thousand strong. They ousted Coronado, who agreed to leave, and there was a truce.

Then they began to trade; the Zuni would swap food for a metal pot that wouldn't break. "The events that happened here opened up North America to exploration by the Spanish," Bowekaty explained. "For 500 years, my ancestors traded sheep with the Spanish, and I grew up on a sheep farm as a shepherd who worked the cornfields. There was no electric light, no running water. We were hunters and farmers. We lived off the land. We call ourselves '*ii*,' or children of the earth."

Bowekaty was as open about his beliefs as he was about his family history. "I don't believe in God or Jesus; I believe in my religion, my gods," he said. "If you are born a Zuni, you are weaned into this religion. In the womb you are taken to ceremonies with drums and stomping of feet. If you are male, by the age of twelve you are initiated and appointed into one of six kiva societies. It never ends."

He told us about the language the Zuni speak, and how it is an isolate, different from all other languages. Some Zuni traveled to different places across the southwest and they learned other languages; some of them came back to Zuni and became interpreters and middlemen for trading. Their payment was in whatever was being traded—parrot feathers, basketry, turquoise, bells, textiles, pottery, obsidian, salt, tools, and defensive weapons. "It was like a Sam's Club here," he said with a chuckle.

He told us about Zuni traditional practices for igniting grasses and weeds to prevent wildfires and how the tribe is both matriarchal and patriarchal. He explained that the A:shiwi are patient people, and that they are not afraid of the future. We listened intently to every word of the stories and myths he told and the history and archeology of his people.

When we left Bowekaty, we returned to the Visitor Center where the woman at the desk said it was our lucky day. A Zuni fetish carver named Jimmy Yawakia was willing to teach us. He would meet us at the center the following day. I asked if I could hug her, and she acquiesced.

For more information: Zuni Visitor & Arts Center is at 1231–1245, NM-53, Zuni; www.zunitourism.com; 505-782-7238.

If Kenny Bowekaty isn't available at the Visitors Center, you will learn from any of the local guides.

You may also want to visit A:shiwi A:wan Museum and Heritage Center at the Pueblo. It's located across from Halona Plaza Market and restaurant.

Jimmy Yawakia, Zuni fetish carver, with a rough outline of a piece.

Make Your Own Animal Fetish with a Zuni Carver

Takeaway: Search for opportunities to discover and express your inner artist. No experience needed.

Several decades ago, I wanted to visit an ancient indigenous site in Utah that sounded intriguing. It was out of the way, but my excitement increased as I neared the ruins. When they were within view in the distance something stopped me in my tracks: an old, swinging, bridge made of wooden slats that crossed a river; I had to walk across it to get to the site. I'm acrophobic. I shudder when I see the point of view of a film actor looking down from a tall building onto the street below. I simply could not cross that bridge. I stood there for half an hour wondering if I should turn back and forget about the ruin. I felt like such a coward. Finally, I tentatively stuck one foot out and began the dread crossing. Step by step, with my heart pounding, I did it. When I arrived at the other side, I felt something hard under my foot. I picked it up, and it was a small, black stone bear carving, worn smooth from use. It fit easily into the palm of my hand, and I knew that it had been in someone else's palm many years before. That was my first encounter with a stone animal fetish. And I secretly felt as though it were a reward for facing down my fear.

At Zuni Pueblo, I met a member of the Zuni tribe in a store that sold fetishes. He explained to me that "the Zuni know that fetishes go far back to ancient Zuni history. They can be described in so many ways and used for multiple purposes and reasons. Most were always made of different types of natural stone. They were used ceremonially or individually for personal use; for prayer, protection, and blessings."

The day after our experience with Kenny Bowekaty, we were fortunate to meet one of the remaining Zuni fetish carvers—an award-winning contemporary artist named Jimmy Yawakia—outside of his home and studio on the pueblo. We told him that neither of us had ever carved in stone before, but we're always looking for new artistic modalities to try.

The tall, lean, bespectacled artist with salt-and-pepper hair, a neatly trimmed mustache and small beard, and wearing a khaki T-shirt and light blue jeans, both of which were liberally dusted with powdered stone from his carving, invited us to sit with him in a small indoor reception area next to his studio. He told us how he had been an EMT for twenty-three years and retired when he was haunted by terrible memories of accidents and illnesses. His life began to unravel, and he spiraled downward. And then something turned it all around: he began carving in stone and, in his words, "It calmed me down, and I realized I had an art I could explore into."

"Fetishes were used traditionally for protection during the hunt, and that's why they're called hunting bears," Yawakia explained. "Pueblo Indians come here to get a fetish before the hunt. The hunting bear has an arrow for protection and a heart line for healing so the hunter will not catch diseases from animals and will not lose his sense of direction." He told us there are six traditional animals that were depicted, and they represented the six cardinal directions: Mountain Lion (north), Bear (west), Badger (south), Wolf (east), Mole (ground); Eagle (sky). In addition to these animals, Yawakia's contemporary pieces, which draw collectors from England, South America, Japan, and the United States, are detailed and multidimensional. "Our ancestors never advertised Zuni art, but now, through technology, the reach has expanded. People find me on Facebook or my website. I get to travel, do art shows, and meet collectors of all ages."

What made our visit memorable, is that Yawakia agreed to teach us to carve animal fetishes of our own. Paul decided on a fish, and I opted for a lizard. The sculptor led us into his small studio, where he sat in one chair and beckoned us to occupy the other two. In front of us were electric grinding machines, hand tools, and a selection of shells and stones. We watched as he thoughtfully and carefully selected pieces of abalone shell to use for the material: in one he envisioned a fish and in the other a lizard. "I got the legs, and I asked the lizard to come out and play," Yawakia said. Of course, we saw nothing, but we would soon enough.

Yawakia began grinding Paul's piece of abalone and said, "It's a rainbow trout." He paused and said to us, "Now it's your turn." The stone grinders operated by pedals seemed a bit daunting, and I told Yawakia I wasn't quite ready to sacrifice any of my ten digits. He laughed as I winced, grimaced, and finally threw finger caution to the wind as I held my shell to the grinder and stepped on the pedal. Yawakia was vigilant and attentive, and we soon were so absorbed in the process of turning mother-of-pearl into little animals that we forgot everything else.

Paul was gaining confidence and working well with a little Dremel drill, when he

Jimmy Yawakia with a completed piece.

had an oh-no moment: part of the little marine animal's tail chipped off. "Nothing is perfect in life," Yawakia offered. Ever the optimist, Paul cheerfully decided it was a prehistoric armored fish rather than a modern one, and he actually knew the name for it—dunkleosteus. He was guided by Yawakia as he used a polishing wheel to bring out the fish's color. My lizard took shape with Yawakia's skillful assistance, and the iridescent little reptile was clearly defined with a tail resting on top of its body and tiny turquoise eye. "Now you have carver's pants," the sculptor exulted.

People I've met have had experiences with shamanic journeys, meditations, or insights where they discovered their power animals. Others have a special affinity with an animal or species. Many are cat or dog owners or lovers. I know kids and adults who have burros, turtles, fish, hamsters, snakes, or birds. All of them would know what to answer when Yawakia asks them "Which animal would you like to make?"

The sculptor said that telling his personal history is part of what he likes to share with visitors. "I'm here to share my story and my artistic talents—that's my 'mela'—corn. It's my name in translation. My three children's names translate as sweet corn, small corn, and seed of corn."

I told Yawakia that my inner artist thanked him and as soon as we left him, our inner stomachs let us know that they were hungry.

To learn more and arrange for a fetish carving lesson: http://jimmyyawakiacarvings.com.

Dinner with Shelley Morningsong and Fabian Fontenelle in their home at Zuni Pueblo.

Fabulous Food at Zuni Pueblo

Takeaway: Food is an appetizer to meeting local people.

After we left Yawakia with our shell fetishes in two little white boxes, we stopped briefly at a few trading posts to admire Zuni arts and crafts, and then headed for Major Market and its gourmet Eat & Go takeout section. We had been feasted before by excellent Native American cooks in their houses and could still recall the generosity and the aromas and satisfying taste of chile and mutton stew, posole, and fresh bread baked in outdoor *hornos*. But we'd never had memorable takeout food that we bought at their local stores. For this reason, we were surprised—shocked, actually—that the takeout food at Major Market really was gourmet. It was completely unexpected.

The menu included a grilled portobello and roasted pepper sandwich with sun-dried tomato tapenade and spinach-basil pesto. But we didn't decide too quickly because there was also *ragu alla Bolognese* and *pasta primavera* with jumbo tiger shrimp. And it was hard to pass up a Reuben sandwich with shaved pastrami, Swiss, and Thousand Island dressing served on marble rye or pumpernickel, so we opted for that. We hesitated for a moment before ordering it because a roasted butternut squash and wild rice salad sang to us as well. The custom drink menu was also enticing, but we finally selected the iced chai with apple juice and four pumps of raspberry puree.

A woman from Taos who stood behind us on the short line, exclaimed: "I've never ever seen anything like this on Native American land. And it's all Native owned. It's so exciting!"

The culinary excitement of Eat & Go is the brainchild of chef David Tsabetsaye. He worked in restaurants in Albuquerque (Seasons and Zinc Wine & Bistro) and hatched the idea of bringing gourmet food home to Zuni Pueblo. "My parents owned a market here," he explained, "and then Walmart came, and they sold it. My siblings and I wanted to come back to Zuni, and we know it will take time to introduce this kind of food to people here, but we're patient."

We took a look around Major Market while we were waiting for our food—it's an upscale shop with healthy, varied produce and meats, and sourdough bread baked on the premises.

And we came back to Zuni two nights later for dinner that the woman in the Visitor Center had told us to reserve in advance. We had the rare treat of going to the home of Shelley Morningsong and Fabian Fontenelle and having intimate and personal time with this remarkable couple in the heart of Zuni Pueblo.

After a brief advance food consultation with Morningsong about dietary restrictions and preferences—either contemporary, traditional, or a blend of both, she decided on a main course of stewed buffalo meatballs with yellow and green squash and piñons. Next came roasted lamb with sweet potatoes, garnished with fresh mint and cilantro and beautifully served on a large white ceramic platter. As we ate, we sipped dandelion tea sweetened with agave. And dessert was a slightly sweet blue corn pudding with blueberries. The bread was sourdough Zuni oven bread.

Fontenelle sat the head of the table, his hair plaited into two thin braids, in the style of Plains Indians. He is part Zuni and part Omaha. Morningsong is part northern Cheyenne.

As we savored the meal, we looked around us at Fontenelles' ancestral adobe home, which Morningsong has designed with paintings and pottery, books she authored, and CDs with music she wrote for the couple's performing life.

Fontenelle is a natural storyteller and regaled us with tales about stealing his first horse from his grandpa when he was nine, scoring a saddle from the 1920s at a yard sale in Wyoming, and how his grandfather said, "He came out kicking so he's gonna make a good dancer." Grandpa turned out to be right; Fontenelle grew up in a traditional Zuni dance family, and he performs both Zuni- and Plains-style dancing. Morningsong performs and composes songs in a variety of styles that even includes rock and soul to traditional rhythms so Fontenelle can dance to them. He is also a Native percussionist and a contemporary, self-taught drummer. And she plays Native flute, guitar and piano. "She's really smart," he said of his wife. "When I proposed to her, I said, "Honey, you do the thinking for both of us and I'll dance." Morningsong smiled and added, "we're medicine for each other."

After we had consumed the last morsels of dinner, we were longing to see the couple perform, and a few weeks later they were booked for the Pueblo Cultural Center in Albuquerque as a prelude to their tour in the United States and

Germany. It was a blisteringly hot day, but Fontenelle, in full regalia, made the crowd forget the heat because they were so captivated by his fancy footwork and the pas de deux between his moccasins and the earth. Morningsong has the voice of a star, and her lyrics are soulful, poetic, and evocative. I watched with the secret knowledge that I had been in the house of the performers, eaten Morningsong's gourmet dinner, and heard their captivating stories.

On the way back to Gallup, we had the car window open and thought we heard a coyote howling. A few days later, we would hear the chorus of an entire canid world.

For more information: Major Market menu and ordering: https://www.clover.com/online-ordering/major-market-inc-zuni; 505-495-1053.

To reserve a private dinner with Fontenelle and Morningsong: shelleymorningsong.com or shelleymorningsong@yahoo.com; 505-508-8104 .

Brittany McDonald, executive director of the Wild Spirit Wolf Sanctuary in Ramah.

Dances with Wolves and Singing Dogs, a Forest Sculpture Garden, and Breakfast All Day

Takeaway: Spending time with another species is good for the heart and soul.

Three decades ago, we visited Candy Kitchen in Ramah, where Jacque Evans and her friend Barbara invited us into the former's remote, rustic, country home. When she opened the back door and led us outside, I gasped audibly: a fenced-in area was inhabited by rescued wolf hybrids and pure wolves. Several of them leapt towards me, and as I froze in terror and then relaxed, I realized they were greeting me and not eating me. I also noticed that none of them went to Paul. Jacque said she thought they were traumatized by the genetic memory of having been hunted and shot by men, and so preferred women.

I have never forgotten that experience and was thrilled to learn that although Evans has passed on, her work with wolves has grown, expanded, and transformed into The Wild Spirit Wolf Sanctuary, about seventy-five minutes from Gallup. It's the largest wolf sanctuary in the United States and also includes wolf dogs and other wild canid species. I loved the fact that it's still remote, isolated, at the end of a four-mile gravel road and visited by in-the-know wolf lovers from around the world.

We tagged onto a small tour of the expansive outdoor property led by Hong, an animal care intern. He walked us to a large, fenced-in area and introduced us to a white wolf and then remarked that playful Kiska and her mate Zeebie were happy to see us because the former wagged her tail. He led us to another enclosure where three pure Australia dingoes—Glacier, Lulu, and Aussi—were kept, and pointed out the heart-shaped faces of these beautiful hunters who travel in packs like wolves and go after everything from rabbits to kangaroos. "They have a bad reputation, and many have been brought to the U.S. for crossbreeding purposes," Hong explained. "But they are calm. They were related to dogs in the past but split off. They howl; they don't need to bark here because they're not hunting. Their bark is a lower sound, so they don't reveal themselves to prey."

"How is their howl different from wolves?" a woman from Germany asked. "Wolves have a long baritone howl that can be heard ten miles away," Hong replied. And then he led us to the oldest and rarest canine species that have not evolved for at least 6,000 years: the tiny, cat-sized, long-bodied Papua New Guinea singing dogs named Bono, Reba, Bowie, and Foxy. They make a short, song-like sound that the dingoes sometimes answer. And speaking of Foxy, besides wolves there are even two red foxes who Hong calls to in a high-pitched voice. "They sound like a woman who is screaming," Hong offered, even though they were quiet during our visit.

We spent quite a while talking to Brittany McDonald, the bright and exuberant executive director, who said the mission of Wild Spirit is "to provide rescue, sanctuary, and education pertaining to wolves and other wild canine species. Most of the animals' stories are tinged with sadness—like the coyotes that were taken from dens in nature when they were puppies. People bought them and thought they were little dogs. But when they took them to vets, it turns out they were wolves, and one of them was even sold in an auction as dog bait."

McDonald said that most of the animals come from the pet trade and also from the wild, zoos, and other sanctuaries. "Our mentality is that the animals come first, so sometimes, even if a guest wants something from the animals, I tell them that we are here for the animals, and they're not here for us. And money shouldn't drive or motivate decisions for the animals' care." Surprisingly, 90 percent of the revenue is from donors who have never visited the sanctuary, and who live in other countries and other places. They just love wolves.

McDonald told us that when she was eight years old, she saw a photo of a wolf, and she was hooked. "In northern Minnesota we'd go to the Duluth area, and I'd howl to the wolves, but they never howled back at me. I would write letters to wolf sanctuaries, zoos, rescues, saying I was eight and I wanted to know how I could work with wolves. They sent me brochures and letters—like what do you tell an eight-year-old?"

We learned from her that "wolves have gone back on the endangered species list, except for a few states, where they can be hunted almost to extinction. I think the thing that makes them special is that they are very similar to humans; they are very social and live in family groups that function like human families do. They leave when they want to start their own family or can't stand mom and dad's rules any more. They rely heavily on each other for hunting, protection, territory. They hunt together, eat together, establish trust, communication, and loyalty. In the wild, the pack is always a family, and generally the males do the hunting." She said that, like humans, traumatized wolves may self-mutilate; they have hot spots where, sadly, they have gnawed at themselves. And occasionally there's a wolf divorce. Sometimes couples don't get along, and have to be separated at the sanctuary.

I asked McDonald if she thought lycanthropy was in her future. She laughed and replied, "If I could transform and become a werewolf, I definitely would. A huge twilight wolf."

There are no restaurants in the area, so after our hearts has been filled by the wolves it was time to pay attention to our empty stomachs. We drove about ten minutes to Ancient Way Café in El Morro. We had a tasty breakfast scramble of two eggs, hash browns, green chile and Cheddar cheese, with green chile apple pie for dessert. Salads, burgers, and breakfast are served all day.

Then it was time to walk the Ancient Way Sculpture Trail, which starts outside the café and goes into the woods. We unexpectedly experienced a wonderland of objects hanging from trees, made of car parts, carved into stone, created from charred wood, or hiding shyly and waiting to be discovered.

The short walk made us long for a longer one, so two days later we came back to the area for a hike over stones and up and down stairs at El Morro National Monument.

For more information: Wild Spirit Wolf Sanctuary is open Tuesday through Saturday; https://wildspiritwolfsanctuary.org; 505-775-3032.

For an experience with the wolves, you can take a tour or spend a day there volunteering at the sanctuary. Plans are afoot to offer evening tours and overnight camping. There is no direct contact with the wolves to prevent them from getting anxious or aggressive.

Ancient Way Café: https://www.elmorro-nm.com/ancient-way-cafe.

Hiking the trail at El Morro National Monument.

El Morro National Monument

A Hike over Stones, up and down Stairs, along a Narrow Path, and past Signatures in Stone

Takeaway: Hiking on fascinating and sometimes challenging terrain provides an opportunity to become fully immersed in the present.

Four of our favorite Diné women weren't at all sure they wanted to go when I asked them. "Navajo don't say no," Meredith Marianito said with a laugh. "They just say, 'I'll think about it.'"

Raina Marianito, her sister, with whom we had visited T&R Market, declined because she had another engagement. Her other sister Sunnye Marianito was reluctant to go because she has physical limitations, and Meredith shook her head no because she was concerned about the heat. I was about to stop asking when their niece Silver Marianito volunteered "I'll go." With that, Sunnye reluctantly agreed, and Meredith laughed again and added, "I guess I'll go too." And Silver, a bright and sensitive thirteen-year-old, agreed to be a travel journalist for a day, equipped with a pad and pen, and ready to ask questions.

Accompanied by their Chihuahua-pinscher mix Sushi, we headed for El Morro National Monument. I wondered why Native Americans, Spanish conquistadors, Mexican colonists, and wagon trails stopped at El Morro, and the answer lies at the base of the high mesa (flat-top elevation isolated in the landscape). A twelve-foot-deep, spring-fed pool holds about 200,000 gallons of water and is the only water source for thirty miles around, according to an on-site ranger. A series of hand-and-toe steps going up the mesa also suggest that the ancient Puebloans who settled in Atsinna Pueblo and other, smaller sites on top of the mesa, also used the water from the pool. "When did the ancient Puebloans live there?" Silver inquired. "About 1275 to 1340," the ranger replied. He further explained that water came from rains in the summer and melting snow in the winter.

With two trails to choose from, we asked Silver which one she preferred: the easy half-mile loop or the harder, more strenuous two-mile one. "Both," she said, and the ranger suggested we start from the end—the more challenging trail—rather than the beginning, with the easiest trail. "When you get to the top," she said, "you'll understand why. It's a lot easier to work your way down than it is to climb up."

The more difficult Headland Trail is along an ascending gravel path past oak, piñon, and juniper trees and up irregular stone stairs to reach soul-stirring views of the El Morro Valley below and the Zuni mountains and remnants of volcanoes in the distance. We passed by the ruins of Atsinna Pueblo, thought to have housed 500 to 600 people, and includes round and square ceremonial spaces as well as 355 interconnected rooms. The folks who hiked down from the pueblo to the pool to fetch water and carry it back must have been in great shape.

The hike was quite dramatic, with ever-changing terrain that required us to be present and pay attention to our steps. I love it when that happens because it is in the present where magic and connection take place and where the mind is liberated from its prison of thinking and overthinking. It was a delight to see how present Meredith, Sunnye, and Silver were. When they shouted into the canyon, their echo came bouncing back. They shouted again, softer, louder, and the echo responded to them in kind.

The temperature was rising, and at times it was uncomfortably hot. We stopped to drink water. Meredith and Silver took turns carrying Sushi and bounded up ahead; we hung back with Sunnye, who said several times she didn't think she could make it, but she always did. There was one other hiker on the trail, a doctor with a chocolate Labrador dog. She said she was lost, and we invited her to join us. Sushi and the Lab sniffed each other out and became fast friends. Now a group of six adults and two dogs, we hiked over white rocks, following a trail that was pecked out in the 1930s. Meredith looked in a distance and sighed at the sight of dead piñon trees. "We go gathering the piñon," she said. "People shake them, but that's not fair. "We get them from the ground." Sushi, cradled in Silver's arms, barked her approval.

As we negotiated our way down from the sandstone bluff along a twisting and turning path, we were glad we listened to the ranger and started with the more difficult trail because otherwise we would have been climbing up steep switchbacks in the heat. Of course, if we were more gonzo hikers, we might have enjoyed that.

We arrived at the easier, half-mile, paved trail, where Sushi was allowed to run free. Inscription Rock has over two thousand historic inscriptions that span over a thousand years of human history. The earliest were petroglyphs, etched by unknown Native Americans. The known inscribers included Juan de Oñate, who, in the words of a guide who appeared, “was a Spanish conquistador who arrived in 1598 to settle and conquer New Mexico and is notorious for a massacre at Acoma Pueblo.” He carved his name in 1605. Don Diego De Vargas left an inscription here as well; he led the military effort to reclaim New Mexico in 1692, after the Spanish had been driven out by the Pueblo Indians twelve years earlier.

The Spaniards chiseled their names and messages in run-on words, with no spaces between them. Anglos, who had also camped out near the water source, left their names and dates behind in the sandstone. Inscription Rock is like a great outdoor visitors’ book, which the French call a *livre d’or*. That seemed especially appropriate as the sandstone cliff shone golden in the afternoon light.

The doctor and her Lab bid us goodbye, and our friends poured water over their necks to cool off. They proffered the water bottle to us, and we laughed and said, “I guess we’ll cool down your way,” and doused our necks. Sunnye was especially pleased that she had made it; “I didn’t think I could do it,” she said as we all congratulated her. Meredith declared she was glad they had agreed to come. “Navajo are always afraid to go places; they’re afraid there’ll be something bad,” she explained.

“It’s gorgeous to come here in the winter, when it has snowed,” the ranger said to us before we left. We all nodded and added it to our “To Do” list.

And for the entire adventure, the Marianitos and we had all stayed in the present, out of our heads, and into each other and the magnificent surroundings.

When we returned to Gallup that evening, we had learned from locals where we should go to dine.

For information on where to eat near El Morro National Monument, see the previous story entitled “Dances with Wolves and Singing Dogs, a Forest Sculpture Garden, and Breakfast All Day.”

Meet the People

We have a trick for finding the best places to eat when we arrive somewhere. We go right to the source—locals and repeat visitors. We generally say something like, "Hi. We're visiting and is it okay if we ask what your favorite restaurant in Gallup is?" They always answer "yes."

We met Mary, a local dressed and accessorized in various shades of blue, at ArtsCrawl, which takes place on the second Saturday of the month. She and her partner were handing out fliers and seemed super friendly.

"Ha, ha, ha. We have two favorite restaurants in Gallup. Jerry's and Jerry's. He uses his own Mexican recipes, and the line is sometimes out the door because people love his food and him."

It was a quiet time of day at Towneplace Suites by Marriott, and the staff was chatting with guests. We asked a business traveler, an amateur cook who was born in Gallup, about his preferred eatery.

"I go to Oasis Mediterranean Restaurant for shawarma, tabouli, and falafel. It's Palestinian comfort food and the owners are great. You don't expect to find that kind of food here, but I'm never disappointed. I didn't try their Kunafa dessert until last week. I'm hooked now."

When we finished our WPA art tour with Rose Eason, her husband Jimmy Thomas, a Diné school counselor, was waiting for her. He was happy to tell us about his fave place.

"I've been eating at Jerry's since I was a little kid and it's always been my favorite restaurant in Gallup. It's owned and operated by one of the nicest humans on the planet, and you can taste it in the food and feel it in the service. Jerry's will fill you up and make you happy!"

A few times we asked people who were going into a restaurant why they enjoy eating there. In one case, we were walking by Earl's Family Restaurant and saw a young couple emerging with two happy-looking kids. Steve Greene, the dad, told us a charming personal story.

"Eating at Earl's was a nostalgia trip for me because my folks took me there as a kid and I wanted to take my kids. It's like a big ole classic diner, and it's all about friendly service. I can't remember what I ate when I was my son's age, but this time I had spam for breakfast for the first time in my life. Would I eat it again? Nah. Maybe. Why not? My son had a big breakfast burrito. My wife bought my daughter a beaded bracelet from a guy who came to our table."

We asked Raina Marianito, our new Navajo chef friend, about her favorite restaurant in Gallup.

"The Railway Cafe!! They serve breakfast, lunch, and dinner all day. American Comfort food. Mexican. They won best salsa. . . . And sometimes we go to the flea market to get a roast mutton/lamb sandwich for home. We don't butcher lambs ourselves, which is how you usually get it traditionally. We don't buy it either with the exception of lamb backbone for our *nischizi* stew. And that is why we go to the flea market to get roast mutton sandwiches, especially when we crave it because we don't get it very often . . . except during traditional Navajo ceremonies. A long time ago my grandma would buy an arm or leg or lamb ribs when we would come to visit. It was a symbol of a special occasion. For big family gatherings, it's economical to butcher a whole lamb."

Lighting

How to Light Your Way

The sun shines in New Mexico close to 300 days a year, but to keep us from getting bored by predictable constancy, especially in high mountain areas, it can be blazingly hot one moment and freezing rain or even snowing the next . . . sometimes both at the same time. The weather can vary from one part of a city to another and a forty-degree difference between day and night is possible all year round. When visitors inquire "What should I wear?" we locals always answer, "Layers."

The lighting conditions that accompany these changes can be as rapid and surprising—from bright sun to overcast to . . . snow. So how do you deal with such uncertainty? The answer is to always be prepared and have the gear and know the techniques you *might* need.

A flash. When the sun is strong, cowboy hats provide shade, but when you try to take a photo, the subject's face is in a shadow. That's why, in bright sunlight, I turn on my flash to kick in some added light and reveal the face beneath the hat. Flash fill also illuminates other objects in heavy shadows. Another way to overcome this problem is to use a reflector.

A reflector. Since the earliest days of movies, filmmakers have been using these to bounce natural and man-made light to where they want it. I always carry a small, lightweight, folding, and inexpensive one with several sleeves to change the nature and color of the light being reflected. It can also block unwanted light reflections.

The two examples below demonstrate how a reflector and flash *in combination* overcame the deep shadow from an overhanging roof outside of Fabian Fontenelle and Shelley Morningsongs' house; and blocked unwanted lighting glare to capture a glass showcase filled with Zuni jewelry.

Many times, a great photo can be ruined by dappled light caused by the intermittent shadows of foliage and passing clouds. If you can neither wait nor move the subject of your photo, filling in light via flash and reflector is the only way to balance out the difference and save your image.

A reflector can bounce light to fill shadows . . .

(*below*) . . . or block glaring reflections while shooting through glass.

But sometimes an overcast day can give you your best photos. Clouds provide a soft, diffused light similar to that created by expensive gear in professional photo studios.

Whatever condition are you in, just smile, have fun, and be glad you have a flash and reflector. If you face a challenge, keep experimenting, and your persistence will make for photos you are proud of.

Part Two

NORTH CENTRAL

El Rancho de Las Golondrinas presentation of New Mexico wines made the old-fashioned way.

Introduction

We have lived in north central New Mexico for almost thirty years but our travel writing work took us abroad and to other states for many of those years. During the pandemic, we were too travel-addicted to spend all our time at home, so we set out on day and half-day trips that were filled with joy, beauty, culture, nature, food, soul, art, learning, history, mystery, majesty, and novelty around our home state. We kept exclaiming, "I can't believe I didn't know about that," and "We want to tell everyone about this!" From the moment we first set out to explore New Mexico until today, we have never stopped discovering, and the wow factor has never dimmed.

Our backyard discoveries included labyrinth guides; a girl who is a marvel of tattoos and traditional weaving skills; a Spanish historical site where the inhabitants explored sexual fluidity in the 1930s; stone temples with portals to other realities; the exact places where the world-famous Georgia O'Keeffe painted; cool cruising with an authentic lowrider; artists who work in kinetic sand, collage, and invite collaborative interactions; a shimmering, little-known lake; the banks and bed of the Rio Grande; and a few of our favorite, easily-accessible hikes. We've also included memorable take-out food and local eateries.

Whether you live here or are visiting, pick and choose what appeals to you, and do it. It's that easy, and it's all there, waiting for you.

One of many labyrinths in Santa Fe.

Life Is a Labyrinth; a Labyrinth Is Life

Takeaway: There's no time like now to take a meditative look inside yourself, and sometimes a guide can help you do it.

I've probably walked thirty labyrinths in my life, and, I say with a sigh, the result is always the same: as I step slowly around the spiral dirt path that is bounded by stones, I become aware of how busy and noisy my brain is and how hard it is to quiet it down.

Perhaps you, too, have walked one, or maybe you don't know what a labyrinth is. According to Chris Harrell, who generously shared his teaching slides with me, it's a "meandering universal path with 'most often' a circular singular path leading to and exiting from the center."

When I walk a labyrinth, I sometimes think about the mythological story from about 4,000 years ago about King Minos of Crete who ordered the architect Daedalus to build a labyrinth; dwelling at its center was the growling, earth-shaking, half-bull and half-human Minotaur monster. Harrell said the story may have been created to explain the frequent earthquakes on the Aegean Island of Crete.

The image of a spiral, which is associated with labyrinths, can be found on the entrance slab of New Grange in Ireland; the structure is older than Stonehenge and the Great Pyramid of Egypt. It appears at the ruins of Chaco Canyon (850 to 1200 CE) and throughout the southwest. And today, in Santa Fe, multiple labyrinths await the curious pilgrims who go in quest of peace of mind, insight, answers to questions, self-reflection, prayer, grounding, heart-opening, or just a new experience. The labyrinths come in different shapes and sizes, and the most unusual one I've heard about is definitely the Canned Food Double-Spiral in Eldorado; why would you expect any less in this zone of extraordinary creativity?

When I enter a labyrinth, which is usually a spiral-shaped dirt path lined with stones, I generally pose a question or ask for help in making a decision: What should I do about work, life, or relationships? What should I say to somebody who has acted poorly? Each time, I hope that walking the path will lead me to an answer. Most of the time it does, and then my mind resumes its usual washing-machine-load of swirling thoughts.

Everything changed when I learned that there are labyrinth facilitators around the world who have been trained by an organization called Veriditas. They learn skills to help people focus, enhance, and expand their labyrinth walks and perhaps open up to new experiences. Two of them in Santa Fe certainly made an impact on me.

Barbara King, who works as a family practitioner and urgent-care provider, was formerly a nurse, massage therapist, aromatherapist, and yoga instructor. Wearing a bright, colorful summer dress that was accessorized with matching shell earrings and necklace, a fringed white sweater, sandals, and a straw hat, she was kind and accessible. "A lot of my life has been about healing and facilitating healing for others, so being a labyrinth facilitator fit in very well," she explained.

She suggested we might try the Relationship and Friendship Labyrinth, which is located off Highway 599, on the grounds of the interfaith Unity Church, in a tree-shaded area. It was designed and constructed by Len Meserve and a group of volunteers, and, according to Meserve, it combines the wave and the spiral—two forms found in nature. The center of the labyrinth is like the eye of a hurricane—the still point.

Two people can walk this labyrinth at the same time although they are on different paths. King handed each of us a red key on a red ribbon and said, "perhaps this will open up an experience for you." "Sure, sure," I thought. "It will open up another lane in the busy freeway of my mind." But that was far from what happened. My feet took off of their own accord. They zigzagged along the dirt path, moved sideways, backward, diagonally. I stooped to gently strike a rock with my key, and I listened to the pinging sound. I thought of nothing else except the unusual spectacle of how my body was advancing along the spiral path. When I came to the center of the labyrinth, which is usually where people pause to reflect, receive, or let go of burdens, I focused on a

Julie Bastine guides visitors through a labyrinth.

metallic silver heart and a star that had been placed there. And I unexpectedly heard the voice of a recently deceased friend tell me how those objects related to my life.

When I began the path out, the same thing happened as before. My feet took off and did their thing while I observed. When I exited, walking backward, I understood that I had to do things differently in dealing with a frustrating situation in my life, and I became determined to do so. My mind never wandered; I was focused on what I learned, and I applied it to my life with almost immediate effect. King commented that Paul also walked out backward, and he hadn't seen me do it.

Another time, we walked a labyrinth with facilitator Julie Bastine. We parked on a paved road and climbed down a short way through an arroyo (dry river bed) and into someone's very large and open backyard. Bastine, dressed casually in a white shirt, jeans, and hoop earrings that peeked out from her long, flowing, brown hair, smiled broadly when she introduced herself. She knew a lot about this labyrinth because she had helped build it. She said it was open to the public, but without her I never would have found it, and I am not sure I could find it again.

Bastine said that labyrinths help balance the brain and are great for kids as well as adults. Like King, she facilitates walks for individuals or groups. "There's no right or wrong way to walk a labyrinth, and you can't get lost," she said. She is also a healthcare provider whose specialties include reflexology, hypnosis, and integrative nutritional coaching.

I had no expectations and decided that what happened the first time with King was a fluke. Bastine invited each of us to stand under a wooden trellis on the "pause" stone (a kid gave it that name) and then perhaps close our eyes, pose a question, ask for something we want, or just begin. As each of us started, Bastine gently struck two small cymbal-like chimes together, and the sound was like a balm to a busy mind. She selected music to accompany us on our walks. Paul went first, and I followed a few minutes after him. Immediately I heard an unseen voice invite me to join "a procession of good deeds." The last time I was part of a procession was my college graduation. Right foot forward. Left foot joins it. Right foot forward. Left foot joins it. This time, it was a silent acknowledgement of good deeds I had done in my life. It made me feel buoyant and great. Paul looked very relaxed after his walk and said the experience was calming for him.

I think a guided labyrinth walk would make a great gift for a lot of folks I know. It takes about an hour. "You could even make a labyrinth party," Bastine said with a smile. I can't think of a better way to celebrate.

We wanted to spend a longer time getting to know her better, but we had tickets that night for the Santa Fe Opera.

For more information:

https://labyrinthresourcegroup.org; www.veriditas.org; labyrinthlocator.com

Julie Bastine: jbintegrativewellness@gmail.com; 505-670-1106; juliebastine.com

Dramatic stage set at the Santa Fe Opera.

Why You Should Go to the Santa Fe Opera—Even If You Don't Like Opera

Takeaway: When you learn more about something you've dismissed, you may find that you really like it.

I have a personal involvement with opera. I can't sing or read music, but I have written librettos for two operas, which means I wrote all the story, words, action, and lyrics. An opera song by one performer is an aria. Two people make it a duet. A trio is when three sing, a quartet is when four sing, and you can probably guess that a quintet is five. A large group of people singing together are a chorus.

That's about all I knew when I got started, but I have a theater background. I thought of opera as a performance where singers stood still and belted out tunes.

Boy, was I wrong. Opera is *total* theater—song, dance, acting, orchestra, costumes, sets, lighting, and glorious music. Famous operas are reinterpreted to speak to contemporary audiences. Old and new operas are written about ideas, concepts, people, and events. Like film, they excite viewers with stories and emotion. Unlike film, they are live. It all happens right in front of the audience. When an opera is in another language at the Santa Fe Opera, they have simultaneous translation appearing on a private screen in front of them. Opera can be funny, tragic, or anything in between.

At the Santa Fe Opera, the parking lot is filled with tailgate parties and on opening nights, patrons may come in costume, set up a candelabra, and dine on elegant and elaborate open air meals in full few of the Sangre de Cristo Mountains that are bathed in the glow of a setting sun. And before each performance, ticket holders can attend a free, lively, informative talk about the opera they are about to see. Although folks sometimes fret about the cost, tickets range from expensive to affordable, and both fans and newbies can score discounts for students, seniors, first-time attendees. The opera even offers a few free outdoor performances in Santa Fe and Albuquerque on large screens, so everyone can stick their toe in the opera waters. And I neglected to mention that the operas are performed on a stage that is open on three sides to magnificent vistas of northern New Mexico. When there's summer lightning or thunder, the audience hears and sees it and it adds natural production value to the spectacle onstage while they are protected under a roof.

Many people attended an opera or had it shoved down their throat as children and found it boring. That's possible if the spectator is focused on the unfamiliar style of singing and what may be a frivolous story. But there are ways to watch an opera and leap right over boring. In fact, I was never bored for a moment during the productions in a recent summer season, and here's why.

Carmen is an 1875 opera by the French composer Georges Bizet. It's a humorous and tragic story about a sexy, flirtatious, independent, feisty woman (Carmen) who practices serial monogamy. Men can't get enough of her, but she tires of them and starts up with her next lover. Carmen is a factory worker and a Roma (Gypsy) who hangs out with a colorful bunch of smugglers. Don José is a soldier who falls passionately in love with Carmen and loses everything to follow her.

While I was watching the opera, these are the questions and issues that occurred to me. What does a society do to powerful women? How can you be free when everything in your society tries to imprison you and make you conform? What does love mean? Is Don José a codependent, and why is that dangerous? How are "exotic" (i.e., Roma) people portrayed? What's the connection between power and sex? Why does Carmen long for her lost innocence? Is this boring? I think not.

Next up was the comic opera *The Barber of Seville*, by composer Gioachino Rossini about the shenanigans of Figaro, a wily barber. The farcical plot twists and turns with disguises, thwarted lovers, nobility, subterfuge, and revelations. The most notable singing style is *bel canto*, and it requires great breath control, vocal range, vibrato, and trilling up and down the music scale at dizzying speed.

Stephen Barlow, the director, milked every moment, prop, piece of scenery, interaction, costume, music, and song for comic effect in the styles of Laurel and Hardy, Mel Brooks, Monty Python, and the Three Stooges. The audience howled at the physical agility of the performers, and the inclusion of laptops and selfies alongside of period costumes. The cast was diverse and multicultural, the choreography was eclectic, and the chorus had a great time hamming it up.

I'll admit that *Tristan and Isolde*, written by Richard Wagner and premiered in 1865, is not for everyone, even though I am a loyal and somewhat obsessed Wagner groupie. Based on a medieval love story (with possibly an earlier Celtic origin), the 4.5-hour production about forbidden love is short on action and plot and long on sublime music and singing.

I had only seen *Tristan and Isolde* performed once and was bored to the point of irritability. How could anyone sit through four hours of expository declarations of love while performers flopped meaninglessly and aimlessly around the stage in a cringey attempt to enhance a static story?

And then there was the staging at the Santa Fe Opera. Co-directors Zack Winikur and Lisenka Heijboer Castañon stripped the story and characters down to their bare essentials. Every gesture, step, change of lighting, use of shadows, color, costuming, sparse elements in the stage set, vocal or instrumental moment, was imbued with significance. Nothing was superficial or superfluous. The singing was magnificent, and we were drawn into a world of intense, passionate emotion which swirled with eroticism, violence, death, love, longing, loyalty, betrayal. Long after the opera ended, the feelings it stirred remained.

The Santa Fe Opera is known for its world premieres, and *M. Butterfly*, by celebrated playwright David Henry Hwang, was the latest. Its first incarnation was a highly successful Broadway play, the second was a film, and the earlier inspiration was *Madama Butterfly*, the famous opera by Giacomo Puccini. *M. Butterfly*, the new opera, with music by Huang Ruo, is based on an incredible but true story about Gallimard, a French diplomat, who fell passionately in love with a Chinese opera star, whom he called Butterfly. She was modest and asked that they make love in the dark. Unbeknownst to Gallimard, his beloved "perfect woman" was a man, and he even faked a baby they had together. Butterfly was also a spy for the Chinese government, and, after their discovery and subsequent arrest, a trial resulted in public ridicule, prison sentences, and Butterfly standing naked before Gallimard and forcing him to acknowledge that she is a he and that he was blinded and deluded by love. Tormented by pain, passion, confusion, denial, and despair, Gallimard himself transforms into and becomes Butterfly.

The opera, which ends tragically, deals head on with identity, sexual fluidity, masculinity, racism, imperialism, revolution, domination and submission, love, and loss. The audience members walked to their cars while animatedly discussing what they had just seen and giving their own interpretations.

So, for folks who are still sure opera is not for them, I wonder if they'd be willing to give it a try. They might like what they see, hear, and feel . . .

For another experience that evoked feeling, I went to meet Isabelle Sandoval, one of New Mexico's formerly secret Jews.

For more information: https://www.santafeopera.org

Isabel Sandoval, crypto-Jewish poet.

A Formerly Secret Jew Shares Her Life and Some Sweets with You

Takeaway: It is a great gift when someone with long historical, spiritual, and mystical roots invites you into her formerly secret world.

In 1492, Columbus sailed the ocean blue, and it was a terrible time to be a Jew. The Edict of Expulsion in Spain gave 300,000 Jewish people—a quarter of the population—a choice to either leave (and leave everything they owned behind) or convert to Catholicism. Over half converted sincerely, while many others kept up their religious practices in secret. And among those who fled, thousands went to Portugal, where they were promised safe haven. Five years later, Manuel, the Portuguese king, married the eldest daughter of Catholic monarchs Ferdinand and Isabella of Spain. The marriage was conditional upon Manuel agreeing to expel all of the Jews from his country. He started with expulsion and then forcibly converted all of them to Catholicism. As in Spain, some of them kept up their practices in secret and didn't even tell their own children for fear the information would be leaked, and they might be tortured and burned alive at the stake.

This is where Isabelle Sandoval's modern-day New Mexican story began. Although she was raised in Wyoming as a Christian, she went to a nondenominational church. "My mother said the one thing she wanted me to do was memorize the Ten Commandments. She gave me a silver dollar for doing it and said, 'You need to know the Ten Commandments so you will have a foundation in your life.'"

Her older brother bought a *l'chaim* necklace (it means "to life" in Hebrew) at the Holocaust Museum and wore it. Her other brother gave her a silver ring with the star of David on it. Her older sister called herself a Sephardic Catholic and her younger one became Evangelical. "After doing a lot of research and studying, I started putting pieces of my family history together. My Catholic grandmother celebrated the Feast of Esther, but there is no Saint Esther in the Catholic church. She is a star of the story Jews tell during the holiday of Purim. My grandmother didn't drink alcohol, but on Friday night—the start of the Jewish Sabbath—she had a small glass of Porto. My aunt made buñuelos on Christmas eve—like Jews make latkes for Hanukah. My mother would travel to give any baby born in the family the first bath, which is a Sephardic tradition. I told my family that I thought we had crypto-Jewish roots. We had never discussed it until that moment. My Sephardic Catholic sister said, 'You are just finding out now?'"

When DNA studies became widely available, Sandoval traced her Sephardic ancestry to Portugal where, in 2013, a law of return was passed that offered citizenship to descendants of the Jews who had been expelled during the Inquisition. Sandoval had the family genealogy and the science to prove she qualified. After three years and tremendous persistence and tenacity, she finally got her Portuguese passport.

Several decades ago, when the story about descendants of Spanish and Portuguese *conversos* or crypto Jews began to surface, there was worldwide interest in them among people of different backgrounds and religions. Throughout Central and South America, thousands of Hispanic Catholics were finding out and coming out about who they were. And one of the loci of crypto-Jewish presence was and is New Mexico. Secret Jews had fled to Mexico and historians uncovered that a sizeable number of them came to New Mexico to escape the Inquisition that had pursued them, and to seek opportunity and wealth. Many of their descendants still kept up the clandestine practices here, even if they were never told what the origin of those traditions were.

Today, Sandoval, who has lived in New Mexico for twenty-five years, is true to her crypto-Judaic origins. "I always light my Friday night candle and clean the house on Friday like my mother did. I keep Passover and Chanukah. I did a *mikvah* (Jewish ritual bath). I always wear jewelry with coral to protect against the evil eye. I can reluctantly say that some rabbis and synagogues have not been friendly to us, even though we have proof of our origins. Luckily, I have met a few who are."

For many years, visitors to New Mexico have contacted me asking to be introduced to crypto Jews. The latter were tired of being studied and picked over like specimens. But Sandoval, who is a poet and educator, has always been a groundbreaker. Her willingness to meet and share stories with visitors—*share* being the operative word—provides a unique and moving opportunity to learn about crypto Jews first hand. She has researched, studied, connected with other *conversos*, and lived what she talks about.

Sandoval bases the reciprocal experience with visitors on eighteen questions; eighteen being the numerical equivalent of the word *chai* (life) in Hebrew. She asks them things such as: What do you remember about your grandparents, or how do you define yourself? Both the visitors and Sandoval answer the questions, which provides a basis for communication and getting to know each other. It a conversational opportunity for Sandoval to talk about her life as a crypto-Jew.

Then she reads guests one of her poems about the reality of being a *converso* and offers them a sample of homemade secret Jewish sweets. A recent visitor said it was like tasting history.

When we left Sandoval, my phone pinged with a message: "Do you know about hiking at Galisteo Basin?" My answer was an enthusiastic affirmative.

For more information: isantadoval@msn.com

Galisteo Basin Preserve.

Galisteo Basin Preserve— A Choice of Trails

Takeaway: Hikers, bikers, and equestrians may be inspired to feel good by doing good and giving back.

The Galisteo Basin Preserve is like a delightful multiple-choice test for hikers, bikers, and horseback riders. They can select from numerous trails and they're unlikely to be disappointed with the one they pick. Many first timers are enchanted and sometimes want to go back the next day, and maybe the day after that. Although most people don't know about the site, the Commonweal Conservancy proudly claims it has constructed the largest privately owned, publicly accessible network of trails in the American Southwest. And it's all thanks to outdoor enthusiast volunteers.

This is how we decide on a trail. We drive twenty minutes from Santa Fe to the clearly marked preserve. We turn in at the trailhead that has the fewest number of cars in the small parking lots. It's that easy.

The first time we went, it was afternoon, and we could hear the lonesome wail of a distant train barreling down the tracks in nearby Lamy. We parked at the Thumb Trailhead. The dirt path curved gently through a landscape that is dotted with cholla cactus and juniper bushes. In all directions there were seemingly endless vistas. We were alone on the trail except for a few mountain bikers. In the magical glow of an iridescent New Mexican sky, the clouds and the daytime moon seemed to be within easy reach.

The trail splits off at several different places, and there is a choice between uphill and flat. Frankly, life felt a little uphill that day, so we opted for flat. We deduced from the fresh tracks in the dirt that before we came, a horseback rider made the same decision. To the side of the trail, dead fallen trees got a second life as natural skeletal sculptures and then a third life as they decomposed and provided nourishment for new growth. "Thank you very mulch," Paul quipped as he photographed the trees.

The flat trail turned upward, and a little pine tree basking in the sun pointed the way. The view changed, and we saw a few hilltop homes and mountains in the distance. I rubbed my eyes to be sure we were not in Egypt because one of the mountains looks like a pyramid.

Then the trail curved downward along a narrow arroyo. I saw splashes of color from the bright garb of mountain bikers and heard the soft voices of owners talking to their beloved dogs. Near the end of our two-mile hike, we were at the entrance to a private neighborhood. A sandstone sculpture called "Moon Over Thumb" commemorates a lunar event at the place we had just been exploring.

When we reached our car, a young woman hiker arrived and told us that she downloaded maps from the Galisteo Basin Preserve website before she hiked. "I love it here. I've become a Friend of the Preserve to help maintain the trails and assist with land restoration projects. It makes me feel good to be doing good." That statement got me thinking in earnest about the volunteers who built and maintain the trails.

On our second visit, we chose the farthest trailhead, appropriately named Cottonwood Trail. Three mature cottonwood trees that were sleeping all winter stood with open branches to welcome us.

The earth seemed to change colors under our feet as we walked along: it was red, then gray, green, white, beige, or tawny. We weren't the only happy ones in the area; nearby, two horses stopped for a vegetal snack and one of them looked out over the land and neighed his approval.

The flat trail was lined with juniper trees, the occasional proud pine, and the sculptural skeletons of fallen trees that were once robust. As the path curved and winded, cholla cactus popped up, showing off their yellow buds. And near them, small, tight-knit communities of paddle cactus huddled together, as though they were gossiping about the few hikers and bikers who passed by.

When we reached a crossroads, we turned right onto trail number 45. It's humorously named Bob Was Here on one of the maps that dots the trail. We followed it towards Richard's Ramble, smiling as we conjured up images of volunteers named Richard and Bob who worked hard to clear the trails and ensure their posterity.

The path was lined with grayish white stones, and gently went uphill and down. Sometimes we walked over the rocks and although we were the only ones on the trail, we saw from tracks in the dust that bikers enjoyed 45 too. In the distance we could see the great expanse of the Galisteo Basin with the outline of foothills beyond. Suddenly the earth became red for a brief time, and then we faced an arroyo. Walking through the steep gully triggered memories of carefree strolling on beaches when I was a child. And our adult calves loved the workout they were getting because the dry riverbed sand was fairly deep. We stopped for a moment at a map that indicated we were on the Arroyo de Los Angeles Trail, and the angels clearly provided us with the perfect weather.

Paul's phone indicated that we had walked three miles, and mine was sure it was three and a half. So, as they say in French, you can cut the pear in half and decide it was three and a quarter.

Speaking of edibles, we got take-out delights from Arable restaurant for our picnic. We began with a large, fresh, homemade German Style Pretzel, which we dipped in French Dijon mustard. Then we slurped our Organic Butternut Squash Soup, which was sprinkled with spiced, roasted pepitas. I opted for Shrimp & Grits, which is an ode to New Mexico with its red chile butter and Tamaya Blue Corn Grits. And my secret pleasure was that the color of the bed of grits evoked the rich sand of the arroyo. Paul loved every baby green leaf, plump baby potato, olive and caper of his generous Veggie Niçoise Salad. And then, to celebrate the colors of the Cottonwood Trail, we had the tricolored Butterscotch Budino for dessert. It's an irresistible indulgence of organic creamy custard, sea salt caramel, and whipped cream. And we figured that the leftovers would easily provide us with another meal or two.

Before we left, we smiled to see the same hiker who had told us that she feels good by doing good, and I will pass her life hack on. If lovers of the outdoors want to have fun while getting down and dirty, they should contact the preserve in advance of their visit to be included in trail building and maintenance or attend workshops. They'll be paying back providential nature and honoring the volunteers who blazed trails. Maybe someday, like Bob and Richard, they'll have a trail named after them.

Or maybe they'll be so inspired by the trail builders that they will decide to build something extraordinary with earth and stone, like James Jereb at Stardreaming.

For more information: https://www.galisteobasinpreserve.com/trails or www.galisteobasinpreserve.com/contact to volunteer.

A colleague of mine says the Shepherd's Trail, which originates at the Cowboy Shack parking lot, is his favorite. It climbs through white and red canyons up to a rocky point with stunning views.

James Jereb, creator of Stardreaming.

Stardreaming among Twenty-Two Standing Stone Temples and Labyrinths

Takeaway: Where and how to indulge your inner mystic, wonderer, and esotericist.

"How many business cards do you have?" I asked James Jereb, whose penetrating eyes sparkled above his gray mustache and beard and underneath a beige bucket hat. He was dressed simply in a billowing, blue shirt and khaki trousers. "Well," he replied, "I do a lot of things. You could say I'm artist, cosmic architect, stone mover, ant whisperer, magician, sorcerer, and sacred geometrist." He laughed good naturedly, but Stardreaming is no joke. Like a modern-day Hercules, he moved 300 tons of stone with a pipe and a crowbar and built nineteen open-air temples on twenty-two acres of wide-open country under cotton ball clouds in an azure sky. He designed the site to potentiate transformation and healing. And most people in Santa Fe (about thirty minutes away) have never heard about it.

I will disclose at the outset that I am not a very woo-woo person, although I am open to almost all adventures that do not harm anyone else or myself, and I have definitely had powerful mystical experiences. But I have never been in a temple complex like the one Jereb describes as "filled with energetic portals or doorways that are opportunities to connect to the cosmos and higher consciousness."

Each of the temples is aligned to the sun, moon, and stars. Many people walk through life looking down, but Stardreaming invites visitors to look up and sense their relationship to billions of stars and galaxies. Our physical bodies connect heaven and earth, what is above to what is below. And depending upon their intention and willingness, guests may have a very personal and perhaps magical experience. "I learned from ants," says Jereb, in his intense, giddy, voluble way. "They are my allies, and I built the temples from the ant's point of view. I was very childlike when I began to construct Stardreaming twenty-two years ago. I always wanted to do what made my heart sing."

Stardreaming.

Today, Jereb is clear as one of his crystal skulls about his belief that human potential is unlimited and that when they come to Stardreaming guests can do whatever they need to do, and they will get what they need. His goal is to connect visitors—who are limited to ten a day—"to One Mind, or the higher vibration of humankind." He limits the number of visitors because, in his words, "it's a sacred place, and not a public installation."

There are two ways for guests to experience Jereb's creations: one is outdoors, with a map of the temples, letting instincts and desires guide them to and through temples of stars, the moon, the sun, the heart, the pyramid of light new earth that is embedded with crystals, and the Faery Ring, which is a bower with the energy of play. They may meditate, empty their minds, follow their breath, commune with spirits, sing, get insights, or just walk, be curious, and enjoy.

The second way is inside the enclosed Temple of Illumination, where visitors are limited to one hour "with many options and portals for them to explore." They can, for example, move around a circle of stone and crystal skulls, and put their hands on one that calls to them. They may get a burst of energy, or a vision. Paul felt a strong pulsation from the back of one skull that he touched. Guests can look up at the ceiling of the Maji, which contains the symbols of civilizations, or handle specially designed balls that Jereb claims are chakra activators. They may leave the temple, walk outside to a mystical garden, and sit on Merlin's wooden, throne-like chair, where they may be transported to the past or future. Several years ago, I sat in that chair and saw a vision of two lines of ancient people in long, white robes, marching forward. One line was for males and the other for females. Their arms were outstretched in front of them and laden with offerings of grains that had recently been harvested. I was transfixed. I sat there for a long time, watching what was like a private screening of a film. I had told Jereb about it at the time, and I was sure he had forgotten the incident. "Do you recall the last time you were here and what you saw in Merlin's chair?" he asked me.

Jereb says that he leaves people alone in the room or in Merlin's chair, and when he comes back at fifty-five minutes to lead them out, some have fallen into trance or simply fallen asleep. The energy is very strong.

When I told a few people about my experience, I could generally tell by their reaction—which ranged from smirks and looks of disbelief to wide-eyed fascination—if Stardreaming was for them.

"When you enter the grounds, you leave crap behind," Jereb says with characteristic candor, 'and you're on your own.' You may experience tears of grief or joy. You may be transported or just feel peace. You may look around and appreciate the silence with nothing but the sound of your steps and breathing. There is no light pollution here. This is ancient energy, and ancient knowledge of connecting to the cosmos. What I am doing is what people did thousands of years ago. I've been creating portals and gateways and doorways for twenty-two years. These portals and gateways are entries to other realities and dimensions, a trip that is drug-free."

Outside, for several hours, we wandered past and through open-air temples that were often spirals and labyrinths built on the earth or lines of standing stones. I didn't feel much except admiration for what Jereb has envisioned and realized, and then I came to the Temple of the Milky Way. It's a spiral made in the earth and bordered with shimmering black obsidian stones interspersed with rose quartz. It was dazzling in in its beauty and symmetry. I began to walk inside the spiral, and I distinctly heard a voice say to me, "Stay steady. Speed up for no one."

When we left, James came riding by in his truck and stuck his head out the window. He said he knew I had a message for him. I told him, "Stay steady. Speed up for no one." He nodded, and left, waving goodbye.

I'm still not woo-woo, but when powerful energy knocks at my door, I answer it. And Jereb's art inspired me to get creative with two other Santa Fe artists.

For more information: To reserve a visit inside, outside, or both: https://stardreaming.org.

Jereb's paintings and prints sell for many thousands of dollars, but he is now producing affordable greeting cards and a limited-edition photographic series of his paintings.

Workshop with Darlene McElroy.

Two Artists and Three Art Experiences for Everyone from Rank Beginners to Established Artists

Takeaway: It's one thing to *see* art, and another to *be* art.

Darlene McElroy led Paul, me, and her friend Beau to her art arbor outside her home; it was draped in purple Russian sage and wisteria. It was an impeccable summer afternoon, and McElroy, who defines herself as a *coyota* (a local New Mexican term for half Hispanic and half Anglo) and "an ageless wild haired mad art scientist," wore a vibrant Mexican apron. She's a well-known and respected artist, with works in galleries around New Mexico and Mexico.

With white hair, sparkling eyes, and an impish smile, she introduced us to Kinetic Sand, a type of sand coated with silicone oils. "It's very cool," she said. "It doesn't dry out and you can mold with it and then it goes back to its original shape. It started out as something for kids, but I've been working with it for 10 years. It comes in different colors, and today we'll be using the shades of pink and natural."

McElroy laid out a box of small objects like beads, keys, a doorbell button, an earring, and a small metallic hand. "Choose the color sand you want, moisten it and put it in the container I'm giving you. Then select the pieces you want to press into the moist sand," she instructed us.

I chose vibrant pink, and easily pressed a string of tiny beads into it. Paul preferred the natural color, and he began by inserting a little wooden doll hand into his. It was easy and playful, and within a few minutes we were completely absorbed in creating our sculptures.

Next, we poured plaster into the stamped sand and set our pieces aside to dry. McElroy said that when the plaster cured and hardened, it would be removed from the sand. The stamped shapes would show up embossed on the plaster and that would be our work of art. "You'll be surprised when it comes out because it's reverse. What you have pressed into it will come out at you," McElroy promised.

While we waited for our pieces to cure, we started on a second art project—collage, a technique for which McElroy is famous. "A lot of people don't know how to start with a large blank piece of paper, so I'm giving you a photo to use as a base. It's of my friend Daniel Martinez who died eighteen months ago. You can make an abstract figure by painting over it and adding collage elements."

She set out a large array of acrylic paint tubes and a collection of paper ephemera—bits and pieces of colored paper and paper objects—and glue. And if we wanted to scratch or scribe into the paint, there were porcupine quills.

As we worked, McElroy offered a few encouraging words like "nice design," or an occasional "good color choices." I thought back fondly to when I first saw McElroy's striking, colorful, witty collages in her booth at the annual, curated Contemporary Hispanic Market art fair in Santa Fe. Each of her pieces seemed to tell a story and the longer you looked at them, the more elements emerged. "I may not look Hispanic," McElroy had said with a grin, "but my family came here in 1692 with Don Diego de Vargas, and my ancestor was his scribe. You're a writer so I thought you'd like that."

When we finished, just as McElroy had promised, we each had a flat, colored plaster sculpture with raised images of the objects that we had embedded. I thought they would make great paperweights. She asked us to hold up our sculptures and opine on what we saw in each other's work. Beau's looked organic, Paul's resembled the floor of a seabed, and McElroy jokingly said mine "showed the Divine feminine. . . . but watch out for that claw."

Then she requested that we hold up our collages to see how the others responded. The group consensus was that Paul's was splattered like a Jackson Pollack piece. It was an accurate expression of his spontaneous, creative nature. "It looks like the escutcheon of King Sborn of Latvia," McElroy said with her characteristic humor. Beau's piece suggested the elegant mystery of art Paul and I had seen in Arab countries, and revealed his love of exploration, cultures, and new experiences. And my original image was broken up with a large blue eye set against red petals. According to the others, it reflected my out-of-the-box attitude towards life.

We left with two objects of art, and a great, smile-inducing memory.

A few days later, we went to Linda Storm's home studio. An energetic woman with sparkling eyes and passion when she speaks, her apron was printed with an image from one of her paintings called "Viola ladder." I met her many years ago,

Linda and Gary Storm offer an art and music experience.

when she opened a gallery on Canyon Road, Santa Fe's storied street that is lined with former houses that have been transformed into art galleries. After a few years she closed the gallery and rented a small nearby studio to focus on her work. She and her husband Gary, a musician and radio DJ, began to feature live concerts in the little studio; famous musicians on world tours performed there. Now they combine their work, and we had come to experience what they do.

Gary sat on a sofa with his guitar. "He's going to play original music for you while you create art," Storm said. "You're kidding? Live music?" I asked incredulously. The duo nodded in synch, and Storm said this is part of the multisensorial experiences they offer.

"Look out the window at the trees and the sky, and observe the shapes of things," Storm told us. "Everything we see is light and shadows bouncing back to our brain." I looked at the streaks of sun across the trees and the darker shadow areas below them. In Storm's paintings, light or the absence of light bestow a magical sheen to earth goddesses and birds, musical instruments, snow clinging to barren tree branches, and the mysterious world of nighttime. She beamed when I told her that I loved her use of bold color and then she led us to the tables where we were to work. The soft guitar playing accompanied us for the entire session.

"Today we're going to work with three primary colors—magenta, yellow, and blue," Storm said. "Magenta makes a true purple when mixed with blue and a true orange when mixed with yellow. When I paint, I think about where pigments come from. Science can mix chemicals, but the chemicals come from the earth. To honor that, I use rainwater in my paintings that is mailed to me from all over the world." She held up a small glass vial she had just received from an unknown admirer in Norway.

She handed us sponges to spread water and color on art paper that that she placed in front of each of us on a table. "Paint your impression of what you saw out the window. Leave no white spaces," Storm suggested when I asked her for advice. I glanced over at Paul's soft, evocative painting of abstract elements whirling around a tree. Influenced by our experience on the Navajo Nation with painter Jerry Brown, mine was completely abstract—splashes of vibrant color with bouncing drips and dabs of paint. I painted yellow over blue stripes to create green. Then I couldn't find exactly what I need to pull the whole thing together. "Don't worry about that," Storm advised, "just let it go."

When we finished, Storm said we should let our work dry, and she and Gary served us watermelon slices, the perfect snack for a hot summer day. As we ate, I asked Storm about the multicultural goddesses she paints. "When I was five or six, I started questioning the religion I was taught to believe in, and why the Creator was a male. The only powerful female I knew was Alice the Goon, an Amazon warrior in Popeye cartoons. She was tall and muscular. I believe that what we are meant to do comes to us naturally as children. Whether I am teaching adults or children, I offer the supplies and wait until the person is immersed. Then I step away. Their art is them in the moment, who they are, who they are meant to be as humans. It's a sacred state."

When our paintings were dry, Gary continued providing the music, and Storm gave us black markers, and black-and-white paint. Surprisingly, she asked us to play with light, shadow, and shapes on our *partner's* art! "You can also use words," she said to me. "They can cast a spell and create depth."

Painting on top of each other's work was certainly unexpected, but I was curious to see what happened and how our paintings would change.

Paul drew small, shaded faces on one side of my painting, and a block of partially discernible words on the other side. Miraculously, they pulled my painting together into a satisfying whole. On Paul's work, I calligraphed the word "Swirl," and highlighted the letters. "I love it!" Storm exclaimed. When she got excited, so did we.

Many people come to Santa Fe to see and buy art. But perhaps their most memorable art will be what they created with accomplished artists and brought home with them. And maybe Storm's love for nature and spirits will inspire them to get outdoors and walk . . . even in the canyon of the devil.

To arrange for a class: Darlene McElroy: https://www.darleneoliviamcelroy.com; info@darleneoliviamcelroy.com; text: 505-660-8326

Linda Storm offers team building art classes for two to fifty people: https://www.lindastormart.com; lindastormartiste@gmail.com

As of this writing, the Storms are selling their house and building The Stormhold, their dream project: a haven for creatives that holds a gallery/event space for fifty; a radio studio and Gary's record collection of 35,000 albums; Linda's art studio, and retreat rooms.

Diablo Canyon.

Diablo Canyon

Hiking with a Unique Point of View and a Gourmet Picnic

Takeaway: If you hike in the winter, you may have a usually busy destination to yourself.

Anyone with a pair of hiking shoes, boots, or even sneaks with adequate grip knows the pleasure of walking in the temple of nature. Something sacred happens when mountains, plains, trees, birds, valleys, meadows, and forests welcome visitors as though they have been waiting for them to arrive.

One of our favorite ways to hike is finding different perspectives from which to see the world. In Las Cruces, we walked in the dry bed of the Rio Grande, exploring how a fish or a clam might see the shore (p. 219). In Los Alamos, we felt as though we were on top of the world on the edge of a mesa (p. 197). In Santa Fe, when I looked up at Diablo Canyon, I saw vertical basalt cliffs on either side of me. It's only about twenty minutes from downtown and is so uniquely dramatic that it's been featured in western films and photo shoots. Although it is sometimes a popular destination for local hikers, on a sunny day when there was snow on the ground, we wore waterproof hiking shoes and had it to ourselves.

Under a delft blue sky dotted by a few cotton-ball clouds, Paul and I left the city behind. We turned onto Old Buckman Road and as we drove along the long, occasionally arduous, washboard dirt road, we immersed ourselves in the unexpectedly rich, complex history that lingered around us. A thousand years ago, the bumpy road was one leg of a vibrant trade route that extended from Mesoamerica to the Rocky Mountains. We imagined ancestral Puebloans exchanging turquoise, pottery, seashells, feathers, and stones as well as news, customs, and technology.

In 1598, Spanish conquistador Juan de Oñate's expedition from Mexico traveled through here, hoping to find great mineral riches and establish a settlement in the region. The riches never materialized, but the impact of the meeting, conflict and eventual coexistence of the European and Puebloan cultures still echoes today. The trail became part of the Camino Real de Tierra Adentro (Inland Royal Road), the historic trade route between Mexico City and Ohkay Owingeh Pueblo that lasted until the nineteenth century. At one point, we thought we saw the ruts of a mule caravan that once ground noisily along the dusty road.

When we arrived at Diablo Canyon, we gasped audibly from the unanticipated beauty and majesty of the two gigantic volcanic rock walls and the snow-dappled, sandy riverbed that snaked between them. It was warm enough for outdoor dining and we unfurled our small, light-weight, rolled-up aluminum picnic table, opened our folding chairs, and settled under the canopy of a tree that grew smack in the middle of the arroyo (wash) that led to the mouth of the canyon. Then we unpacked our gourmet take-out picnic lunch from Doctor Field Goods' restaurant and Butcher Shop. We began with New Mexico comfort food: green chile stew flecked with sharp cheddar cheese.

We tasted and fell in love with the *patatas bravas* enveloped in house-made kimchi and miso aioli. We felt nobly healthy as we sampled a Vegetable Stuffed Handmade Burrito, which was rich in sautéed cabbage, onions, and fennel and given color and depth with carrots, beets, quinoa and of course a dollop of green chile. For an island treat developed in Florida, we took a few bites of our El Cubano sandwich, a hearty mix of pork, ham, Swiss cheese, and cabbage salad. And we didn't even try to resist the bread pudding with raisins and pine nuts complemented by caramel sauce and frothy cream for dessert.

As we ate, a park ranger passed by, stared at us, broke out in a huge smile and said, "You guys sure have it figured out."

After a leisurely lunch, we tucked at least half of our picnic into our cooler, and figured we'd have a great dinner or two at home. Then we walked through the wash into the canyon itself. The sand beneath our feet was studded with pieces of nature's jewels: basalt and quartz. There were several choices of paths that paralleled the main thrust of the arroyo, and a few times we had to step over large rocks on what is otherwise an easy trail. The patterns in the cliffs are dazzling and suggested everything from rivulets to sculptures to corrugated stone.

The dramatic scenery accompanied us as we walked through the deep canyon that was carved by wind and water erosion. Around each bend was a new and unexpected vista and the cliffs changed color with the light. I wondered how the place got its name—Diablo Canyon means Devil Canyon. Maybe it's because it's hotter'n hell in the summer. Or perhaps an early visitor saw a devil's outline in the

Climber in Diablo Canyon.

rock. Another possibility is that someone gave it that name to dissuade people from coming and spoiling the glorious destination.

On our way back to our car, we stopped to watch two rock climbers scale the cracked basalt cliffs. They invited us to use their gear and give vertical rock climbing a try. When I declined their offer with a bit of a shudder, one of the climbers said, “I guess heights aren’t your thing, right?” We all laughed as I nodded vigorously.

For rock climbers, the canyon is definitely a sweet spot. For ground huggers like I am, it’s the ideal place for an unforgettable outing that’s close to Santa Fe. We could have walked as far as the Rio Grande, but the wind was coming up we turned around before we got there. We loved going there in the winter when it was our private playground. We remembered to pack out whatever we carried in . . . or we might have had the devil to pay.

Which brings me to another place where there are spirits both of the ghostly and drinkable kind.

For more information: https://www.blm.gov/visit/diablo-canyon

Making chile ristras at El Rancho de las Golondrinas.

El Rancho de las Golondrinas

Wine? Ghosts? Chiles? Wild Foraging? Jousting? Native American Hoop Dancing? Pick a Festival

Takeaway: You may want to return to places you know and love to discover new aspects of them.

One of the great pleasures of travel is going back to our fave places at different times of the year. In autumn we crave visual bursts of golden aspen, and in summer we feel creative and want to try our hands at a new craft and then slip into a bathing suit and glide through the water of a pristine lake. In winter, our hearts are warmed by hiking, cross-country skiing, or snowshoeing in the lap of snow-capped peaks, and in spring we can't get enough of the sudden greenery and blossoms on the trees.

As soon as someone says, "I've done it," about a destination, I may not say anything, but I'm thinking, "I'll bet you haven't. You've probably only seen a fraction of it at a particular time of year."

When I'm home in Santa Fe, I always plan several visits south of the city to El Rancho de las Golondrinas—the top living history museum in the Southwest—during their annual festivals. It was early July when I first attended Viva México and stood, slack-jawed, as four of the Mexican *voladores de Papantla* leapt off a ninety-eight-foot-high platform in mid-air and spun around a central pole, upside down, tied only by an ankle rope, until they reached the ground. The fifth remained on the platform, simultaneously playing a flute and dancing. The audience held its collective breath as it watched the ancient Mesoamerican spiritual ritual, and only exhaled when all five of the men had landed safely.

Afterward, I sampled Mexican food and bought an armload of handcrafted gifts and clothes from a variety of Mexican artists and vendors. Then I had a private massage by a Mexican *curandera*, or folk healer.

Before July was over, I had gone back for the Wine Festival and as I sipped and sampled, I learned that New Mexico has more than sixty wineries and a bunch of award-winning wines. It is also the oldest wine-making region in the country—140 years before California. Of course, the vino was accompanied by a choice of foods, and it was there I first discovered Fusion Tacos. Their food truck has a devoted following of Santa Fe foodies for tacos, tortas, quesadillas, burritos, bowls, breakfasts, salads, smoothies, green juice, protein shakes, and all served with a big dollop of love. And because of their popularity, they now are in several locations.

In September, we've attended a Renaissance fair and watched medieval tournaments like jousting and swordplay, while we gnawed on a turkey leg the size of a warclub. If we had kids, the Fiesta de los Niños would delight them with Native American dancers, young Hispanic folklore performers in brightly colored traditional clothes, and the chance to make crafts and learn about other cultures.

In October, I followed my nose to Golondrinas for The Harvest Festival. The aroma of roasting chiles permeated the air, and I had to decide whether I wanted to stomp grapes by foot, make a corn husk doll, visit a blacksmith's shop, watch the women stringing *ristras* of chile in the courtyard of an adobe house, suck on a piece of sweet sorghum (New Mexico's answer to sugar cane), pick a pumpkin, watch an Indian hoop dancer, sample local traditional foods, photograph, shop, or do it all.

The last time I was there, the free tour with Dryland Wilds (from Albuquerque) was a highpoint of the day. They led a group of us on a sustainability and foraging walk and started with some ground rules for newbies. Only take one quarter of a plant or less and make sure there are many similar plants nearby. Don't harvest on cement roads and be 100 percent sure of the safety of plants you gather; they may be on protected National Forest land or sprayed with toxic products. If you live in New Mexico and want to get rid of invasive Russian olive trees, think again: in a drought they hold water; the olive acts as an antiviral and provides collagen; the wrinkled berries, when dried, make a fine tea; the leaves, berries, and flowers can be used for wound healing. Yes, they are invasive, so they must be kept in balance with native plants that get priority. The Siberian elm, the most hated plant in northern New Mexico, produces leaves that are a probiotic; they can be eaten raw or used to make kimchi or sauerkraut.

I learned that cattails are a calorie-rich wild food that tastes like cucumber and can be consumed unless they come from contaminated water. Coyote willow? It's good for pain and acne but it shouldn't be eaten by those who are allergic to aspirin. I knew nothing about sweet clover, but in the sixteenth and seventeenth centuries, it was used to get rid of the smells of body excretions and can still be used as a bathroom spray unless it is moldy. And *verdolaga*, which grows in our yard, is a relative of spinach and shouldn't be eaten raw because it's high in oxalic acid and can cause gout. Ouch!

When it comes to allergy sufferers, it may help them to learn that the more they hate juniper, the more it affects them allergically.

No matter when I visit, I never feel that I have "done" El Rancho de Las Golondrinas. Au contraire, I urge culturally curious tourists and local friends to head over there and start making plans for when I will go back again.

Another place we have gone back to many times is Chimayo, and we were drawn by other things besides the famous healing chapel.

For more information: https://golondrinas.org

For private guided tours and workshops:
https://www.drylandwilds.com

Chimayo weaving.

Beyond the Famous Healing Sanctuary

Takeaway: When visiting well-known destinations, explore the vicinity surrounding them to discover little-known or unknown attractions.

Like many travelers, we are drawn to famous attractions and after visiting one, we stay in the area to discover what other folks usually miss because they leave immediately afterward.

One example of this is Chimayo, nestled in the Sangre de Cristo Mountains on the High Road to Taos. Native Americans lived in the region for almost a thousand years before the Spanish founded the village in the early eighteenth century. Conflict ensued as many Indians resisted the efforts of the missionaries to convert them to Catholicism. The famous sanctuary was built from 1813 to 1816, and many people refer to this pilgrimage site as the "American Lourdes," because of the sacred dirt claimed to have healed many afflictions. It's very moving to see all the discarded crutches and braces of pilgrims who gained mobility after a visit.

On Good Friday, Chimayo is the destination for tens of thousands of pilgrims who walk from as far away as Santa Fe (thirty miles) or beyond, joining the largest religious pilgrimage in the United States. The faithful come to offer thanks, complete a vow, or pray for healing for themselves and their loved ones. I have met many participants of diverse religious backgrounds who come from all over the world.

What is less well-known is that Chimayo has been a center for Spanish weaving for several hundred years. It is also the only town in New Mexico where you can still see a historic fortified plaza (town square) constructed to defend against Indian attacks.

Ortega's is the largest of the weaving shops, and Robert Ortega obliges visitors by demonstrating family weaving traditions on a large, wooden, two-harness walking loom, operated by foot treadles. "This is the Rio Grande style. Most weavers sit, but we 'walk' by using the treadle. It's a very creative outlet," he explained as he showed us how he weaves a multicolored woolen textile. "My ancestors came here 300 years ago. There are two other weaving families here, and we are all related," he said. Although, ironically, he is allergic or sensitive to some wools, including local wool from churro sheep, he has nonetheless been weaving for sixty years.

Churro sheep were first brought to New Mexico with the Coronado expedition in 1540. The sheep thrived here and in addition to providing food, they carried on their backs the raw material for what would become much-valued trade items: Rio Grande blankets. At first, they were worn and used on beds for warmth on cold mountain nights, but their popularity gave birth to an entire industry of sheepherders, spinners and weavers who produced both functional and decorative items. The designs often include stripes, stars, diamonds, a central area, and borders.

In the adjacent shop, visitors buy handwoven clothes, household items, and the popular newbies—cellphone and eyeglass holders. "Imagine getting a healing and a woven fashion statement in one destination," said one excited woman from Abilene.

From there, we sometimes stride into local history. Near the Ortega shop is a walking bridge, and water flowing under it is part of the acequia that dates back to the founding of Chimayo and is one of the oldest continually used irrigation ditches in New Mexico. It still fertilizes the ancient fields in the fertile valley.

On the other side of the bridge is the Chimayo Museum, which was formerly an ancestral adobe home of the Ortega family. It houses wonderful old photos, locally made Hispanic pottery, nineteenth-century artifacts and weaving devices, and unique New Mexican tinwork. Tin was the poor man's silver ever since it was introduced here by the US Army when they occupied New Mexico in 1846. Local artists crafted decorative objects from the military's discarded cans. We also learned there that ancient Native Americans considered Chimayo a special place with dirt that had curative powers.

Walking out the back door of the museum on a recent visit, we entered the rare architectural remains of the fortified plaza; the museum was part of it. It's an enclave with a post office, a chapel with a wooden bell tower, and long rows of adobe houses facing a central plaza—all designed to protect the Hispanic villagers against Comanche raids. Apparently, the latter group also raided Indian villages, so fear was widespread, and fortifications were de rigueur.

Today, what's de rigueur for us is checking out the automobile masterpieces that sometimes cruise the main street of Chimayo, which, along with Española, bills itself as "the Lowrider Capital of the World." Many thousands of dollars and hours go into designing and rebuilding classic cars and transforming them inside and out into paeans to Hispanic culture, love, religion, family (living and deceased), art, and design. With hydraulic technology, the drivers can make their cars jump and dance.

Many visitors to Chimayo reserve in advance for their traditional New Mexican meal at the pueblo-style Rancho de Chimayo. They opt for indoor or outdoor dining and appreciate the award-winning local and ancestral recipes. An alternate dining choice is El Parasol Tacos in Española—it's a simple taco stand with outdoor picnic tables. Locals line up for their tacos, burritos, tostadas, even tortilla burgers and vegetarian specialties along with other New Mexican and Mexican specialties. "It's real *autentico*," said one guy who drove up in a two-tone lowrider that looked like it had cruised out of the 1950s. After eating, he drove slowly to show off his designer ride.

On our way back to Santa Fe, I decided that even though I knew little about Chimayo weaving and lowriders, I wanted to have experiences with both of them. For starters, we found a cool new spin on an ancient weaving tradition.

For more information: http://www.ortegasweaving.com; 53 Plaza Del Cerro; 505-351-4215

Chimayo Museum: 13 Plaza del Cerro; 505-351-0945

Workshop with Emily Trujillo, Chimayo weaver.

A Cool New Spin on an Old Weaving Tradition

Takeaway: You can open your mind and heart to new spins on old traditions.

Emily Trujillo was not what we expected of a Chimayo weaver: age twenty-nine, purple hair, sixteen tattoos, and sporting anime boxer shorts under a short skirt, she bounded outside to greet us. Her curriculum vitae includes figure skating, long boarding, digital painting, long distance running, writing, climbing a tree and doing a cartwheel in her wedding dress and, relating to the purpose of our visit, weaving and creating in the world-famous Chimayo tradition since the tender age of five. She is the eighth generation of weavers in the internationally famous Trujillo family—the accolades and awards garnered by her father Irvin and mother Lisa extend over the length of wall in the Centinela Traditional Arts gallery and workshop in Chimayo—and she blends a cool, confident, contemporary sensibility with a 400-year-old tradition.

After studying ethnology and human neuropsychology in college, she realized that cultures, including her own, were dying with globalization. She returned home to Chimayo to pass on the knowledge of traditional weavers to the next generation. She did an internship in the gallery and then wove half a day with her father. "I was doing inventory and I found pink yarn hidden away in the back of the yarn room. I said I wanted to weave a piece with it, and my father said, 'Ugh. Cerise. Nobody buys cerise.' I waited for him to go to lunch so he couldn't tell me no, and I made a skein into spools. It is my most popular piece to date. It sold the day it went up on the website. I named it, 'Can you take me cerise-ly now, dad?'" she laughingly recounted.

She explained that in the fertile valley of the Sangre de Cristo mountains where Chimayo is located, a mere forty minutes from Santa Fe, weaving began with the coarse wool of hardy Churro sheep brought by the first Spanish settlers in 1598.

Her own family established themselves as weavers in the early to mid 1700s. Known generally as Rio Grande weaving because it was produced along the mighty river that sustained the villages, a twentieth-century local outgrowth and development of the tradition is often referred to as Chimayo weaving today.

Trujillo gestured to the family rugs and tapestries displayed on the gallery walls—in colors ranging from subtle earth tones to bright neon colors—and explained that there are four basic styles of weaving. Rio Grande contains stripes and was purely utilitarian for a long time. Spanish looms were used to make saddle blankets, couch covers, and blankets. Saltillo is complex and valuable. "If a man showed up with a Saltillo over his shoulder his future in-laws would exult, 'He's rich!'"

Vallero can be identified by its eight-pointed stars known as Vallero stars. And Chimayo—which was developed in the early 1900s—has geometric designs. "You have to know how to weave, and then they can be done quickly. You do half and then flip it over to do the mirror image. They were traded everywhere. Now there's modern too, and, sadly, it's the most popular style. I want to pass on the tradition and the traditional style and history of my people. There are less than twenty weavers who still live here in Chimayo."

With this introduction, Trujillo turned to the task at hand—teaching a total novice how to take two skeins of wool and feed them onto two spools by using a spinning wheel as a spool winder.

As she demonstrated what she wanted me to do, I stared at her as though she were Rumpelstiltskin. "I can't do that. I have no skill," I protested, and ten minutes later my skein was wound around two spools and ready for weaving.

I gingerly approached the hundred-year-old loom her grandfather made, and it looked like an elliptical trainer made from wood. The weaver stands while working and operates foot pedals or treadles; it is a physically demanding way to produce art. Trujillo handed me a boat shuttle made by her grandfather and explained that I had to push it from one side to the other to pass the spooled wool through the open shed.

I stumbled and bumbled my way through it but within a few hours of arriving at Centinela, and with a little help from co-weaver Paul, I was the proud owner of a teal and peacock colored standing loom woven bookmark that I will treasure in disbelief for many years. Trujillo is a terrific teacher, highly entertaining, and I will never again look at a weaving the same way because I have some understanding of the skill, patience, artistry, and labor that goes into it.

Trujillo agreed to offer classes to weaving virgins like myself as well as to somewhat experienced or even very experienced weavers. The classes range from a few hours to a day or several days. And even if they don't want to spin and weave, visitors to Centinela can watch demonstrations or buy a vest, shawl, rug, or wall hanging made by masters.

I was feeling proud that I had a taste of weaving and was preparing for my second goal: entering the world of lowriding.

For more information: https://www.chimayoweavers.com or call 505-351-2180 and ask for Emily.

Ridin' high with a low rider in Española.

Cruising through a Northern New Mexico Lowrider Experience

Takeaway: Whether or not you're a car fan, you will love the art and cool of this part of our New Mexican culture.

"I haven't gotten married yet because it's hard for a woman to be in a relationship with someone who shares his attention between her and his car. And my car named Española is pretty demanding," said "Orlie" (Orlando) Martinez.

Española (her firm and curvy body is a 1983 Monte Carlo) is no ordinary car, and Martinez is no ordinary man. He drove up to meet us behind the wheel of Española, and when he alighted, he was sporting a black mustache attached to a black goatee and dressed in a long, robin's egg blue Majestics T-shirt, black Majestics cap, baggy black pants that reached down to his calves, and open-laced high-top black sneakers. In his forty-four years, he has won more than forty awards for his mechanical ability and aesthetics, and he is one of only nine New Mexicans invited to join Majestics, which is the elite club for lowriders. Prospective members are not only required to have super clean, high-quality, traditional lowriders, but they also have to be good human beings who are desirable additions to a family of car lovers who go from showing in the streets to bringing the streets into the shows. Who wouldn't want good-natured, bright, affable, Martinez as part of their car club family?

Upkeep on his car is a part-time job for Martinez. With a polishing rag in hand, he is always on the qui vive for a bit of dust, a drop of rain, or anything that mars the perfect beauty of candy-pattern-painted Española whose name is a tribute to the town where Martinez grew up and learned about the world of lowriding from his uncles. It also happens to be the town that bills itself as "The lowrider capital of the USA," and that's why we went there to meet Martinez.

Before scoring an unforgettable ride in Española, I did a bit of background reading about lowriding. It started in the mid to late 1940's in Los Angeles and continued through the prosperous l950's. Inventive, young Mexican Americans created height-adjustable suspension systems capable of raising and lowering their cars. The style of driving was cruising—"low and slow" is the motto—and the artistically decorated cars became paeans to Hispanic culture, family and faith. The car hobby has only become more elaborate, creative, competitive, and expensive since.

Martinez was drawn to lowriding because, in his words, "I was attracted to the positive energy. I saw it made people happy and am fascinated by how people react to cars. Española is a magnet. She's my jewelry, my art, my work in progress since 1999. I guess you can say it's an obsession, an addiction. The only spot of rust on her is my VIN number."

Lowriding has exploded in popularity all over the world—from Japan to Brazil to the French Riviera. Lowriders pour tremendous amounts of time and money into their gorgeous cars, and Martinez explained why he does it: "I want to inspire people. When I take them for a ride, they laugh, are happy, and enjoy it."

Martinez is not only a car owner and driver, but he also functions as a tour guide to his home turf. "I grew up in the Santa Cruz River Valley right here," he said with pride as we drove towards the historic section of Española, crossing the Rio Grande and passing through groves of cottonwood trees. He pointed out the adobe Mission y Convento, a replica of the original San Gabriel Mission that was built nearby in 1598. We also cruised by Sacred Heart Church, which Martinez said was "where I played bingo with my grandma on Wednesdays. These were the neighborhoods where I cruised with my uncles on the backstreets because we didn't have licenses. And here's where I skipped school and hung out with girls."

Martinez is one of hundreds of lowriders who gather on Good Fridays to "bring out what they've been working on all winter. We're all driving around in our art work. And May 11th has been declared Lowrider Day in New Mexico. There's even a lowrider from the Española-Chimayo area in the Smithsonian. It's called 'Dave's Dream.'"

We headed to the main street to see the murals of local New Mexican culture. They included lowriders, lowrider bicycles, conquistadors, Native American dancers and drummers, a quinceañera (a celebration for a girl's fifteenth birthday), images of Mexico, farming, green chile roasting, and a homage to the city in the words "100 percent Spaña"—Spaña is what locals call Española. Then we cruised through Chimayo in style, admired the famous *santuario*, and came back to Spaña for eats at a local taco shop.

Everywhere we cruised and parked, people of all ages and backgrounds were drawn to Española and asked Martinez about it. They looked at it as though it were the *Mona Lisa*. And as we drove, Martinez confessed that he's a lowrider 24/7, even in his dreams, his house is full of lowrider car parts and wheels, and although he has two formidable speakers and an amp in his car, he doesn't blast them because he "likes to hear the car." He explained some of the wonderful, evocative lowrider terms: bouncing (it's like cruising); hopping (up and down, like a rabbit); surfing or dipping (going over bumps in the road); three-wheeling (the car turns on its side with one wheel raised off the ground); high lockup four link suspension (something incomprehensible that has to be welded and fabricated to do three-wheeling). He also said that the word "lowrider" refers to both the car and the person who owns it.

And then I was treated to the demo I had been waiting for. As I laughed, howled, and squealed with surprise and glee and a little bit of apprehension, Martinez made Española hop, bounce, dance, and then show off with some fancy three-wheeling. Normal cars are not built to do this, and even regular lowriders just go up and down. From the force of all that slamming, twisting, bending, and bouncing, breakage is common, and repairs are costly. But love is blind, Martinez is the coolest, and Española wants to make her lover, riders, and admirers happy.

I can't imagine a more unforgettable, experiential gift to offer friends, family . . . or oneself.

There was one more experience I wanted to have in the area, near Chimayo, and I knew it was a well-guarded local secret.

For more information: "Orlie" Martinez owns several lowriders and can be reached at 505-929-4942.

Santa Cruz Lake.

The Lake I'm Reluctant to Write about Because It's so Beautiful; Can You Keep a Secret?

Takeaway: What you find when you get lost and why getting lost can be a good thing.

Some of the best and most memorable experiences we have had in New Mexico are the result of getting lost, turning onto a random road, or a chance discovery. We used to be so destination oriented; now every trip is a voyage of discovery, a lost and found experience. We love telling people about what we find. But sometimes we stumble upon something so special that we are reluctant to spill the travel beans.

Santa Cruz Lake is one of those secrets. When I tell any of our friends about it, I always start with "I've decided to trust that you will go there yourself or recommend it to a dear friend, but please don't spread it far and wide on social media. Deal?"

We first discovered the lake when we were driving north from Santa Fe, turned right onto NM 503, continued past the Chimayo exit to CR98, saw a sign that said, "Overlook Campground," and turned there. We found ourselves on a sinuous road that offered unexpectedly gorgeous mountain and desert views and culminated in a panoramic vista over a clear blue lake hundreds of feet below. Frankly, we were stunned. We're landlocked in northern New Mexico, and when we visit a lake it's often a sad puddle of its former self because of years of punishing drought. But there it was, unmistakable, below us . . . Santa Cruz Lake in all of its shimmering glory. It was blessed with water, while many of the sister lakes thirsted.

After we had finished inhaling the beauty, we got back on 503 and continued for 5.5 miles, past the picturesque rural church, ranch lands and cattle of Cundiyo, to Santa Cruz Dam Road (CR98A). Although there was no sign for the Santa Cruz Recreation Area, the road took us there.

We parked in the upper lot and had a snack at a picnic table under a sun-protecting canopy, with a different, closer vantage point over the lake than the overlook had provided. It was as though we had seen a filmic long shot, and now it was a medium shot. After lunch, we drove down and parked at the lake itself. Richard Tafoya and Ernie Trujillo, two friendly fishermen, were carrying out their day's catch of rainbow trout, and said they had reached their limit of five each. They described to us in mouth-watering detail how they planned to cook them. They suggested we walk the Laguna Vista Trail around the lake, which starts near the restrooms. We always take suggestions from locals when they offer them.

We were lucky to be there on a weekday when there were very few visitors. Laguna Vista is the perfect dirt trail for all skill levels—especially for folks who are craving a view of water and a shoreline. The path slopes up gently and all along the trail we had panoramas of the lake. We listened to the wind whispering through cottonwood trees, enjoyed the secluded areas with shade, and discovered that there were several side trails that led right down to the lapping water.

We arrived at a series of embedded log steps that led to the top of a hill for an overview over the lake and two kayakers who had it to themselves. It was tranquil for them and us as well. We looked up at a hawk circling overhead. The only other sound besides our breathing was the call of the birds.

The next time we see fishermen with their catch, we'll remember to ask them for recommendations. And the next time we go for a drive, we'll remember that the land will reveal its secrets if we allow ourselves to wander on roads less taken and even embrace getting lost.

Another time we got lost, and we ended up in Los Luceros, a historic site with a surprising history.

For more information: https://www.blm.gov/visit/santa-cruz-lake-recreation-area

Parking is $5.00.

Los Luceros Historic Site in winter.

Los Luceros

A Spanish Colonial Site that Heralds Its LGBTQ+ Heritage

Takeaway: History is much less straight than you thought.

If the Rio Grande could talk it would tell us about Indigenous people who sustained themselves along its banks for millennia. At least 700 years ago, the Tewa village of Phiogeh was established, and farmers grew the three sisters—corn, beans, and squash—as well as cotton and amaranth.

In 1598, the controversial conquistador Juan de Oñate led an expedition of Spanish colonists who settled in the area. In 1680, history changed forever when Popé from nearby Ohkay Owingeh organized a Pueblo revolt that drove the Spanish out of New Mexico. Twelve years later they came back to reconquer the land, and the Spanish Crown made a land grant of 51,000 acres that included the Los Luceros property. The native people were paid to dig an *acequia* system (irrigation ditches); the "salary" was parcels of their own land that had been taken from them. As a sign says in the hacienda (ranch), "The first European colonizers to usurp the land from Indian Tewa people was the Sebastian Martín Serrano family in 1703." Although Phiogeh lies silent and unexcavated under the site today, the *acequia madre* or mother ditch the inhabitants built is still being used.

In the eighteenth century, the massive adobe hacienda was the heart of the Sebastián Martín land grant. In the nineteenth century, the hacienda got a Territorial-style makeover and shone as the architectural gem you see today. The original eighteenth-century church was destroyed by a terrible flood and rebuilt by the Ortiz family—the owners at that time—and named for La Sagrada Familia, the Holy Family, to give thanks for having survived the flood. Inside the church, visitors admire the *retablos* (paintings of saints) and the information posted under each of them. Some of my personal favorites are Saint Gertrude, the patron saint of cats, travelers, gardeners, and those with mental illness; and Saint Clara de Assisi, the patron saint of eye disease, TV, good weather, and extrasensory perception. The altar piece and small statues of saints were created by a *santera* (a woman who makes religious images) named Clare Villa.

In the words of Instructional Coordinator Carlyn Stewart, "We have Indigenous and Spanish influences here, and also wealthy white women who came and contributed to the site in the twentieth century." By the early 1930s Boston heiress Mary Wheelwright (who later founded the Wheelwright Museum of the American Indian in Santa Fe) completed the purchase of Los Luceros Ranch, which had fallen into disrepair. "Many visitors come here today because of Mary Wheelwright. They admire that she came out alone from Boston and contributed so much toward saving the property. Sometimes they expect the entire site narrative to be devoted to her. But we try to highlight all of the other historical narratives here as well," Stewart explained. "There are so many of them."

The hacienda, eighteenth-century chapel, Victorian cottage, carriage house, and guesthouse have been lovingly restored. A free self-guiding map indicates the sites and buildings, but our imaginations filled the land with illustrious visitors who walked the land from the time of Mary Wheelwright onward. Renowned artist Georgia O'Keeffe, Santa Fe painter Olive Rush, Mabel Dodge Luhan, and Maria Chabot (a rancher, advocate for Native Americans, and close friend of O'Keeffe) topped the list of women. As for men, D. H. Lawrence admired the scenic and historic site, and Leonard Bernstein filled the two-story hacienda with piano music. When Mary Wheelwright lived in the hacienda, Hastiin Klah occupied the room next to hers. He was a Nádleehi (someone who is born male and has a feminine nature and demeanor), as well as a Diné Medicine Man and weaver. Recently a Navajo lecturer at Los Luceros said that a Nádleehi was considered an elevated person and was revered.

Signage around the property reveals that in the early twentieth century, Los Luceros residents defied cultural norms of gender, identity, and sexuality. Today it's a draw for the LGBTQ+ community, just as the site also attracts people of Spanish and Indigenous heritage and those who are interested in architecture and history. And wherever visitors wander or explore, beauty accompanies them throughout their visit.

The first time we entered the property, which is north of Española and near Alcalde, we drove down a dirt road bordered by cottonwood trees that extended their branches in greeting. Several short trails (about three quarters of a mile each) led us through the bosque (woods), along the river, past the pond, through the apple orchards (where visitors can pick their own heritage apples during the fall harvest festival), and across the fields and to the farmyard. I was delighted to meet some very friendly churro sheep, curious goats, and a persnickety donkey.

Walking in the fresh air made us hungry, and we had a choice of picnic tables near the visitors' center or ingenious benches along the river that transformed into small picnic tables. For our Bosque banquet, we chose to dine near the river with the Sangre de Cristo Mountains in the distance. Fernando Olea, 2022 James Beard award winner for Best Chef: Southwest and owner of Sazón Restaurant in Santa Fe, was inspired by his own prior visit to Los Luceros and provided our take-out lunch. His culinary homage to the historic site illustrated why he was named 2019 Restaurateur of the Year by the New Mexico Restaurant Association.

The tribute meal began with a delicate Sopa de Milpa ("farm soup") made of succulent corn kernels, poblano peppers, squash and squash blossoms and bits of zucchini floating in a homemade vegetable broth. It was followed by a Rack of Churro Lamb surrounded by a colorful burst of silky sweet potatoes, swirls of shaved beets, crispy white rice noodles and a splash of persimmon reduction. The entrée was served with chef's original apricot-base mole. "Everything is made from local ingredients that would have been traditionally available at the hacienda," chef explained, "except for the rice noodles and sweet potatoes." I'll bet my shaved beets that the wealthy farm owners never had such inventive cuisine.

For dessert, Olea tipped his cowboy hat to little Natilla, the friendliest of the churro sheep at Los Luceros. He prepared traditional New Mexican Natilla—milk custard with roasted pine nuts, caramelized apples, meringue, and a sprig of fresh mint. I am sure I saw the sun winking at us as we savored the last bit of our riparian repast.

Back in our car, we were listening to 1960 Ray Charles rendition of "Georgia On My Mind," and we started talking about Georgia O'Keeffe and decided to head next to the place where her spirit still hovers.

For more information: https://www.newmexicoculture.org/historic-sites/los-luceros; 505-476-1165

Nearby places locals like to eat:

Sugar's BBQ: https://www.facebook.com/BBQSugars/

El Parasol at Ohkay Owingeh Pueblo: https://elparasol.com/Española-north/

The precise places where Georgia O'Keeffe painted at Ghost Ranch.

Ghost Ranch

On the Trail of Georgia O'Keeffe, the Triassic Coelophysis, and Caribbean Food

Takeaway: Stories, legends, history, and good guides can greatly enhance the quality of your travels.

Sometimes, I get a yen to go on the trail of famous people, especially wildly talented and groundbreaking ones like Georgia O'Keeffe. We've seen her dressed and undressed in hauntingly beautiful photographs by her husband Alfred Stieglitz, we've wondered about the austere looking woman who dressed in black and rode on the back of a motorcycle, and we've been drawn into her vibrant, energetic, unconventional vision of New Mexico's singular landscapes, flowers, and sun-bleached bones. She was the most famous woman painter of her era, and the years have burnished her reputation as a groundbreaking modernist artist. I wanted to know why the woman who was born in Wisconsin in 1887 decided to live in New Mexico and what drew her here.

In 1934, Georgia O'Keeffe arrived in her Model A Ford at Ghost Ranch in Abiquiu, New Mexico. When she beheld the spectacular beauty of the red, ochre, gray, and white cliffs, and the impeccable blue skies splattered with dramatic patterns of lily-white clouds, she declared that "this is where I wanted to live." She rented a cabin, then bought a house, and created 120 paintings of the landscape in what she called her "backyard." She gathered and painted the bones of long-gone animals and considered them to be living objects filled with vibrancy. For the woman who has become one of the most beloved female artists in the world, Ghost Ranch was visually, spiritually, and inspirationally home.

We decided to spend a full day there, experiencing a few of the numerous unique and exciting experiences provided for visitors. The Landscape Tour offers the biggest "wow" factor. A guide named Karen drove us in a van to the actual sites O'Keeffe painted. When she held up replicas of the paintings, we saw the specific dead cedar O'Keeffe depicted in Gerald's Tree (1937) and the hills, valleys, and majestic Cerro Pedernal Mountain that haven't changed since she immortalized them on canvas. Karen was a knowledgeable and unabashed Georgia fan, and when we weren't gaping at the paintings that came alive before our eyes, we learned about the artist's ideas, personal life, and work.

By the end of the tour, we knew more about Georgia's past, and we took the history tour to find out about the checkered, colorful past of Ghost Ranch itself—which goes way back to a period 10,000 years ago when hunter-gatherers first roamed the land. It is thought that Native people found gigantic animal bones from the Triassic Period and believed there were fearsome monsters in the hills. After Spanish settlers arrived in the sixteenth century, Indigenous people told them about the monsters, and no one made a permanent settlement in the area until two horse-rustling brothers hit upon a brilliantly perverse scheme. They stole horses but spread and amplified the monster story so people were too frightened to come and investigate them. One thieving brother eventually killed the other, and the remaining one was hanged from a tree by a posse from nearby Abiquiu. The next incarnation was a dude ranch for some of the richest people in the country. And because we wanted to know if there are ghosts at ghost ranch and who the illustrious visitors were, we had to sign up for the thirty-five-minute walking tour.

We were intrigued to learn that the New Mexico state fossil, the carnivorous and perhaps plumed Coelophysis, was found on the Ghost Ranch land. A 2.2-mile paleontology hike, led by an exuberant guide, went to the actual site where hundreds of Triassic skeletons from 200 to 220 million years ago were uncovered, quarried, and protected in enormous plaster blocks. Along the way, we learned about the plants, geology, and terrain as it existed when dinosaurs roamed what was then lush land.

At the end of the tour, we were greeted by Gretchen Gurtler, the paleontologist who helms the Ruth Hall Museum of Paleontology on the property. She showed us a huge, quarried block that contains several Coelophysis specimens and explained that only one third of it has been painstakingly excavated. She guided our wide-eyed looks to the bones of a strange Triassic armored swimming reptile that are still embedded in it.

Having traveled into the remote past, we then ventured across vast culinary distances when we hungrily unwrapped exotic picnic food we had brought along from Jambo Café in Santa Fe, where Executive Chef Ahmed Obo from Kenya is the king of international cuisine. He serves up Caribbean cooking with strong roots in Africa and the southwest. Obo's hearty, complex rendition of island goat stew with succulent bone-in chunks of goat was poured over a bed of perfectly cooked, fluffy yellow couscous. It was followed by a burst of flavors in our three-dish selection from the combo plate: Moroccan lamb stew with raisins and apricots over curried couscous, Ethiopian chickpea stew, and golden-hued chicken curry. The first two were Obo's delightful spin on some traditional out-of-Africa flavors.

We shared the small cornmeal plantain crab cakes with Caribbean spice sauce and a surprising chermoula-rubbed salmon topped with shaved swirls of crispy sweet potato and mango mustard dressing. We happily dipped the harissa lemon fries in our sauces. We sampled the award-winning curried black bean and sweet potato soup and savored the colorful and flavorful curried chicken salad wrap with the pineapple, peanuts, celery, and raisins bursting out of the homemade roti.

When we had finished and packed away the remains of our leisurely lunch, we headed to the Welcome Center to see the two free, excellent videos that round out a Ghost Ranch experience. In the room with us were two women with three kids, and the minute the videos had finished the women took the trio on a self-guided Scavenger Hunt around the property. "We couldn't get the kids excited about Georgia O'Keeffe, but you bet we'll be back for the tour when they're in school again," one of the women confided as she headed out the door.

In the gift shop, we met a woman from Abiquiu who asked if we had ever taken a road trip to Velarde and Pilar. We told her we had and had vivid memories of it.

For more information: https://www.ghostranch.org; 505-685-1000

Book the day tours in advance as they fill up quickly.

Ghost Ranch also offers multiday and week-long workshops for hands-on art creation (i.e., painting, jewelry making, mosaics, metal sculpture, photography, and writing).

For local take-out food, visit Bode's (pronounced Bode-ees) General Store in nearby Abiquiu. Besides food, the store is a one-of-a-kind shopping experience: https://bodes.com; 505-685-4422.

To visit Georgia O'Keeffe's home and studio in Abiquiu, reserve well in advance: https://www.okeeffemuseum.org/homes/.

Preparing to raft the Rio Grande.

Slow Road Trip with a Gourmet Picnic, Scenery, Hiking, a Winery, and Fruit Nirvana

Takeaway: If you're willing to set out without a fixed destination, even a short, half-day road trip can lead to multiple unexpected discoveries.

It was Friday, and the sun was smiling on our favorite day of the week to drive north from Santa Fe on the Low Road to Taos. We passed through Velarde, where we would later return, and saw several buses and vans carrying excited visitors who were embarking on guided river rafting trips along the Rio Grande. At turn-in spots, they were outfitted and given instructions before they gripped their paddles and hoped for the thrill and adrenaline rush of rapids. It's a wonderful watery way to experience the mighty river.

We drove north for about thirteen miles along curvy roads with the river, wineries, and orchards providing a bountiful backdrop. And then it felt like a 3D ride with mountains popping up and appearing all around us. When we arrived at the tiny village of Pilar—identified by a casual eatery and gift shop—we turned left and entered the Orilla Verde Recreation Area that is part of the Rio Grande National Recreation Area. It's a popular site for camping and picnicking, and it's easy to see why locals and exploring tourists are attracted to the peaceful spots along the banks of the Rio Grande.

But it wasn't always peaceful there. It was home to Jicarilla Apache residents before the Spanish came to settle northern New Mexico. In 1680, there was a Pueblo Revolt, and the Spanish were driven out. In 1692 they returned to reconquer the land, and in 1694 the conquistador Diego de Vargas burned the Apache village that was situated where Pilar is today.

We were looking for a less populated spot and found it at Lone Juniper site, where a picnic table awaited us on the shore of the river, in the shade. A row of

Canada geese swam by. They were followed by local Katrina Kaeck who paddled along on a raft with Gnarly, her beloved shelter dog, and I think the pooch waved at us.

People customarily don't think of barbecue as fine dining, but that's a perfect description for our picnic banquet from The Ranch House in Santa Fe. We began with crispy taquitos enveloping a texturally rich fusion of robust smoked turkey, soft cream cheese, corn, and chile. After a refreshing salad of smoked chicken and a Tex-Mexy mixture of beans, corn, and Tillamook Sharp Cheddar, we sampled three delicate tacos crowned with sautéed salmon and remoulade and served with green chile slaw.

Ranch House fans are mad about the ribs and brisket, but we're more the chicken and buffalo types with a few dalliances that include pulled pork. The Half Chicken Plate was brined in-house and finished in the smoker. It begged to be eaten with our three favorite sides: sassy waffle fries, cornbread made edgy with green chile, and slowly baked beans, the ultimate barbecue comfort food. The pulled pork sandwich was topped with green chile slaw and served on a brioche bun, and The Ranch House thoughtfully packed the meat separate from the buns and sides, so there was no wilting or sogging—even later on, when we got home.

After lunch, we headed back towards Pilar and stopped for an impromptu hike on the La Senda del Medio Trail, which is part of the Pilar Campground. The well-maintained and easy dirt trail wound though land that is rich in boulder-sized volcanic rock, sage, juniper, pine, and colonies of cactus. It offered views over the river and the surrounding mountains. We started heading down into a canyon when the skies opened up and it began to pour. The hike was cut short, but we decided we'd definitely return.

The rain stopped and so did we at the Black Mesa Winery in Velarde, which hosts a mini farmers' market with live marimba music every Friday from 3 to 6 p.m. Local vendors sell fresh farm produce and handmade crafts and it's a perfect place to sit in the shade of a tree, order wine or cider and schmooze with locals from the valley. Paul sat next to two oenophiles in cowboy hats and boots, and the three of them had a heady discussion about the poor quality of wine in ancient Rome and how vast Rome's distribution channels were in Europe. I, on the other hand, listened to a harpist in a flowing, flowery, ankle-length dress, who said she channeled angelic music when she played.

Black Mesa is a working winery, and guests are invited to walk through the vineyards and to do a tasting in the barrel room. Insiders know that behind the winery is a petroglyph trail—where ancient hands chiseled mysterious images in stone—and a homemade labyrinth which visitors can walk while pondering or emptying their minds—depending on their disposition at the time of their visit. As we strolled among the Montepulciano de Abruzzo grapes on the vine, a couple was arguing loudly behind us. They apologized for disturbing us, and I saw how unhappy they both were. "May I suggest something to you?" I asked. When they nodded in the affirmative, I told them that perhaps they could find a solution by walking the labyrinth. Neither of them had ever had the experience, and they concurred that they would try it. I don't know what happened after that, but I was relieved to see that even their talking about the labyrinth seemed to have a calming effect on them.

We ended our afternoon at the Fruit Basket stand in Velarde, where the Velarde family has been farming since 1598. Fifteen generations back, their ancestor came to New Mexico with the Juan de Oñate expedition and served as the conquistador's secretary. When he saw the valley he said, "I'm tired of conquering, can I stay here?" The Spanish king granted him permission.

The Fruit Basket is our favorite place to stock up on seasonally grown, organic plums, peaches, cherries, apricots, pears, melons, and apples from their three orchards. We also loaded our basket with preserves, salsas, blue corn *atole* and flour for pancakes, and vegetarian tamales.

It didn't take us long to get back to Santa Fe, and we marveled that without ever rushing and without any prior planning, we'd enjoyed a gorgeous drive, a gourmet picnic by the river, a hike, a stop for vino and a walk through a vineyard, shopping in a local, organic market, and meeting locals. It was so New Mexico.

For more information: Orilla Verde Recreation Area: https://www.blm.gov/visit/orilla-verde-recreation-area

Fruit Basket Velarde: 505-852-2310

Facebook page: https://www.facebook.com/Velarde.Orchards/

Black Mesa Winery: 505-852-2820

A trusted colleague recommends Los Rios River Runners for rafting: https://www.losriosriverrunners.com.

Meet the People

While visiting the historic site of Los Luceros, we asked Carlyn Steward, the instruction coordinator, to tell us what she loves most about the property.

"Spring here has the apple blossoms and perfect picnic water. In the summer, everything is green and lush. There are a lot of wildlife—bears, mountain lions, deer. The monarch butterflies are usually here in September. That's also when we have the Fall Harvest and Apple Picking. You just pay the admission, and you can pick a bag of heritage apples. Fall is all about the leaves. In winter we get the sandhill cranes and birding is spectacular. *Farolitos* [lanterns created with candles in paper bags] line the walkways down to the river and flameless ones are on historic buildings."

At Fort Union, we walked by a man doing preservation work on a nineteenth-century structure. We began to talk, and we wondered if his ancestors had told him anything about the area.

"When I was young, my grandpa told me stories about fighting Indians. He said they used to go up into the mountains to gather wood and they fought with Indians. His own brother was killed by an Indian arrow as he stood by a cross. I guess it was a misunderstanding over the fire wood. But when you think about it, it was the Indians' land."

My modern sensibility was ruffled when our guide told us something about the wives of the soldiers at Fort Union.

"The soldiers were very lonely. They had to get special permission to bring their wives here who then had to work as laundresses. Each laundress cleaned the clothes of nineteen soldiers."

When we parked our car to walk to a trailhead along the Jemez River, we met a man whose job was stocking the river with little cutthroat trout and whose mind was philosophical.

"We should all be stocking the river of life for the future with our words, thoughts, and deeds."

We got more than organic fruit from the fields at The Fruit Basket stand in Velarde; we also got the recipe owner June Velarde uses to make posole.

"Put the posole in a pan on the stove covered with water. Cook at medium heat for forty-five minutes. Drain and rinse until the water is clear. Put it back on the stove with more water until it opens like popcorn. It should not be mushy."

When we talk to locals, we often get invaluable tips, like this one from a woman we met while we were driving to Penasco.

"You must stop there for a photo at one of the world's smallest casinos. It's the size of a gas station."

We always seek out Park Rangers when they are nearby, as they are an invaluable source of insight and information. When we asked one if he had seen any elk at Valles Caldera, he gave us a thoughtful reply.

"You probably won't see any elk today because hunting season ended yesterday, and the elk are wary now. They heard the hunters' shots or the echo of shots. They could feel the vibrations. They've gone up into the forest and they may come down at sunrise or sunset. There are also animal predators out, so they don't go out into the open fields during the day . . ."

He also told us about some of the history of Valles Caldera:

"There used to be cowboys and ranchers here . . . originally they had sheep but with the World War II development of synthetics it knocked out the wool market, and they started with cows . . ."

We loved the response we got when we asked a woman who was fishing at Santa Cruz Lake what the best day of the week was for visiting.

"For visiting most places, everyone who comes to Santa Fe is a little bit psychic, so they can tune in to when it's best to go. Weekdays, and certain hours are best for avoiding peak traffic and a lot people."

One afternoon, when the trees at the Santa Fe Ski Basin were wearing their golden autumnal leaves, we met a volunteer who was collecting trash in a forested area he loved.

"I have a bum knee, but I want to help the forest service out. . . . You might want to look up now. See how when the wind blows the trees begin to dance?"

A father and son were gathering red willow by a stream near Abiquiu, and they said they were using it to decorate their hand-made wooden furniture. As we spoke, they also told us more about themselves and their lives.

Father: "We raise cattle—an Angus-Simmental mix. The calves are so big that the heifers have trouble birthing and we sometimes lose a calf."

Son: "I want to be a rancher and stay here. It's isolating, and kids my age want to leave. I mostly have older friends, and that's okay with me."

How to Draw Your Viewer into Your Story

Sometimes it's overwhelming to sift through social media photos. Sure, the baby donkey is cute, and the cocktails were fabulous—but do we have to see twenty-five imperceptible variations of the same thing!? This is where story enters the picture—*your* story. How do you create unique images that grab and keep viewers' attention? How do you select diverse photos—even if they come from the same destination—that engage your audience in the experience you had?

Fortunately, New Mexico generously provides you with many opportunities to shoot, select, and then invite your audience in. Because of the quality of light, the varied and evocative landscapes, and photogenic people, "the Land of Enchantment" has a long history as a haven for artists. Following the suggestions in this book, you will not only meet some of them but have opportunities to learn from and work with them. So, using your experiences with artists, how can you most effectively and artistically invite your viewer to come along?

Sometimes you may be inside a studio (as with painter Linda Storm); at an outdoor space (with collage artist Darlene McElroy); or in plein air (with "cosmic architect" James Jereb). The lighting situations vary, and each presents a different challenge. There may be low lighting, or it may come from mixed sources—for example, fluorescent, daylight, and even your own flash. Study the light before you take a photo. Where is the light source and where is it striking? How about the shadows?

By repositioning your subject or bouncing illumination with a flash unit or reflector, you can emphasize what you determine as important. You can create mystery with shadow. Light and dark (*chiaroscuro* in classical Italian painting) can also be used to create the illusion of depth.

I find that lenses you might think of for outdoors have application in these situations as well: wide angle (to capture and establish the surrounding context) and telephoto (for extreme close-up detail) help tell the story. Both are available for phone cameras. And I've used them when photographing jewelers, clay artists

Emily Trujillo at one of her family's hundred-year-old looms.

painting small seed pots, and with miniature glass blowers to show where they are, what their working environment is like, and how skilled and detailed their art is.

It's important to find the focus of the story that *you* are in, regardless of whether you are an active participant or an interested observer.

Remember to tell a story (using the establishing image, medium, and detailed close-up techniques mentioned in the photo tips of the Southeast section on p. 343) and be totally in the moment—seeing everything around you and selecting the details that draw your eye and will tell *your* story. This hyper-awareness will not only help you create better images but also improve the quality of your travels in general for lasting memories.

For the story about traditional weaving with Emily Trujillo, I wanted the weaver at the center of the story. I chose a low angle on the loom with the threads leading the viewer's eyes toward the weaver at work. The loom functioned as both a framing device and provided context. Lighting was a combination of available light coming through a window plus that from overhead fixtures.

One of the more difficult things to achieve is naturalness, documenting a people moment unimpeded by stiff posing. Featuring a person in your photographs is a gift to you from that person. When I've caught a truly candid moment, I always approach the person directly afterward to ask permission to use the image already taken, then I shoot another photo. Invariably, they'll pose rigidly with a fixed smile the second time. I have never used one of those. Another way is to involve your subject in conversation. The result is a natural expression at a particular moment, which gives sincere emotion to the image and allows the viewer to feel they are right there with you at that time. There is real viewer involvement as they are engaged, pulled into a story and, in effect, share the captured moment with you. When the subject of your photo remains cognizant of the camera, I ask Judie to engage them in conversation. This switches their concentration away from me as photographer and takes the pressure off them to "perform." If the artist is working intensely, I let their focus shine through and, if not, I'll tell a joke to evoke a laugh—anything to avoid that dreaded frozen antique tintype appearance. Don't be afraid to ask your subject to move to a different angle or where the light is better.

Of course, all of this applies to anyone you photograph, not just artists. Remember that, when photographing children, always ask their parents' permission first.

Once you have an interesting subject, the best lighting, and a series of photos that show the progression of the experience, your work will intrigue, amuse, and invite the viewer in to your story.

Finally, never let photography interfere with your having fun. The photo is for everyone, but the moment is for you. Life comes first.

Part Three

NORTHEAST

A *major domo* cleaning an acequia, Mora.

Introduction

It's said that everything is a trade-off, and when we went to Angel Fire in the off-season, we experienced neither the bonhomie of all the skiers who converge there in the winter nor the frolicking families that choose it as their playground in the summer. Many restaurants were shuttered for the season, and there was no raucous nightlife.

What we did get was the joy of discovery and the feeling that we had it all to ourselves. Everything we did felt special and unique. Our days and nights were structured by what sang to us, and we never had to stand in line or call in a reservation.

We stayed in Angel Fire for ten days and fanned out from there. We visited an authentic, undoctored, wild western town where we could still see the bullet holes from gunfights in the tin ceiling of a bar and the remains of the nearby stone jail where sodden gunslingers had plenty of time to sober up. It was hard to believe that this charming, sleepy town was once one of the bawdiest and baddest in the nation. We discovered a ten-acre art installation created with found objects and one artist's vision. We saw boxes of Kleenex for vets at a war memorial and talked with a man who had fought in the Vietnam war and had never spoken about his experience at length before. At a wildlife preserve, we saw the ruts from covered wagons that carried merchants and merchandise along the Santa Fe Trail in the 1800s and then got a ranger-led tour to a stunning geological surprise. We hiked in rare high-altitude wetlands. And we picnicked by a bubbling mountain stream in the shade of dramatic stone cliffs that towered hundreds of feet above us.

We took other northeastern day trips from Santa Fe. At a nineteenth-century fort, we learned about the women who lived there and why they were accused of being too raucous and about the terribly misguided policies that resulted in the building of forts to fight the infamous Indian Wars. Then we went to an almost-ghost town where the soldiers went to decompress, drink, gamble, go AWOL, and get syphilis—which was the principal illness treated at the fort infirmary.

We were the only ones on a tour with a historian, and together we climbed a mountain pass that was the site of a Civil War battle called the Gettysburg of the West. Was the name accurate? We talked about it over gourmet takeout from—really—a gas station.

Whether you have an afternoon, weekend, or week-long stretch of free time, you'll want to explore and enjoy the little-known treasures and pleasures of New Mexico's northeast.

Whatville experience, Angel Fire.

Art in the Middle of Nowhere

Takeaway: You unlock surprises when you simply ask, "What's that?"

Every day we were in Angel Fire, we drove by a far distant array of brightly colored structures surrounded by empty fields. Every day one of us said, "What's that?" or "I wonder what that is." When we ask that question and shrug, nothing happens. When we ask and follow up, something happens.

After about four days, we found a road that led to the mysterious colors of Whatville, a ten-acre installation of Outsider Art. Generally speaking, insider art is work that appears in galleries, is often considered fine art, has commercial potential, and appeals to contemporary taste. In contrast, Outsider Art, or Raw Art, is most often done by untrained or non-mainstream artists and isn't mediated by demands of current aesthetics and marketplace. I have been collecting Outsider Art for most of my adult life, ever since I first encountered it at the Musée d'art Brut in Lausanne, Switzerland, which was founded by artist Jean Dubuffet.

In the middle of a vacant, weed-strewn field, we parked near a huge sign that said "Welcome" and another, on an orange building and written in bold green, pink, blue, and red lettering, read "Stay Lost." I loved that, as sometimes getting lost is a prelude to adventure.

We walked into the site—which is always open and free—and followed a dirt path that revealed the evocative hulks of rusted cars, customized old trucks and cars, a plane propellor, the supports for tipis made of branches, boldly colored wooden spirit sticks and arrows, wooden sculptures of seated figures, a manual typewriter, a chandelier hanging in an empty wooden barn. Every time we thought "what is this?" we were going deeper into the experience of Whatville, and we were the only ones there except for the prairie dogs who squeaked in the distance and the hawks that circled overhead. The path led to an American flag made of dots, a snowmobile, antlers, ramshackle buildings with signs that read "Ballou dog" and "Love."

Whatville detail.

Intrigued, we came back the next night when we saw purple, orange, red, and green neon lights in the direction of Whatville. Elements of the collection were illuminated, and, as we walked under a full moon, the site became a dramatic living theater set. The play was our own response to the experience.

Texas-born Ray Renfroe is the sole creator of Whatville. His background is in carpentry and home building, and he has no art training. "I started working on it five years ago," he told me during a long phone conversation. "I brought in little tipis and rocks to carry on the Native American presence here in the Moreno Valley. It used to be part of Taos Pueblo, and the flute player Robert Miraval said men came here to prove their manhood. They circled three trees that grew out of a rock. Those trees have died since, but they marked the place where the men turned around to go back to their pueblo. It would have been dangerous to proceed any farther into Cimarron and the Plains because of hostile Indian tribes. These were the last peaceful mountains they encountered. At Whatville, I honor them."

The tipi at the entrance to Whatville is Renfroe's story of creation. And the typewriter signifies the written story of mankind. Renfroe grew pensive when he spoke about the nighttime illumination at his installation. "I had a tragic loss of my seventeen-year-old son Cody, and at night I light Whatville up for him. He was such an inspiring person, and I wanted to inspire others. I was always fascinated by the night sky, and I want people to share that and to see the good and be inspired by Cody."

Because of visitors like us, who kept asking, "What's this?" Renfroe named his site Whatville. And his dream to is have other artists displaying their work there while musicians play. Maybe there could even be food vendors. Renfroe hopes the town of Angel Fire realizes that Whatville could benefit them too.

None of the folks we met in Angel Fire knew about Whatville, and we kept asking until we found a woman who told us about Ray Renfroe. Once we had his name, we persisted until we connected to him. Our phone call was inspiring and when we told artist friends about him, several said it bolstered them in their belief that you don't have to follow the pack on the path to creation. And they loved the idea that the simple act of asking "What's that?" can lead to Whatville and other unplanned discoveries and adventures.

Another of these chance discoveries in Angel Fire also turned out to be much more than we expected. We thought it was a simple monument, but it was a doorway into a haunting world for those that inhabited it.

For more information: Whatville is located at the intersection of Camino Grande and Mountainview. At the time of this writing, there is no website or phone number. Renfroe suggests you just show up.

Vietnam Veterans' Memorial State Park.

Vietnam Veterans Memorial State Park

A Meaningful Destination about a Terrible War

Takeaway: It can be deep and powerful to learn history from the mouths of those who lived it.

In the past, I met veterans who returned, broken in spirit and body, from combat in Vietnam. When they descended from their transport planes, antiwar protesters spat at them, hurled insults, and blamed them for the war and for crimes that others had committed. Many had been drafted and were shipped off to Vietnam as teenagers in an unpopular war. They were not honored for their service or recognized for their sacrifices. It took us many years, as a country, to realize that they didn't start the war, and a shocking number were suffering miserably from afflictions like PTSD and Agent Orange exposure. Some killed themselves, became homeless, wandered the land like hungry, lonely ghosts. Some survived and even thrived, but none forgot what happened in Southeast Asia half a century ago.

Most people who drive by Vietnam Veterans Memorial State Park on a hill in Angel Fire think it is just a stark, abstract, white sculpture that rolls like a frozen wave and juts upward toward the sky. But when we stopped, slowed down and entered the site, we realized it's a memorial, a highly evocative museum with unexpected artifacts, an event space, and a place to meet Vietnam vets and those who lost dear ones in a hellish war. It's one way to honor those who were never honored. Here's what one of them had to say . . . through his tears.

"My name is David Powell." He sat on a bench and introduced his wife, Wilma. "Are you a vet?" I inquired. He nodded, and as we spoke, he pulled up a Google Earth image of where he was in Vietnam. He was Air Force. His family had fought in the Revolutionary War, War of 1812, Civil War, and WWII, and with that ancestry it was logical that he volunteered in Vietnam, the Gulf War, Iraq, and

Afghanistan. “I had to do it,” he explained. “When he left, I was left alone with a five-month-old baby,” Wilma added.

As he spoke, his eyes grew misty, and his mind carried him back to Vietnam. “We had zero news of antiwar protests in the USA or Agent Orange exposure in the foliage. But I don’t talk about it because unlike others I came home with both legs and with a reel-to-reel tape of Otis Redding.” He paused for a moment before realizing, “This is more than I have ever spoken about Vietnam.”

“He lost his hearing,” said Wilma, “but he wouldn’t claim it at the VA until 2017; he felt that others had it so much worse.” David looked at Wilma, sighing, “My wife is a veteran too for what she went through with me.”

One of the veterans who never made it home was Lieutenant David Westphall, who was killed in action in May 1968. At a time when supporting troops was unpopular, his parents Jean and Dr. Victor Westphall started a memorial to honor their son, the sixteen men who died with him, and the 58,000 members of the military who perished in the war. It was the first major memorial to honor Vietnam vets, and it inspired the creation of the memorial in Washington, DC. In 1994, Doctor Westphall took a handful of dirt from Angel Fire and scattered it at the ambush site where his son lost his life. And he brought back earth to mix it with New Mexico soil. Today Lieutenant Westphall’s parents are buried on the grounds of his memorial.

Visitors are greeted by a Huey (an actual helicopter used in the war) next to a peaceful flower garden, where running water cascades downhill over rocks to settle in a pool. Benches provide places to sit and contemplate. Visitors stop in front of a bronze statue of a kneeling soldier who writes a letter to his parents, but his haunted, blank eyes look away from the page. The words on the bronze plaque that accompanies the statue explain what it was like for the soldier to write the letter, and how much he couldn’t tell them. “Dear Mom and Dad are written. Now what? He can’t tell them what he is seeing, he can’t tell them what he is doing, his eyes see a foreign land, his heart sees the other side of the world.”

A concrete walkway is lined with bricks that are dedicated to fallen soldiers, and one has even been placed for Pepper Scout, a dog. Nearby, a woman sits on a bench, quietly wiping away her tears.

Outside of the museum, leaves on an aspen tree fluttered sadly, reminding us that nature is life, and war is death. Inside the museum, a bulletin board invites visitors to leave Post-it Notes for those who served.

The museum displays include striking photos of soldiers tenderly examining a local Vietnamese child, dog tags worn by soldiers, canteens, a K-bar fighting and utility knife, a tropical survival kit with anti-malaria pills, water purification tablet, anti-fungal ointment, medals, Vietnamese currency, military uniforms, POW bracelets of those who came home, a Vietnamese zip gun, stick grenades made of wood, and information about Hueys that once triggered either anxiety or relief at the arrival of supplies. A breastplate rests near a flute and a medicine pouch—a reminder that 42,000 Native Americans served in the military in Vietnam. The objects evoke a war half a world and half a century away.

I had never heard of Montagnard friendship bracelets before; they were gifts from Indigenous Vietnamese in the Central Highlands to US fighters. It was considered a great honor when they were given to US military. Not far away is a pair of Ho Chi Minh's sandals that were made from recycled tires and worn in combat. Although vilified in the United States during the war, he was a revolutionary, politician, poet, and iconic North Vietnamese military leader. The former capital of defeated South Vietnam was named in his honor: Ho Chi Minh City.

A movie room is lined with chairs. A box of Kleenex sits on each chair, a clear indication of the grief that viewers feel and release. The museum is a place where veterans can connect, feel safe, and be understood. And we can try to comprehend what they have suffered.

The monument provides dignity and recognition to the US forces who fought in the Vietnam War. When we were in Ho Chi Minh City (Saigon) in Vietnam we visited The War Remnants Museum about what people we met referred to as "The American War." It is one of the most popular museums in the country for tourists from around the world, and I found it to be terribly disquieting. Exhibits dealt with the horrors endured by Vietnamese soldiers and civilians—the effects of Agent Orange and other defoliant sprays, napalm bombs, and the infamous massacre in the village of My Lai. I mouthed aloud, "Humans should never ever make war. It's a scar on our species." A Vietnamese man who stood next to me heard me and repeated, "We should never ever make war."

Today the two countries have a productive and positive relationship. The monument in Angel Fire acknowledges the hell of war, and the deep human desire for peace. It is a safe place to learn, to understand what occurred, and perhaps think about what we can each do to prevent it from happening again.

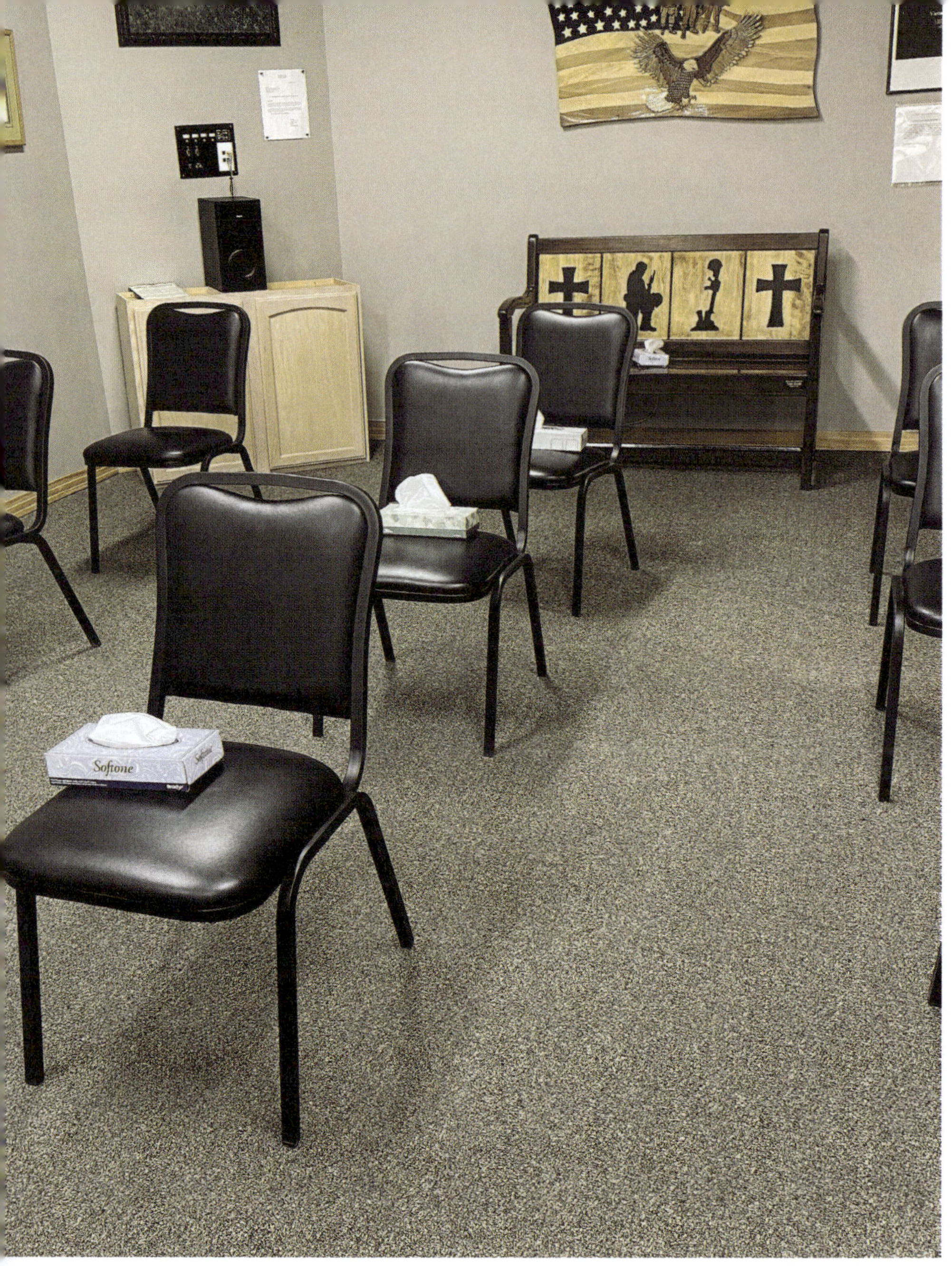

Emotional reactions are common at Vietnam Veterans' Memorial State Park.

Sometimes travel destinations are unexpectedly personal and meaningful; they cause us to stop and reflect on our lives. This is especially true when we learn about war from those who have lived through the violence and danger of combat far from home.

Although those who lived it are long gone, we decided to go to a town which we learned was once one of the most violent and dangerous places right here in the United States.

For more information: https://www.vietnamveteransmemorial.org; 34 Country Club Road, Angel Fire, NM 87710; 575-377-2293

St. James Hotel, Cimarron.

An Authentic, Uncommercialized Way to Experience the Old West

Takeaway: Off-season and shoulder season travel make everything more intimate and enjoyable.

Angel Fire is a winter hotspot for skiing. In the summer, the draw is outdoor mountain recreation and family travel. But in the autumn, the crowds are gone, and it quiets down. That's when we decided to visit the town of Cimarron on a road trip.

It was about a fifteen-minute drive from Angel Fire through Eagle Nest, a New Mexico state park where the shimmering blue lake and sun-dappled mountains looked so artfully designed that we felt as though we were in an oil painting. Several Native American tribes go there to get ceremonial feathers, fishermen are drawn by the trout, and campers relish the beauty, boating, and wildlife viewing.

We continued driving through the wooded Cimarron Canyon State Park till we reached the Palisades Sill—spectacular igneous rock cliffs carved by the Cimarron River. The rock is composed of monzonite which was emplaced a staggering 40 million years ago as the Southern Rocky Mountains were being uplifted to an elevation of 8,000 feet. We walked down to the river to sit on rocks and contemplate the geological marvel of the Palisades.

Then it was wide-open western country before us as we headed to Cimarron. Fire had devastated swaths of the forest and black, charred tree skeletons stood as mute witnesses. We arrived at the place where the Plains meet the Rocky Mountains and walked through the Mountain View Cemetery in Cimarron.

Some people are spooked by gravesites, but I am not. There is no actual death in cemeteries. They are places of honor for ancestors, notables, artists, children, and the great variety of folks who peopled the west. Reading tombstones is like perusing pages in history books. You learn about lives, loves, losses, and what mattered to the living and the dead.

The Cimarron Cemetery was a riot of colors, with plastic flowers of every imaginable hue festooning the graves. One of the latter was decorated with an intriguing religious symbol: a Jewish star inside a cross. Another memorialized a two-month-old baby, and near it a farmer was honored with an image of a tractor. One tomb was shocking pink, and another had one word: Love. The grave inscriptions were personal and tender testimonies.

A little farther on, in the old part of the cemetery, many of the markers were just slabs of wood with the names of the deceased worn away. One man mourned his thirty-five-year-old wife and a few markers bore barely legible dates like 1872 or 1880. Others were painted white. Several had been replaced by modern granite markers for ancestors who died 120 or 140 years ago. People tell a lot about themselves in their cemeteries, and it was obvious that Cimarron doesn't forget its past or its forebears.

When we arrived in Cimarron, less than an hour from Angel Fire, we were delighted to find self-guided tour brochures of the Historic Walking Trail. From the first few steps, we loved it. No fake recreations. No hype. Just the real wood and stone buildings from the Old West. We started at the Colfax County Jail, built in 1872, which included the remains of a ten-foot-high outer stone wall that was four feet thick. This jail meant business. Cimarron was once one of the most dangerous places in the nation. We looked inside, through the iron bars set into an old wooden door, and imagined guards parading down the stone corridor that was lined with individual cells filled with outlaws, murderers, and criminals of all stripes.

Our next stop was the St. James Hotel, with its photo gallery of images from 1870 to 1930 and its collection of original room tags for names that live on in history and legend: "Bat" Masterson, Buffalo Bill Cody, General Lew Wallace, and Jessie James.

The hotel had a reputation for being rowdy, which is a polite way of saying there was wild drinking, gambling, and gunfights. The walls are lined with stories of outlaws and cowboys, commercial travelers along the Santa Fe Trail, pioneer women, and gunfighters. A local gave us a tip about talking to the bartender in the saloon and asking her to show us the bullet holes in the tin ceiling; she generously complied. If there's no bartender when you visit, look above the mounted antelope head, and you will see the holes that are evidence of some serious gunslinging.

Outside again, we walked to the water-driven Aztec Grist Mill. It originally provided wheat and corn flour, but later became a staging ground for dispensing blankets, meat, flour, beans, and rations to Indians and locals. It was the Indian Agency headquarters from 1861 to 1876 and land was designated for the Utes and Jicarilla Apaches. After the Gold Rush of 1867 attracted a large influx of people, the Native population was treated poorly and unfairly. Eventually, the agency was closed, and the Native people were relocated to northwestern New Mexico and Colorado.

We continued to the Colfax County Courthouse, and The Immaculate Conception Church (a gift from the Maxwells to honor their deceased children). The original 1864 church was dedicated by Jean Baptiste Lamy, the first bishop of Santa Fe, about whom you may have read in Willa Cather's famous 1927 novel, *Death Comes for the Archbishop*. When a new building was constructed, Lamy got the deed for one dollar.

At the old Plaza, a well was dug in 1871 and used by freighters who were hauling goods along the Santa Fe Trail from Kansas City to Fort Union. The Plaza itself was reconstructed in 1962 from old photographs. It was an overnight campground for wayfarers on the trail and a watering place for oxen and horses. When the railroad came in, the trail was history.

Next to the Plaza are the graves of the Maxwells' daughter and grandma. Overhead, about 15 vultures circulated. They added to the ghostly feeling of the place.

After touring the town, we drove to Dawson Cemetery. We were greeted by a herd of pronghorn antelope at a spot where the largest mining town in New Mexico was once located. A series of devastating underground explosions in the mines were the reasons for the rows of iron crosses. Farther on, there was a chilling area filled with identical white crosses and discrete sections for Slavs, Italians, Catholics, Knights of Pythias, and Masons. The lugubrious cemetery is the opposite of the Cimarron Cemetery, with its bright colors. The one at Dawson honors the immigrants who came to America, where 383 lost their lives in the explosions of 1913 and 1923. They were two of the worst disasters in American coal mining history. A huge panel lists all their names and the location of their graves. It ensures they will not be forgotten.

As we drove back to Angel Fire, we spoke for a long time about the Old West, outlaws, architecture, bullet holes, immigrants, and miners, and we were grateful

Dawson Cemetery.

that we had been able to visit the sites with no fanfare, whitewashing, or crowds. It helped a lot that we were there in the autumn, which is the off-season. For us, it's always the best time to travel.

Another autumn venture took us to an isolated wildlife refuge, where the only other visitors were a pair of inland nesting sea birds called curlews.

For more information: www.cimarronnm.com

At this writing, there is no website for Dawson Cemetery, but you can find it with your GPS.

Impressive overlook, Rio Mora National Wildlife Refuge.

Rio Mora National Wildlife Refuge

For Lovers of Birds, Mother Nature, Conservation . . . and Surprises

Takeaway: If you love the land, you can discover what different sites and destinations are doing to restore it to the way it used to be.

It's remote—between the Great Plains and the Southern Rocky Mountains—virtually unknown, and dedicated to the wild ones, especially those that fly. If folks are lucky, they'll share their visit with an osprey, sharp-skinned hawk, black-chinned hummingbird, golden eagle, and a wigeon or shoveler. The 4,224-acre Rio Mora National Wildlife Refuge, twenty-five miles northeast of Las Vegas and two hours from Santa Fe, has only recently been officially open to the public, and we went there when the main Juniper Trail was completed. We were drawn by rumors of a stunning surprise.

When we arrived, we walked through the prairie and saw ruts where the wagons on the Santa Fe Trail once carried intrepid travelers and merchants westward from Independence, Missouri, with vast quantities of desirable goods. Today's prairie travelers are more likely to be elk, birds, and bison. The latter belong to the Pueblo of Pojoaque, which maintains ancestral and cultural ties to the land by grazing the animals at the refuge.

Because the words "conservation" and "restoration" speak to our love of nature, it was a great place to learn about the unusual restoration of the historically overgrazed land that is being done with rock dams; they help to hold sediment and filter rain water that nourishes both flora and fauna. We were fortunate to spot a long-billed curlew couple who had built a nest in the grasslands. It's uncommon for these shore birds to feel at home in far-away New Mexico, and the construction of the new Juniper Trail was postponed until the babies had fledged.

We followed the cairns (piled stone markers) along the Juniper Trail through a

Rio Mora National Wildlife Refuge offers gentle hikes.

ponderosa pine forested area with Anna Blades, the refuge manager. If she is on site and giving tours, visitors should just say yes to taking one. She's like a mother to the preserve, and she protects and nurtures the wildlife during her waking and sleeping hours.

"Now . . . are you ready for the surprise?" she asked. Suddenly, after emerging from the woods, we stood at the edge of a vast, magnificent canyon with views over the meandering Rio Mora. As far as we could see, green lichen glowed in the sunlight as it clung to the rimrock around us. A black turkey vulture flew overhead. Blades pointed out a peregrine falcon nest, showed us her favorite spot for listening to the sounds of nature, and told us stories about the surrounding sites: Seven Sisters pasture (and why no one could figure out exactly how many sisters there were); Orphan Hill; and the hooch house. Blades loves talking about these legends and filling in details that locals tell her from their family stories.

"Anna," I asked, "does anyone know the canyon is here?"

She smiled like the Mona Lisa.

Before leaving, we sat in a shady area and unpacked some favorite Capital Grill dishes that stayed fresh in our cooler that we brought from Santa Fe. I began with spinach salad accented with feta, dried cranberries and candied walnuts, and Paul loved the passion fruit sauce that added extra sparkle to the spicy Cajun shrimp and avocado salad. Then came small but macho bison sliders, tangy crab cakes that were perfectly crisp on the outside and fluffy on the inside. The thick, hearty, house-made veggie burger with mint apple relish would even appeal to a carnivore, and we simply couldn't say no to the sweet chili calamari, which didn't have a hint of grease. Before eating, we asked Mona Lisa if she wanted to join us. She demurred, saying she had already eaten. But we insisted she try one of the crab-cakes, and she wasn't sorry she did.

About a week later, we headed for a site not far from Rio Mora where we encountered some other special women . . . who lived a long time ago.

For more information: The trail is open daily from thirty minutes before to thirty minutes after sunset.

Besides Blades, Jon Erz, assistant refuge manager, is also a terrific guide.

https://www.fws.gov/refuge/rio-mora

https://www.cimarronnm.com; 505-248-6453

If you're hungry: Dining options in Las Vegas, about thirty minutes away, include Charlie's Spic & Span Bakery and Café and the Plaza Hotel, prettily situated on the Las Vegas Plaza.

In the town of Mora, about fifteen minutes away, Main Street Grill offers take-out and dine-in meals. If you're a fan of huevos rancheros, you'll be happy to know they are served all day.

Fort Union National Monument.

Fort Union

Women, Buffalo Soldiers, Indian Wars, and the Life of Soldiers

Takeaway: Something important happens when you ask questions.

Wherever we travel, on-site guides invariably say that most people who take their tours don't ask questions. When we do, it invariably leads to adventures, and one of them was triggered when we toured Fort Union.

When I was growing up, my parents dragged me on a family trip to an old military fort. I have vague memories of climbing the high stone steps and posing for photos with canons, but then I was ready to go. Military history didn't appeal to me—it seemed to be about people in uniforms who shot other people. Wars were fought. People suffered and died. Each side venerated its heroes. At some point, someone "won."

It wasn't until I moved to New Mexico that I understood how compelling forts can be. Each one in our state is a time capsule of a period when trade and commerce were gaining muscle, Native Americans were resisting the occupation of their lands, soldiers were generally overworked and bored, and women, well . . . that's an interesting and little-known part of the true story of the real Old West. And what I learned surprised, delighted, and sometimes shocked me.

Intriguing tales swirl around Fort Union, which is about thirty minutes north of Las Vegas. We stopped there to get a picnic from Adolfo's Food Truck, where a Guatemalan couple serves up gourmet Italian, East Indian, and Southwestern food. They packed up two delicious chicken dishes for us to put in our cooler. I had the Chicken Linguine Primavera with perfectly marinated chicken breast nesting on linguine pasta and supported by tomato, broccoli, pepper, pesto, parmesan cheese, and garlic bread. Paul opted for Chicken Tikka Masala, in a tomato cream sauce, presented with basmati rice and naan bread. They added, gratis, two slices of fresh watermelon.

We ate our international lunch at the fort, where we loved the stark, remote beauty of the arid landscape and the herd of pronghorn antelope we watched in the distance.

After we had finished the last crumbs, we set out on a ranger-led tour along the flat and pleasant trail and got a crash-course in a chapter of unvarnished New Mexico history. According to park ranger Mary Feitz, the fort had three incarnations: the first established a military presence in the southwest; protected travelers and the highly lucrative trade along the Santa Fe Trail; and tried to control and subdue Native American activity. The second was designed to defend the United States during the Civil War when the Confederacy was at the doorstep. And the third, which contained a military post, quartermaster depot, and arsenal, supported US troops and secured supplies.

Feitz guided us around the vast site that included visible wagons wheel ruts from the Santa Fe Trail and the wind-sculpted, cinnamon-colored stone remains of the jail, latrines, crowded barracks and warehouses. We laughed and said it seemed as though the ruins had been perfectly arranged for photographers under a cerulean blue sky with puffs of clouds and the imposing Sangre de Cristo mountains in the distance.

At the officers' quarters, we learned how the "other half" lived. The officers and their wives had every possible comfort, and their needs were attended to by servants. That started me asking questions.

"Servants?"

The answer was unexpected. "Enslaved people."

"Even though this was a Union fort and there were African American Buffalo Soldiers serving here? Some of those soldiers were formerly enslaved people themselves."

She nodded sadly, and then continued, "After the Civil War, the servants were men from China, because all the female servants were wooed away and married by lonely enlisted men. Only Chinese male servants were brought in after that."

"That must've made the enlisted men mad."

"They rebelled."

"And?"

"The women came back."

"Mary, could soldiers bring their wives to the fort?"

The reply was a conditional yes. "*If* they worked as laundresses on 'Suds Row.'"

The old saying was that a women's place is in the kitchen; but, at the fort, their place was among the wash basins. The laundry gals had a reputation for being somewhat unruly and unladylike, which I think means they had boisterous fun. When Mary saw that I was interested in the story of women at the forts, she spoke about a freed African American named Cathay Williams. She changed her name to William Cathay and enlisted as a man. She got away with it until she was finally outed when she got ill, and the surgeon saw the woman behind the male disguise.

When we passed the ruins of the hospital, Mary asked: "What do you think was the most frequent disease here in the mid to late 1800s?" Paul guessed tuberculosis and I shrugged, "Smallpox?"

"Syphilis."

"Where'd they get that?" I asked.

Our guide gave us the lowdown on the soldiers' nightlife. After an arduous day of labor, many traveled five miles from Fort Union to the nearest wild western town to gamble, dance, drink, and have raucous sexcapades.

"Does it still exist?" I asked.

"Yes, but not like that," she laughed.

And that's how we got to Loma Parda, now an evocative ghost town. If I hadn't asked Mary Feitz any questions, I would never have learned about the women of the fort. I certainly would never have known about Loma Parda.

Very often, questions open the door to more adventures. I'm frequently surprised by the answers, so I ask.

And now we're off to the infamous Loma Parda, about which we were very curious.

For more information: https://www.nps.gov/foun/index.htm; 505-425-8020

Self-guided or free ranger tours are available at the fort.

Adolfo's: 505-303-8059. Check Adolfo's on Facebook or Instagram for current location in Las Vegas.

Loma Parda, ghost town.

Loma Parda

"Sodom on the Mora"

Takeaway: When someone mentions a place that sounds interesting . . . go there.

When our guide at Fort Union mentioned a nearby town where soldiers went for brothels, booze, and macho brawls and gunfights, we decided to see what remained of it. In New Mexico, history is as close as a word on the tip the tongue that is suddenly retrieved, a fact that is momentarily forgotten and then remembered, or a jigsaw puzzle with only one piece missing that miraculously shows up. It's right there . . . and with a little patience and tenacity it reveals itself to those who are interested.

It was five testosterone-driven miles on horseback, by buggy, or on foot for the lonely and horny soldiers at Fort Union. It took us about twenty minutes to get there from the fort, via the tiny town of Watrous. We crossed a bridge that spanned the Rio Mora and entered Loma Parda, a picturesque almost–ghost town in the Rio Mora Valley where each of the abandoned stone buildings was a repository of stories.

If necessity is the mother of invention, the isolation of soldiers, cowboys, and teamsters on the Santa Fe Trail birthed a business boom in Loma Parda. When Fort Union soldiers didn't show up for Reveille or roll call in the morning or went AWOL, it was often because they passed out at Loma Parda after a night of saloon, sex workers, dancing, gambling, eating, alcohol, and gunslinging. The town had a hanging tree for serious offenses, and there was no lack of those. Horse rustling? I guess anything NOT tied down could be stolen. Murder? There was plenty of spilled blood. Scandalous behavior? It would take a lot to outdo the legendary cowboy who grabbed a woman from the street, slung her over his saddle, rode into a saloon, and ordered drinks for the house. When his horse wouldn't imbibe, he shot it, picked the woman up off the floor, and, horseless, departed. The town quickly earned the sobriquet "Sodom on the Mora."

Benito C' de Baca, patriarch and part owner of Loma Parda.

Today Loma Parda is considered a ghost town, but numerous signs reminded us that the structures are private property that belong to The Fish and Wildlife Service and also to the C' de Baca family. Benito C' de Baca, the elderly patriarch, still lived in the town when we went. He was sitting outside his house when we met him, and he wore a brown felt cowboy hat with a leather band, a brick-colored long-sleeved shirt with blue stripes, and his hand rested on the painted and carved cane beside him.

In a sense, visitors to Loma Parda are walking on hallowed ground for C' de Baca because he has spent many years of his life buying back and reclaiming property that he said was stolen from his family by crooked land grabbers. As he spoke, he recalled that, as a child, the adults in the town were invited to a meeting where they were told that fences were going to be built for them on their property. All they had to do was sign a paper. They spoke Spanish. The document was in English. They signed, and little did they know they were signing away their land.

C' de Baca's ancestors established Loma Parda in the 1830s, and his great grandmother was a cook in the busy saloon. His grandma was her assistant. When Fort Union shut down in 1891, there was no work to be found in Loma Parda, and the wild days were history. Over time, inhabitants left for the cities, and the town fell into disrepair and ruin. The only inhabitants were of the ectoplasmic kind, as quite a few visitors and former inhabitants have reported seeing ghosts.

C' de Baca's daughter, Louise Moreno, walked with us from the bridge, along the dusty main street. To the left are ruins of a house with a grocery store in front. On the right side, the remains of a hotel with rooms and outhouses. Beyond it is the spot where C' de Baca is rebuilding the church. A little farther on the left are the evocative remains of a huge saloon and the attendant corrals for horses. Inside the saloon were a dance hall where bands played around the clock, a restaurant, and a small shop. We were cautioned by Moreno and posted signs not to enter the buildings because of the dangers of fallen wooden beams, hidden rusty nails, and holes.

As we walked around Loma Parda, my imagination was in active mode: I built walls on the ruins, furnished them, and peopled them with Spanish, Indian, and Anglo locals, soldiers, traders, frontier women, and all the colorful characters who once occupied them. I looked and listened, but nary a ghost. The only sound was the whisper of an afternoon breeze. Paul found the town especially picturesque in the late afternoon, when light and shadows played across the river and darted among the buildings.

I was glad we had followed up on a town our Fort Union guide mentioned that sounded interesting. It's how we found Loma Parda and many other sites as well. It's what brought us to a mountain where a history professor led us to the so-called Gettysburg of the West.

For more information: https://www.newmexico.org/places-to-visit/ghost-towns/loma-parda/

Church ruins at Pecos National Historic Park.

Pecos National Historical Park

Gas Station Gourmet, a Mountain Hike through History, and a Battlefield on a Hill

Takeaway: It can be exciting to discover the truth of a story yourself, but sometimes you need an expert. Was Glorieta Pass really the Gettysburg of the West?

When I learned United States history in school, it was often linked to wars that took place in the past. Of them all, the one that was the most famous, and left the most corpses, was the Civil War where more than 600,000 men perished. The three-day battle in Gettysburg, Pennsylvania, turned the tide of the war and ended in the victory of the Union forces and the and the defeat of the Confederacy.

For many years I had heard that the Battle of Glorieta Pass was the Gettysburg of New Mexico. I had gone on a horseback tour of the Gettysburg battlefield in Pennsylvania where the guide, a retired police officer from New York City, spoke like a character in a TV police show. He pointed out the exact spots, time of day, number of men, weapons used, key personalities, and casualties of the seminal events of the battlefield. All of the other tour members clopping along on horses were highly knowledgeable about Gettysburg, and I, having little interest in battles, was the only tabula rasa. Everything I learned was new, and I found the guide's verbal recreation of the events fascinating. I was also intrigued by the debates going on around me about the most minute details of what actually happened there.

I wondered what all of this had to do with New Mexico. Finally, curiosity drove me to Pecos National Historical Park, twenty-five miles southeast of Santa Fe, where Paul and I toured the site and learned about the history from signage and an off-duty ranger, and then took a free, ranger-guided walking tour of the Glorieta Pass.

Humans have lived in the Pecos Valley for at least 12,000 years. The Towa-speaking trading pueblo of Cicuye was a regional power with about 2,000 inhabitants. Tribes came from the Plains with buffalo hides and slaves, shells and flint, and Puebloan farmers who lived along the Rio Grande brought crops, pottery, textiles, and turquoise.

After the Spanish arrived, the balance of power shifted. Franciscan friars built and rebuilt churches while trying to convert Native people. They destroyed the sacred Native American kivas and forbid ceremonies. Spanish settlers taxed and exploited the locals. Resentment grew and exploded in 1680 with the Pueblo Revolt, which drove the Spanish out of New Mexico.

But all was not peaceful in Cicuye. Over time, raids, disease, and drought had decimated the Indigenous population. In 1838 the last seventeen inhabitants moved to live with their Towa-speaking relatives in Jemez. Visitors can walk around the park, descend a ladder into an ancient kiva, and see the low stone wall ruins of the multistory ancient pueblo buildings and an imposing Spanish Mission church. But I also needed to know what happened there during the famous Civil War battle of Glorieta Pass.

We met our guide Claudia Floyd at the Visitors Center, learned that she is a retired university professor and specialist in the Civil War, and drove with her in the lap of the snow-capped Sangre de Cristo peaks, to the battlefield site. We were the only ones on the tour. "Today I'll compare Glorieta Pass to Gettysburg," she said. "And I also want to address the relevance of Civil War issues to those we are facing today: race and racial violence, states' rights versus national government, and who mandates decisions that affect the lives of people."

As we started the moderate climb up the mountain, Floyd pointed out two different kinds of juniper, and Gambel oak trees, whose leaves turn color in autumn and—this is quite rare—don't fall until spring. Then she began talking about and showed us photographs of the two Civil War commanders connected to the battle that took place there: Colonel Edward Canby (of the Union army) and Brigadier General H. H. Sibley (from the Confederacy). Sibley planned to come from Texas with about 3,000 fighters who were mostly volunteers. About

400 got sick, left, and deserted. The small, ambitious troops won the battle of Valverde, and they pressed on toward Fort Union for more military supplies to win the war. Next, they'd head up to Colorado to the gold and silver fields, and then on to California for more gold and silver to be used as hard currency for the Confederate cause.

In March 1862, they arrived at Glorieta, a 7,300-foot-high mountain pass; it was not a traditional battlefield where a general would choose to fight. It was unplanned, on difficult terrain, but at least there was water from the Glorieta Creek. By the third and final day of the battle, winter had set in, and a foot of snow covered the ground. The Santa Fe Trail went through this mountain pass, and the Union soldiers were coming down from Fort Union while Confederate troops were coming up from Santa Fe, on opposite sides of the trail. It was an unusual battle with bushwhacking and hand-to-hand combat—sometimes with knives. Many Confederate troops brought their own hunting guns. Horses made no sense on a mountain battlefield. I marveled that Floyd was animating our otherwise peaceful mountain hike with soldiers and nineteenth-century combat that emerged from her keen imagination and knowledge acquired over many years.

But was this the New Mexico Gettysburg? At Glorieta, there were 23,000 men fighting. Gettysburg? 165,000. At Glorieta, there were 375 casualties. In Gettysburg, 51,000. Artillery pieces at Glorieta? 11. Gettysburg, 650. And in Glorieta, there were no generals; only colonels led the charge. In Gettysburg, 120 generals. "In terms of size and scope, it's like comparing a mosquito to an elephant," Floyd explained.

So, what did the battles at the two G's have in common? They both involved Confederate invasion of Union territory. Both had a Union victory, and Confederates had to go back home. Both were, however, considered to be turning points in the war. If the Confederacy had won at Glorieta, our history, present, and future might have looked very different. Finally, my curiosity was satisfied.

There were few remnants of the Civil War at the battlefield, but the signage was terrific, and, most of all, we had a guide who knew how to recreate and help us envision history.

Interior of a ceremonial kiva, Pecos National Historic Park.

When we descended the mountain, I stopped to ask a local police officer to recommend a great place to eat. "The Shell gas station in Pecos." "No, seriously, where should we go?" He smiled broadly and said, "Pancho's Gourmet right next to the pumps. You won't regret it."

After we chowed down on a Turkey Reuben bonanza of locally made sauerkraut, applewood smoked turkey, and Swiss cheese on and thick marbled rye bread, we finished the last crumbs of a Garden Burger Smothered Burrito Plate. It was a choice between that and the Borrachera Bratwurst. Pancho's is Germany meets New Mexico. I wished I could find that police officer to thank him. "There's never a cop around when you need one," Paul quipped.

While we were waiting for our take-out food to be prepared, we checked out the building next door—Adelo's Town and Country Store, established in 1919. It's a historic building and the mural on the side was painted by local artists who ranged in age from eleven to sixty-two.

We ate our lunch in a nearby park, and the ranger on duty asked what type of travel we wrote about. We told her about nature, culture, history, hikes, food . . . and she nodded and said that's what interested her too. I could see from her parted lips and the word "but" suspended in mid-air that she had something she was burning to say. "What is it?" I asked. "I like the same things as you . . . but I just got engaged, and my fiancé and I are looking for something luxurious, set in nature. Do you know of somewhere we can go?" she blurted out.

The answer to that is the next story.

For more information: https://www.nps.gov/peco; 505-757-7241

https://www.PanchosinPecos.com; 505-757-2620

Vermejo Park Ranch.

Vermejo, A Ted Turner Reserve

The Ultimate Splurge for Lovers of Nature, Wildlife, and Conservation

Takeaway: Luxury can entail the low-key peace and healing of unplugging, going back to simpler times, and having a meaningful, private experience with nature and wildlife.

We were sitting around a firepit on the large patio at night, inhaling the aroma of burnt marshmallows as we roasted s'mores after a dinner of mushroom hot and sour soup, bison potstickers, Bandera quail, and wild game pasta. In the distance, a herd of bison munched peacefully. Two successful, multifaceted, middle-aged men were extolling their fabulous wives, and, unexpectedly, realizing how jerky male behavior can be. They were comparing themselves and their sex to what they had learned about male elk from their private guides at Vemejo Park Ranch, a Ted Turner property in Raton. "All year long, male elk hang out with the guys. Then, rutting season begins, testosterone surges, and buddies become mortal enemies. They hardly eat, drink, or sleep and make dumb decisions because they have only one thing on their minds. A month later, they're back to the being with the boys again," one of the men mused.

Seeing how personally and deeply guests reacted to the wildlife education they were getting was my first surprise. The second was meeting several guests who had booked a return trip to Vermejo within hours of arriving. It's the allure and the magic of what Ted Turner has created.

Turner is best known for founding CNN—the first twenty-four-hour cable news channel—and being the owner of the Atlanta Braves. He is also a rabid conservationist, and on 550,000 acres he has brought back the original bison that once roamed the land in the millions. He has saved cutthroat trout from extinction. He has preserved every historic structure on the property and is restoring the land to the original state it was in prior to ranching and farming. When we were there, a total of twenty guests shared the property with us, and there was never a whiff of pretension. Everyone talked excitedly about how many bears they had seen that day or how many fish they had caught in a pristine lake or what elk, bison, eagle, owl, or hawk behavior they had witnessed. It was like having a national park to yourself, with all the intimacy with nature that affords.

Our room in a house that originally belonged to Turner's son was large and tastefully appointed. But what was extraordinary was the staff. The first night, Hank, the sous chef, came to our table to introduce himself, and when we chatted, he mentioned his Persian heritage. We told him that we had visited his ancestral land, spent a month there, and fell in love with *fesenjan*, a sumptuous chicken dish bathed in walnut and pomegranate sauce. Guess what we were served for dinner the next night?

When I told a staff member that I wanted to find an elk antler that had been shed, a private guide took us shed hunting in a lush, forested area on the property. I learned from another private guide that elk antlers are the fastest growing body part of any animal on the planet—up to an inch a day of growth. When Paul expressed interest in photographing the remains of the 1891 town of Catskill, we were whisked away to see an array of thirty-foot-high beehive-shaped kilns with Gothic-style entrances where wood was transformed into charcoal for ironworks and copper smelting. The clearcutting of ponderosa pine to meet the need for wood—in the kilns, for use in the construction of houses for 2,500 inhabitants, and for heating in the winter—led to massive flooding that wiped out the railroad used to transport the charcoal. Then the prices of charcoal and wood declined. The inhabitants took the wood from their houses with them and moved on. Today, the feral horses they left behind still roam the property, and they are a reminder that what was a boom town for fifteen years turned to bust, and everything in life is mutable and ephemeral.

Every outing with a private guide was exceptional and highly informative. We opted to go in air-conditioned pickup trucks rather than UTVs or SUVs because they offered the quietest environment for listening. Kevin Cole took us wildlife viewing at night and challenged our stereotypical way of thinking about hunters and hunting. "The elk live in beautiful surroundings and all of my senses are heightened there—the view, the sounds, an overwhelming feeling of gratitude. When I kill an animal, I take time to sit there and take everything in. I am so lucky. I give thanks that I get to hunt for my food."

Tricia Rossettie, another guide, got her master's degree studying mountain lions. "They have the largest historic range of any feline in the world. They use their back legs to make a little mound where they pee and mark their territory. In general, they are solitary, although a mother and daughter might share a kill. Their food preferences are deer and elk," she told us.

Abandoned charcoal kilns, Vermejo Park Ranch.

Eric Cosgrove is a fisherman who said he would never kill a cutthroat trout because they just got off the endangered species list. As a guide, he loves to tout the remarkable qualities of animals. In his words, "pronghorn can run faster than any animal on earth at a quarter of a mile"; "bison are born a dark cinnamon color and can walk within a few hours of birth"; "female elk run the herd and decide where they go and when they go"; and "bison are good for the land because they keep moving and their hoof will crack the earth and then seeds can fall in there and germinate."

By the end of our stay, we had a better understanding of our place in the ecosystem and how to live more sustainably within it. Ample opportunities for activities like archery, horseback riding, fishing, electric biking, hiking, and a Via Ferrata course that's like rock climbing without the technical part are available for guests. But no matter what you do, education is part of the experience, and you learn about the land and species that were here before us and will be here long after us. And you are afforded the solitude, peace, and beauty to contemplate that and perhaps do nothing else at all. "That's the greatest luxury of all," one of the guests told me.

For more information: https://TedTurnerReserves.com; 1-877-288-7637

Meet the People

While walking towards the Lady Slipper Trailhead in Angel Fire we met a woman who spoke to us as she was feeding crackers to the geese and ducks in a nearby lake.

"There used to be a goose here named Gretsky. When he saw me, he would rush to me and eat honey grahams from my hand. He left for the winter and came back with a young lady friend I called Greta. He was getting older, and it was a May to December romance. This year he hasn't come back. Rest in peace, Gretsky."

At Eagle Nest State Park, we stopped to talk to a local fisherman who only fishes for pike. We asked him if what we heard was true—that it's illegal to throw pike back in the lake because they are an invasive, unwanted species.

"Yes, it's true," he replied. "I caught a forty-two-inch pike and left it out for the birds. I fish them, but I don't eat them. They're too hard to clean and have too many bones. The pike are called the poor man's lobster or chicken."

A road worker was holding a stop sign to inform drivers of a delay because of construction. I opened the window and asked him if he had seen any elk. It led to an unexpected exchange that resulted from a small misunderstanding.

"I saw a herd at 6:30 the other morning. But there are eagles and hawks flying," he said. "What does that mean?" I asked. "Well, eagles and hawks are birds, like wildlife." I smiled and inquired, "Yes, I understand, but do they have some connection to the elk?" "Well, I guess there is. They are all spiritual beings."

I asked John Pollard at the Eagle Nest Cabins & Marina shop, where they sell supplies for fishermen and hunters, what the difference is between the two.

"All hunters fish," he replied, "but not all fishermen hunt."

In Angel Fire one autumn day we watched, agog, as bike riders rode 10,677 feet up in the ski lift with their bikes, and then came racing down the slopes. We asked Jacob Steele, the lift manager, if it was dangerous.

"Angel Fire is known for its bike run," he replied, "and people come here for mountain biking on the slopes. I took a bad fall on my bike, and I'm just getting back my range of motion in my shoulder. There are many more accidents among bikers than skiers."

On a Sunday in Eagle Nest, we encountered a few friendly fishermen at the lake. One of them said he lives in Taos.

"I caught one trout," he reported. "Not with fancy lures, but just a worm. The fishing isn't good, but we're out in nature, it's quiet, there's solitude, and it's a timeless activity. We're just observers."

Nearby, another fisherman was listening to a radio. "I hope the fish like this music," he volunteered. A third was fishing while watching a football game on his phone.

On route 64, en route to Tierra Amarilla, we encountered 1,500 sheep coming down from the mountains for the winter and the herders who accompanied them on horseback. While we stopped for them to pass, we spoke to one of the shepherdesses.

"I'm from the Shepherds Lamb family, and I've been doing this all my life . . . for as long as I can remember. We started bringing the sheep down yesterday on horseback, with sheep dogs. In Tierra Amarilla they won't be in pens. They can eat there and on the surrounding ranches."

Another couple was waiting with us for take-out food at a restaurant in Chama near the railroad depot.

"We love this area. We left Santa Fe and moved to Tierra Amarilla and bought a ranch. We will raise cows. We never did anything like this before and we're in our 70s. It just seemed right, and the locals are very friendly."

Notes, Signage, and Logging Your Photos

Your Personal Library at Your Fingertips

As a digital photographer, you may shoot hundreds or thousands of photos on a single trip. When you come home, or years later, how do you easily and rapidly locate and identify what you shot? Although you think you will remember the details of a trip later on, it's impossible to retain it all. If you want to return to a memorable restaurant, show someone a photo of wild horses, or post online, here are two tips to make accessing easier.

The first relies on old-fashioned, timeless technology: a small, pocket-size notebook that goes everywhere with you. Just note the date, and the names of the places you went on that day. In the future, you can refer to the notebook and find the photos by date or place. It will make your task faster and easier and eliminate guesswork. Phones and digital cameras help with dates and geo locations, but only you know what information is important to you.

The second way is to snap shots of signage. It's simple, doesn't take up much space or time, is a visual record, and identifies the places where the photos were taken. As soon as we arrive at a destination, I photograph the sign at the entry. If we drive by road signs that describe the area or its history, I pull over and capture them. It's also a way to make sure you have the correct spellings. In an era of massive misinformation, fact-checking and being accurate are important for you and your credibility. If you post photos on social media or send them to friends and family, you want to be sure that what you say about a place is true. Just as people research in libraries, I often do so in the field—and signs prove invaluable for gathering, recording, and later, using information.

When we became interested in the lives of women who lived at Fort Union, our guide provided general information, and terrific signage supplied the rest. At the Vietnam Veterans Memorial State Park, signs provided precious information which allowed us to enter emotionally into the story and read about the vets in

Information and fun provided by signage.

their own words. We always think we will remember the important things we read, but, most often, we forget over time and can't retrieve what it was that made an impression on us. Recorded signage can also prevent memory tiffs. If your travel partner recalls details that differ from yours, you can check the sign and easily settle the matter.

Going back to reread some signs can be nostalgic, educational, and entertaining.

The poet William Wordsworth described poetry as "emotion recollected in tranquility." If you photograph signs as you travel through life you'll be providing "information that can be recollected in tranquility." There are some things you never want to forget.

Part Four

CENTRAL

Treading the narrow, time-worn trail at Tsankawi.

Introduction

There's something very grounding about the center of the state. The area abounds in hikes for every level of experience or desire. One of our favorites took us along a trail that made us feel that we were literally on top of the world. Another was along a ridge that resembled the back of a dragon. A third was a formed in soft tufa rock by the ancestral Puebloans as they trod in yucca-sandaled feet.

In springtime, we went on a little-known pilgrimage up steep Tomé Hill where many others had climbed for hundreds of years and left behind petroglyphs etched into rock. On a sunny winter day, we picnicked inside the mouth of a massive supervolcano, where we shed our urban veneer and surrendered to the sheer evolutionary power and geological variety of the natural world. We delighted as we made fresh footprints in snowy fields. In autumn we drove to Los Alamos to enjoy locally made Chinese dumplings while we watched elegant water fowl paddle by. And we drove the Jemez Mountain Trail Scenic Byway to see Nature changing her wardrobe from summer green to gold. In summer, when we had a yen for traditional Mexican baked goods and a sandwich on green chile cheese bread, we visited the *panaderia* owned by a man who is planning his 130th birthday party.

At any time of day, and in any season, central New Mexico offers a rich smorgasbord of memorable experiences.

Prajedes Morales, Golden Crown Panaderia.

You Are Invited to a Man's 130th Birthday Party at the Golden Crown Panaderia

Takeaway: Never dismiss someone else's dreams.

Prajedes Morales is a dreamer. But he is also a doer. And the owner of the popular Golden Crown Panaderia in Albuquerque, a casual, cozy, indoor-outdoor dining venue where carb-craving foodies scan the pastries in glass cases and make their selections. Morales proudly proclaims that he is eighty-four years old and "one of the healthiest people in the world. I can do 85 percent of a back flip. My shoulders, leg muscles, and core are incredibly strong because I'm a baker. I pick up fifty, sixty, seventy, or eighty pounds of dough from my mixer and carry it to my table. I make thirty to forty loaves of bread by myself, and on the table, I cut it and roll it. Look at my shoulder and arm muscles. They are rocks."

A *panaderia* is a Mexican bakery that makes breads and cookies. At Golden Crown, the specialty is *biscochitos*—the official state cookies of New Mexico. Morales has created chocolate, cappuccino, sugar free, and gluten free varieties. He also sells *maranitos* (molasses cookies that look like little pigs) and empanadas (stuffed turnovers that are influenced by Spanish and Native American cuisine). In his own words, he laughingly says he "makes a lot of dough" because his uneducated and experience-wise Mexican father told him, "You don't work for someone. You see where there's a need and you fill it. You're the one who gives people jobs." The need Morales saw was for an authentic, old-fashioned, traditional, neighborhood bakery that primarily makes things by hand. And the stream of visitors—including celebrities—who order cookies, salads, and sandwiches on green chile cheese bread prove that his analysis of the need was correct.

When I asked Morales if he was comfortable with bragging so much about himself, he replied, "I know who I am and why. I am happy. I will live to 130. People make themselves old and sick. I only sleep four hours. So why not talk about it? I am not after money—just personal satisfaction. I'm going for longevity with happiness and health."

After a slight pause, during which Paul and I savored our turkey sandwiches on green chile bread and chips dipped into melted queso (cheese), Morales said that his mind is forty-five years old, and it will never get older than forty-five. "I don't like what seniors do with their minds," he added. "I have things to do, and I need another fifty years to do them. I'm a bread artist and a bread sculptor. I can create any object or form based on my creativity and the dough at hand. It took me three to four years to create my pizza dough. It's the only New Mexican pizza crust in the world; it has eighteen to twenty-four ingredients. It's made from blue corn, green chile, and a multigrain peasant dough. The flavor is in the crust. I want everything to be nutritious. Delicious. And Beautiful. That describes what I make. And at eighty-four, I am just getting started."

I inquired what advice he had for others. "We're limited by age," he replied. "I want to break that barrier. You'd better take care of yourself to keep up with me. I'm going for 130. I live a three-minute walk from my work. I don't have to breathe fumes or sit on a freeway. That frees me to be creative. I am my lifestyle. It's not work. I am doing what I love. At the gym they build muscle. I am making a living from doing that. My body responds to the commands of my mind."

"Do you ever get depressed?" I asked.

"When I'm down, I count my blessings and I'm up again. I'm at a 400-degree oven and that takes out the toxicity. I eat nothing that will shorten my life. I want people to live longer and be happier and have the body to do it with. Longevity is living longer than what you thought. Don't stress your body. Don't go to the point where it breaks. I was a runner, but I stopped running because it stresses me."

I listened to every word he said, and my mind bounced back and forth between thinking he was delusional and considering him a guru of aging well. What he said was not theoretical. It was very specific and based on his own experience. I remembered that my ex-brother-in-law, who was a highly successful doctor who helmed a top hospital, told my mother when she turned eighty-five: "When you start to think of yourself as old, you're in trouble."

I finished my sandwich, thanked Morales, and was ready to go when he said, "This is my world. This is my vacation. I put no one else down. I want to unite everyone. I want to be a role model for everyone, and I want them to get better and be role models for me."

I put in my reservation for his 130th birthday party on April 4, 2068. He said everyone is invited.

On my way to our car, a lizard crossed my path. It turned, looked at me briefly, and then began pumping its upper body up and down, as though it were doing pushups. I think it was trying to get my attention or perhaps demonstrate how strong it was and to establish its territory on which I was intruding. It was not to be my last encounter with lizards.

For more information: http://goldencrown.biz/wp/;
1103 Mountain Rd NW, Albuquerque, NM.

Abó, Salinas Pueblo Missions National Monument.

A Highly Recommended Short Documentary Film and Saving a Life at the Ruins of Abó

Takeaway: Embrace the unexpected events that make your travels unique and memorable.

When we visited Tortugas Pueblo near Las Cruces and attended their ceremonies (p. 223), several of the Native people said their ancestors had originally come from Abó Pueblo up north. The ruins of that pueblo, which was once a thriving trade center and crossroads of cultures in the Estancia Valley, are now part of Salinas Pueblo Missions National Monument. We had visited the two other ruins—Quarai and Gran Quivira—but although Abó and the nearby Visitors Center sounded intriguing, we tried to go there three times and couldn't find them. It turned out that our trusty GPS was useless, and the disembodied woman with the British accent had misdirected us. This time, we used an old-fashioned map and relied on the instructions of random folks we met.

The Visitors Center in Mountainair is at the corner of Broadway and Ripley, and their excellent fifteen-minute film is insightful, informative, and deepens your knowledge of Pueblo history. We learned that the inhabitants of Abó practiced dry farming, stored corn for the lean times, and traded hides, salt, corn, blankets, pottery, and, unfortunately, slaves. Everything in their world was considered to be animate, alive, and they had a relationship of reciprocity with animals, the heavens, and the interrelated harmonious elements of the natural world.

The film talks about the Franciscan friars who came to the area looking for a particular kind of wealth: the souls they could save by casting out paganism and converting the Native Americans to Catholicism. The friars followed the way of Saint Francis and embraced nature and animals as the Puebloans did, and the latter could relate to that. They could also accept a new god in their pantheon. Fray Francisco Fonte established a mission in Abó in 1621. The friars instructed the inhabitants to build an earlier church, followed by the magnificent red sandstone mission with European-style buttresses whose ruins we see today. By the mid 1600s, Spanish settlers, Indians from Mexico, and Puebloans had intermarried. Theoretically, it could have worked out to everyone's benefit. But it didn't.

The Franciscans came to convert, and they didn't want their God to be one divinity among many or their beliefs to exist alongside of paganism. They encountered resistance to conversion. Frustrated, the friars eventually burned the Natives' sacred objects, banned their ceremonies, buried their kivas, and whipped the spiritual leaders. They forced the people to provide crops and food to feed the friars, so the farmers' own fields and stores suffered. Then came epidemics, drought, crop failure, famine, attacks from other Indian tribes, and death. Most of the survivors drifted south, never to return.

After our orientation we were anxious to visit Abó, and Kevin, the ranger on duty, directed us to the ruins which were about nine miles away. As we began to walk along the cement path to the church, we saw the well-preserved adobe ruins of a circular, in-ground ceremonial kiva on the grounds of the mission. Did the kiva play a role in converting the Native Americans? What was the relationship between the two faiths? Stone effigies of the Puebloans were found along with a ceramic candlestick and a mother-of-pearl cross.

In the maze of rooms at the religious complex, Native Tompiro people once performed the tasks that kept the mission running: they herded livestock, gardened, rang bells, ground corn, maintained the property, and cooked meals. Tompiro boys had once rushed up a stone staircase to join the grownups in singing in the church choir loft. The words of the Spanish and Latin liturgy echoed off the fifty-feet-high sandstone walls, and the sound of trumpets, bells, bassoons, and an organ provided by the friars made joyous sounds in the mission. Outside the grounds, corn, beans, and squash were cultivated, and game animals provided food. The Spanish introduced apples, peaches, melon, chile, sheep, cattle, and wine.

The day we were visiting, a group of young volunteers and workers had just applied thick black tar to patch cracks in the concrete path around the site. Kevin warned us to watch out for wet areas as we headed towards unexcavated dirt mounds where Puebloan houseblocks once covered an area the size of three football fields, and nearby springs provided water. Suddenly, at our feet, we saw a lizard thrashing wildly, his tail and one foot caught in a tar patch. I tried to nudge him out with a thin branch, and he panicked—biting the stick, writhing, rising up in terror. Paul ran after Kevin, who was leaving for the day, but agreed to come with a screwdriver to help dig the lizard out of the tar. He spoke kindly and gently to the trapped reptile, and was able to dislodge it, although it had to leave its tail and one foot behind. Kevin was optimistic that it would regrow the missing body parts. The three of us had saved a lizard's life.

After Kevin drove away, we were horrified to discover three more lizards who were trapped in the tar and had died. It seemed like a metaphor for the double-edged sword of modernity. On one hand, dirt paths could be paved with cement for the comfort of visitors, and any cracking could be repaired with hot tar. On the other hand, local animal life became victims of the improvement.

When we got home, we contacted Kevin, who promised to alert those in charge to the danger of using tar, and we trust that by the time you visit, another material will be used for repair. Hopefully, something both safer and more aesthetically pleasing.

When folks travel, they have unexpected experiences at places they are visiting. They may evoke strong, personal reactions, and travelers find that they include them, even years later, when they remember their trip and tell others about it. These incidental happenings—both good and bad—are part of what makes each adventure unique and unforgettable.

A lizard, a small reptile, changed my experience of Abó. But a much larger ancient reptile—up to an almost unimaginable 150 feet long—inspired my next trip.

For more information: https://www.nps.gov/sapu/learn/historyculture/abo.htm

Biking in the Ojito Wilderness.

Two Hikes

One Where Dinosaurs Walked and One on the Back of a Dragon

Takeaway: When Nature calls, answer.

Sometimes, in the middle of a busy day in Santa Fe, I hear a faint sound that's like the soft rustling of aspen leaves or the distant love song of a bird. Slowly it gets louder—a rush of wind, a coyote's howl, a raven's insistent caw. It's the call of Nature, and I stop whatever I am doing to answer. It's time to leave the city world of incessant chatter and obligations, and pay homage to the spirits of the earth, air, and water. The only preparation I need is to choose from hundreds of hiking trails that crisscross the land. Nature welcomes everyone to her home among the mountains, forests, rivers, plains, prairies, lakes, and streams.

Some days we want to stay in Santa Fe, and we find hikes in nature at the outskirts of the city. On other occasions, we have more time to explore farther away for a glorious morning or afternoon outing. When the latter is the case, we sometimes drive to one of my favorite destinations where there are trails suitable for all levels of hikers from greenhorn to gonzo.

The very name is exciting and sounds like something out of an old western film: the Ojito Wilderness. The first time we went, we drove over the long, dusty road that is framed by rock formations resembling organ pipes, witches' hats, and the swirl of soft serve ice cream. Finally, after about seventy minutes from Santa Fe (or fifty minutes from Albuquerque), we arrived at a remote destination near San Ysidro. We parked in the small lot, crossed the road, and thought about a seminal paleontological event that happened here: the skeleton of a seismosaurus, one of the longest dinosaurs in the world, whose length measured a startling 120 to 150 feet, was found. The Ojito Wilderness also provides fossil remains of other rare dinosaurs, plants and trees. It was a weekday and on the out-and-back Seismosaurus Trail, we were two of only four hikers.

The fairly flat rock-strewn path, which gently dips and rises, offered dramatic and varied views of seemingly endless wide-open spaces. Along the route, a hiker from Paris called out to us, "I have never seen anything like this in my life," he said. "It's the Old West. *C'est magnifique.*" He loved the large volcanic plug in the distance called Cabezon Peak, which looks like a stocky neck with the head chopped off.

Along the trail, ancient trees had fossilized into petrified wood, and their aligned segments resembled slices cut in gigantic stone baguettes. We sometimes wandered off the main trail to gaze into geological marvels to our left and right: multi-hued mesas (flat-topped hills), canyons carved by long-gone rivers, and hoofprints left in the sand by deer or antelope.

Near the far end of the trail, we saw something sacred and special. Ancient Native Americans had incised petroglyphs in the rocks, eons ago. They were clear and vivid, as though the years and the elements had either overlooked or protected them. I found them to be mesmerizing and mysterious. One looked like a snake, another a human figure holding a rod or staff aloft. Others resembled a long hand or foot, a moon, a frog, a turtle and a shield or the sun. Perhaps the carvers were hunters who stood on the cliff where we were standing and drew totemic figures to bring good luck for their hunt in the valley below.

Aside from the ancient stone record, we had found the perfect place to enjoy our picnic of tacos from Bosque Brewing Company in Bernallilo. The marinated chicken and shrimp ones were drizzled with *pico de gallo* and lime *crema*. Our veggie choice was roasted cauliflower, topped with chopped red onion, *mojo* sauce, and *queso fresco*.

As we finished eating and were packing up, a young hiker named Vanessa came by with a Labrador and a blue healer. She told us that on the way back to our car, off to the right, we would come to a long piece of petrified wood that looked like a vertebral column. Just beyond it was a short trail leading down to the foundation of an ancient stone building. We went, found it, and it was the perfect end to our three-mile hike. Once again, someone with whom we had a brief encounter turned out to be a guide for us.

We were so enchanted by our Ojito Wilderness experience that we returned two weeks later for the Dragon's Back Trail. We climbed up the "tail" of the mythical beast and stayed to the left. Beneath our feet was Jurassic age gypsum. We took the first turnout on the left for a view of Cabezon, the thumb, and then we returned to the main trail and everywhere we were treated to great views of arroyos, valleys, and hills.

At the White Ridge junction of trails, we continued bearing left and had magnificent views of a red, gray and white canyon in front of us, with purple hills in the distance. We were on the dragon's back, and everywhere we looked were spectacular vistas of red and gray hills dotted with green bushes and red peaks in the valley below.

On both sides of the path, we encountered cryptobiotic soil or crust. It is made of cyanobacteria, moss, lichen, and fungi; tiny organisms that play a role in the fragile ecosystem. It looks like an agglutination of tiny little dark towers of black speckling on a desert floor. And it is alive—a living crust that protects the soil and may take hundreds of thousands of years to form. It is chilling to think that if we walk on it, just the pressure of our feet can destroy it. We were careful not to stray from the designated trail, and we invented a slogan as we walked: "It is idiotic to destroy cryptobiotic."

The trail at that point revealed what looked like a *Star Trek* planetary landscape: isolated small hillocks with white gypsum paths snaking through them. We skirted the edge of a hill, and once again, on a weekday afternoon, we were alone. When we looked down, the valley to the left was green and yellow and to the right, red and white. The twisted limbs of dead trees seemed to point out the features of the landscape and the most picturesque cloud shapes in the sky.

We turned around at the two-mile mark and walked the back of the dragon towards our car, but you can keep going.

At the end of the trail, we met a lone biker with his dog. "How'd you guys like it?" he asked. I can't remember my answer because we were emerging from the kind of dream that only takes place in nature.

This brings me to another dream-like adventure we had in Central New Mexico. It included a hike in nature, but the trail was holy, the locus of a religious pilgrimage.

For more information: https://www.blm.gov/visit/ojito-wilderness-area

If you go during the week, there are fewer hikers and mountain bikers.

Pilgrims on Tomé Hill.

Why I Love Pilgrimages, Especially One Most Folks Have Never Heard About

Takeaway: It is a deep and special privilege to walk on sacred land.

Over the years, friends and colleagues have asked why I am drawn to pilgrimages. First, walking outside is an essential part of my life. When I do it alone, the repetitive steps put me in a thoughtful or meditative state. When I do it with others, it invites intimacy, openness, and honesty because nature itself is so honest. And when I join pilgrims who are penitent, prayerful, and thankful, it somehow enhances my own existence; it doesn't matter that I don't share religious beliefs with them. We all need to be grounded by the earth below, elevated by the sky above, appreciative of the natural world that sustains life, and connected to each other. I am drawn to spiritual, religious, and holy sites and events because they are peaceful, and they remind us that humans can—even if only for a short time—live with each other in harmony.

Every Good Friday, the highways and byways of North Central New Mexico are studded with pilgrims who walk from near and far to Chimayo to pray, offer thanks, fulfill vows, or partake in a spiritual tradition. It's the largest pilgrimage gathering in the country.

But to the south of Albuquerque, surrounded by rural farms, is another, less known destination for Hispanic pilgrims: Tomé Hill. When we go, we are aware that the hill was significant to ancestral Native Americans who left behind 1,800 petroglyphs on a high place where they went for their ceremonies and prayers. The Spanish people also considered it a holy place along the Camino Real de Tierra Adentro trade route that began in Mexico City, and they too etched religious glyphs and petroglyphs.

At the park below the hill, a striking 1997 sculptural installation by Armando Alvarez silently tells the layered history of early New Mexico: cattle, churro sheep, shepherds, elderly farmers, Indian scouts brandishing rifles, people praying, railroad workers, cattle skulls, priests, conquistadors on horseback, war dogs, Native American dancers with bows and arrows, deer dancers, and Native women carrying pots on their heads. The last time we went there, as we walked through and around the figures, they induced a dreamy mood, and I imagined them as real and alive.

And then we were ready to begin climbing the Camino Real de Tierra Adentro National Historic Trail, a moderately difficult path which ascends 400 feet above the fields below.

The first time we went to Tomé Hill, the trail was crowded with walkers, and we were carried along by a wave of prayer, meditation, thanksgiving, personal sacrifice, and appreciation of nature. During the pandemic, attendance was sparse, but walkers came for the same reasons. A helicopter hovered in the sky above us, and two concerned Native Americans from Isleta Pueblo said tourists were being charged $300 for an aerial look at the pilgrimage below. One of them said he felt he was cheating. "We're supposed to walk all the way from the church in Isleta to the top of the hill, but we drove today. It's a shortcut, but even without the long walk it increases my spiritual-ness to be here."

As we ascended the hill, we met a young father whose right hand held onto his young daughter and his left held a Bible. Periodically he stopped to read passages aloud to his family. We were surrounded by black volcanic rocks, and we could almost feel the force of the ancient lava flow that deposited them there. We paid close attention to where we were walking, as the loose rocks were sometimes unsteady and shifting.

At the top of the hill, we encountered three large crosses; two red and one white. Close to them was an altar with wooden crosses, votive candles, photos of people for whom the pilgrims were praying. A wooden sign informed the pilgrims about how we can apply the lessons of the holy day to our lives: love, acceptance, forgiveness, giving others a hand, and helping them to bear their crosses in life.

We joined others—including infants in their parents' arms, couples, friends, and families who sat on large rocks and looked down and around at the unbounded 360-degree view of the vast countryside and the distant Sandia Mountains. They spoke quietly in Spanish, English, and Tiwa. We descended a bit on the other side of the hill and saw the petroglyphs chiseled on the rocks. They are still powerful despite being worn by time and weather.

On the way down, walking slowly to avoid tripping on loose stones, we spoke to pilgrims who said they felt renewed, balanced, and less overwhelmed by their problems. "Many people come here for regular hikes during the year, but for me it's all about Good Friday. I'm not Catholic and I'm not religious, but the atmosphere is calm and beautiful," a young woman in a floppy red sunhat said. She pushed back the hat so we could see her eyes and asked, "Don't I look peaceful?"

At another destination, we experienced the peace that comes from walking in the path of ancient Puebloan ancestors and actually entering the cave homes where they once lived.

For more information: https://www.nps.gov/places/el-cerro-de-tome-tome-hill.htm

Tomé Hill is about half a mile east of the junction of NM 47 and Tomé Hill Road. You can climb the hill any time, but remember it's a sacred place, so, out of courtesy, please stick to the designated path.

If you're hungry: Before we go to Tomé, we have a tradition of stopping in Albuquerque to get Korean take-out lunch from one of three places: Seoul Bowl, Korean BBQ House, or Hanmi Korean-Chinese Fusion.

Exploring at Tsankawi, Bandelier National Monument.

Tsankawi

Walking in the Footsteps of the Native American Ancestors

Takeaway: You can time travel by connecting to ancient people on their land.

Sometimes, when the chaos of contemporary life gets too loud, frantic, and obtrusive, Paul and I drive into the past. We find it forty-five minutes from Santa Fe at Tsankawi (pronounced San-Ka-Wee). Hundreds of years ago, at this ancient Puebloan site, inhabitants walked up and down from the mesa, or flat, elevated ridgetop, to their fields below. The constant pressure of human feet began to wear into the rock and eventually carved a narrow path. Today it is both moving and exciting to walk, quite literally, in the footsteps of their woven yucca sandals.

Before a recent trip to Tsankawi, Paul and I decided to combine two things we love: eating great food and hiking. On the surface, gourmet fare and hiking boots don't belong together. But when we eat, we are really present, slowing down to thoroughly enjoy every bite. We admire Nature's décor, feel grateful for our repast and our surroundings, and relax before walking into the scenery. And we always say that food tastes better outdoors.

We made our picnic selections from Tesuque Village Market and dined on the land near the entry to Tsankawi. With a view of the dramatic red cliffs in the distance, we began with crisp, cheesy cheddar quesadillas and a grilled garnished wild whitefish taco with a cilantro *crema* dressing. It was happily complemented by a vegetarian tamale swimming in a peppy, house-made red chile sauce. Our main course was a thick, hearty-as-beef black bean veggie burger that even a confirmed carnivore would love. We savored the idea that tamale, chile, and beans all harken back to traditional foods. For dessert, we indulged in their famous shimmering green key lime pie that was artfully topped with spirals of whipped cream. Needless to say, we carefully packed our copious leftovers in our cooler for dinner so we didn't snooze and miss our opportunity to hike on the land of the ancients.

The time-worn trail at Tsankawi, Bandelier National Monument.

We relaxed for a while, as our everyday life melted away, and then we began to climb. The lichen and algae that covered the rocks around us offered a wonderful palette of colors: ocean green, sky blue and marigold yellow. The 1.5-mile trail through the ruins is of moderate difficulty because it involves climbing three wooden ladders. Descending on one of them may be a bit daunting for visitors if, as in my case, heights are not their thing. If folks are agile, they can sprint through the ruins, but to me that's like speed reading a great book. I suggest people take their time, explore, and feel the breath of the ancient ones who have given them permission to visit their former home.

Often the walls of rock on both sides of the trail are so narrow that we had to turn sideways in order to pass. At some places there was no room for both of my feet next to each other. I proceeded one foot at a time, as I imagined I would do on a tightrope if I weren't afraid of plunging to the ground below. We passed by the central plaza, which once bustled with life. There were 275 rooms on the ground floor of a two-story-high building. When we looked closely, we could see foot and toe holes where intrepid people once scaled the rocks.

All along the trail we were treated to spectacular views of the canyons below. And after we climbed down the last, steep ladder, we entered several cave dwellings that were carved out of volcanic tuff for habitations. Some of the ceilings are blackened by fire. We stayed for a moment and observed ventilation holes for smoke and niches in the walls for personal and household belongings. I gave my imagination free reign, and time magically dissolved. I saw children playing, women carrying water in ceramic pots on their heads, mothers teaching daughters how to grind corn, the sounds of prayer and drumming from ceremonial kivas, and adolescent men flint knapping with deer antlers. I even envisioned farmers who were masters of water conservation, expert potters, and young boys being taught by elders how to hunt and provide sustenance for the community.

When we visit San Ildefonso or other pueblos in the area, we get a glimpse of how the ancestral Puebloans might have lived in Tsankawi. Their ceremonial kivas, pottery traditions, dances, languages, and food are evidence of powerful cultural persistence.

The ancient ones at Tsankawi were not isolated. Besides neighboring pueblos there was extensive trade of items like copper bells, live parrots, and seashells from as far away as the Pacific coast. Turquoise, cotton, and salt were traded with northern Mexico.

Once again, it was the right time of day, and I saw petroglyphs carved into the rock walls as I walked. Sometimes I could clearly see animal forms, and other times I tried to guess at the shapes and their meaning.

When we finished hiking, it was late afternoon, and we weren't ready to go back to daily life. We couldn't get enough of the beauty of the area and drove five minutes to White Rock Overlook. We were alone there, transfixed by the magnificence and expansiveness of the view. Everywhere we looked were dramatic mesas, evocative rock formations, and the Rio Grande meandering through the vast canyon below.

The mental images of our outing lasted long after the easy drive home. And after being immersed in a world of ancient Puebloan habitation, we longed to go back further, much further in time at another site.

For more information: https://www.nps.gov/band/learn/photosmultimedia/tt-vt-intro.htm

https://visitlosalamos.org/overlooks

Valles Caldera, inside an ancient volcano.

Inside a Volcano

Takeaway: Always remember to take your imagination with you when you go exploring.

When I travel, the first thing I pack is my imagination. I can always replace socks, shoes, or a hairbrush, but having my imagination with me ensures that I will not only have a new experience, but I will also "see" how the site was formed or built, what it looked like in the past, who was there before me, and how it might change in the future. It's a way of inviting the past, present, and future into each experience. We are part of a continuum, and when we connect to the long chain of time that brought us to where we are today, the present becomes more alive for us, and the future is ripe with possibilities. Our daily worries and problems dissolve as we immerse ourselves in where we are situated in the endless landscape of time.

About 13 million years before we first arrived at Valles Caldera, there was a long period of tremendous volcanic activity in the Jemez Mountains. I imagined the trembling, shaking, and explosions of the land. A mere one million years before our visit, there was a violent collapse at the center of a volcano that spewed a staggering 500 times the material released by the famous 1980 explosion of Mount St. Helens in Washington State. And a geologically recent 50,000 years before I arrived, magma leaked to the surface and formed hills in an enormous valley that is 13.7 miles wide. Today it is called the Valles Caldera National Preserve, a magical world only an hour northwest of Santa Fe.

Most people think you can only view the site from Highway 4, which runs along the outer rim. Wildlife enthusiasts with binoculars gather there during elk mating season in the fall and are rewarded with eerie calls that sound like shrill whistles; with luck, they sometimes see entire herds. But much of the Caldera valley can't be viewed from the road. Instead, we drive down into the Caldera and experience the raw majesty of the preserve while contemplating that we are nestled inside an ancient volcano.

"We're slower than a snail in terms of marked hiking trails," a park ranger told me, "but there are hundreds of miles of logging roads, all of which are walkable." In the winter or during periods of inhospitable weather, the main road that wends its way through the vast valley may be partially closed, so we leave our car (a four-wheeler that can navigate snow season or inclement weather) in the parking lot and hike the nearby La Jara Loop Trail. Indifferent to the patches of snow and mud, and avoiding fresh elk droppings, which meant they were near, we walked in awe along the easy route, knowing that we were almost alone in this jewel of nature. Some prefer to travel on skis or snowshoes and, if the weather gods of precipitation are willing, the Caldera greets them with seemingly endless open fields of snow. I imagined what the fiery world looked like in the past. I wondered how the land might be affected by a changing climate. I felt fortunate to be there at that particular moment and felt how miraculous it was that nature, time, and the elements conspired to create such a perfect day.

When the weather is fine, we hike or drive for miles along the main road and through the fields, marveling at the changing landscape of mountains, flatlands, forests, streams, ponds, volcanic domes, and old log cabins built by ranchers and cowboys. We pack our binoculars and search for bobcats, black bears, coyotes, and golden eagles, in addition to elk. Then we pause for a moment, breathe in the fresh air, and each time feel lucky to be alive.

When we visited in the fall, nature exploded into brilliant golden hues, and we were often alone as we set out on a long walk into the mystery of the Caldera. We thought of the ancient hunters who visited the site as early as 11,000 years ago. They gathered obsidian to make arrow points and spears and traded them across a wide swath of the Southwest.

In the winter, with only a handful of other visitors in the valley, we marveled at the snowy terrain, undisturbed except for the occasional animal tracks and a lone coyote.

Nature has a way of animating the appetite, and we joyfully unrolled our portable aluminum picnic table at a spot with a soul-stirring view. Award-winning Chef Martín Rios of Restaurant Martín in Santa Fe prepared our picnic as a homage to the Caldera.

The first course was called "Earth," and the rich soil base was created from blackened mushroom-seeded bread. It was the bed for a lush and colorful garden of heirloom beets, asparagus, radishes, and spring pea purée. The entree had two

Valles Caldera.

elements: roasted duck breast with honey glaze, and duck leg confit enveloped in kale and black Thai rice. The dessert was—surprise!—a molten lava bittersweet chocolate cake exploding with salted caramel and organic berry gel. The few other visitors were gawking enviously at our banquet while they munched trail mix.

If the weather is unsuitable for an outdoor picnic, we set out our smorgasbord picnic on the dashboard of our car, and more than one visitor has called out us, "bon appétit."

Each time we go, I remember that that no one ever had the same experience as we did in the past, and no one will ever have it in the future. The day is ours, and only ours. It is forever marked on the continuum of our lives.

On the ride home, after being in the bottom of a volcano, I thought about another experience we had in the area where we felt as though we were on top of the world.

For more information: https://www.nps.gov/vall/planyourvisit/index.htm; 575-829-4100

Kwage Mesa's top of the world view.

Kwage Mesa

A Baozi Picnic and Hiking on Top of the World

Takeaway: Hiking is about place, and not just pace.

Every time we drove the winding and picturesque road north from Santa Fe to Los Alamos, we admired the dramatic mesas, or flat-topped ridges that jut out like thin, extended fingers over the deep canyons of the Pajarito Plateau hundreds of feet below. I always wanted to hike or walk on top of one of those isolated mesas, and we chose a Goldilocks day when it wasn't too hot or cold outside.

Whenever possible, we get local to-go food and begin our adventure with a picnic. We find out which restaurants residents like, and when we follow their recommendations, it connects us to them and gives us a commonality from the get-go. Instead of being isolated inside a restaurant, we breathe the local air, meet people, and discover new eateries that we return to.

In Los Alamos, a foodophilic scientist recommended we try Yuan's Dumpling and Noodle House. They prepared a picnic lunch that included *baozi* (plump dumplings stuffed with vegetables or meat) and *lao mian* (stir fried noodles with a choice of accompaniments), and we headed for Ashley Pond Park to enjoy it. The serene respite place, with mountain views, picnic tables, a small waterfall, and a pond with ducks, geese, and fish has quite a bit of history.

Ashley Pond Jr. founded the nearby Los Alamos Ranch School, which functioned from the end of World War I until the third year of US involvement in World War II. The boys' school was dedicated to educating its students in classical subjects and the outdoors. They belonged to the first mounted troop of Boy Scouts in the country, who canoed, swam, played hockey, and practiced ice skating at Ashley Pond.

But the boys' robust and energizing school experience was unexpectedly cut short when the leaders of the Manhattan Project visited the school and then petitioned the US government to take over the entire property and buildings. They allowed the boys to finish their first term of school in 1942. Then, in early 1943, they transformed it into a top-secret lab in a clandestine city where they developed the atomic bomb.

After watching white geese floating peacefully by during our leisurely lunches, we walked around the pond and then drove to our destination. We instructed our GPS to take us to Kwage Mesa Loop Trail. It led us through remote countryside and a long series of horse stables. We thought we were lost until finally we saw a small sign that indicated the trailhead. It was a windy day and ours was the only car.

The narrow, flat, easy 4.3-mile dirt trail curves along the top of the mesa. It rises high above the surrounding countryside and offers a dramatic view of turquoise sky overhead, snow-capped Sangre de Cristo Mountain peaks in the distance, and a forest of pine trees below. The silence is only pierced by black ravens that make their throaty kraa calls as they fly by. I was thrilled to finally be on top of a hill I had seen so often from the twisting road to Los Alamos.

At a crossroad, we turned right and continued following Kwage Mesa Trail. The path widened, became sandy, and we soon found a narrow, parallel trail that led us along the edge of the ridge. To the left, we marveled at the striated rock of a parallel mesa, a sweeping view into the canyon, and the vast expanse of land and sky.

At the far eastern end of the loop trail, the 180-degree view became soul expanding. We were surrounded by more mesas, mountains, and deep canyons. The color palate ranged from orange, yellow, brown, white, and black rock to yellow grass, hunter green trees, and the white streak of a contrail across the sky. Our eyes followed the flow of ancient lava that once poured out of exploding volcanoes. It seemed as though an unseen hand had created it with a giant paintbrush across the ancient geology.

Standing alone and looking into the canyon below, we felt as though we had discovered the area, but, in fact, starting as far back as 10,000 years ago, Archaic hunters, Paleo-Indians, ancestral Puebloans, and Spanish settlers were there long before us. The word "Kwage" derives from a Tewa Pueblo word meaning "top of." We were grateful specks in the timeline of the Pajarito Plateau.

Heading back to the trailhead, we saw houses in the distance and only passed a girl with a white pit bull, a guy in a hockey shirt on a bike, and a rapidly pedaling woman with gray hair and sexy hot pink shoes. For all of us, it had been a wonderful escape from our daily lives.

Shortly after our visit, I heard that a dedicated, professional group of Kwage Mesa Trail lovers installed information panels and signage. But I'll bet future hikers still feel as though they alone have discovered a trail of such singularly high beauty. And I hope they don't forget those *baozi*.

For more information: https://www.losalamosnm.us/government/departments/community_services/parks_recreation_and_open_spaces/openspaceandtrails/barranca_mesa_trails/kwage_mesa_trails; 505-662-8333

Meet the People

We find so many people, places, and even signs that inspire us as we travel around New Mexico. You never know where the wit, wisdom, and information will show up, so you have to pay attention all the time. Maybe that's the secret to slow, meaningful travel—having your senses alert to sounds, smells, sights, tastes, and the feel of things. Looking at people and knowing which ones have something to tell you or are open to communication.

On one of our visits to Bosque Del Apache National Wildlife Refuge, we saw an arresting sign along one of the paths. It spoke to us as though someone was standing before us, mouthing the written words.

"The motto of John P. Taylor Junior, who worked to preserve native wetland habitats by restoring cottonwood groves, savannahs, and salt grass meadows at Bosque Del Apache National Wildlife Refuge: 'When the birds arrive at Bosque del Apache, they should have corn in the field, fresh water in the river, and a place to rest. . . . The migratory birds that fly to this refuge are the essential visitors. We must preserve and maintain a habitat that continues to welcome them long after we are gone.'"

Paul was putting gas in our car in Socorro when the pump stopped working. A man named Alfonso came out of his car and approached ours to see what was wrong, and he and Paul started conversing. Alfonso was a nature lover, and through the open window I heard him talking to Paul about rodents. I was about to turn away from the conversation when he said something arresting.

"Do you know that Beavers are the biggest rodents in North America? They are sexually mature by the time they reach two or three years old, and when they mate, it's for life. Better than a lot of us guys, huh?"

Another day, while lunching on the patio of Golden Crown Panaderia in Albuquerque, we began talking to folks at other tables. Jessica Bowen, a thirty-eight-year resident of Albuquerque, had only recently discovered the Mexican bakery.

"We came here, and now we are back for the second time. It's the green chile bread. It doesn't matter if it's just a sandwich. You can't get it anywhere else. And the queso dip gives it a New Mexican twist."

Sean Dube, a two-year resident of Albuquerque, put down his turkey sandwich on—what else?—green chile bread, and told us something I didn't know about the local baseball team.

"The Isotopes are famous because of *The Simpsons* There was an episode where they jokingly referred to a New Mexican baseball team named the Isotopes. The local team changed its name from Albuquerque Dukes to the Isotopes. They tried to get the show's creator Matt Groening to throw the first pitch, but he was too busy."

At a lowrider barbecue at USS Bullhead Park in Albuquerque, we met Gilbert Chavez, a lowrider who drives a bus at UNM.

"They claim Española is the lowrider capital of the US, but in my opinion it's Albuquerque. Somebody gave me a ride in one that had hydraulics when I was thirteen and doing dumb things. I thought the lowriders were all about the flashy cars, the gold rims. Now I'm grown up and it's a positive lifestyle—family, friends, the love of cars. For thirty years I've been doing it, fixing it, driving, and breaking it."

Gran Quivira, which is part of the Salinas Pueblo Missions Nation Monument, is the least visited of the Salinas ruins because it's off the main road. A ranger in the museum in the Visitors Center perked up when I asked him if he knew anything about some fascinating objects that were displayed behind glass. He said a highlight of his job is when people ask him questions.

"These are ringing stones—they were used to call men to kiva ceremonies and meetings. And that's a lightning stone. The shaman struck and rubbed large pieces of quartz together during rain ceremonies to produce a flash and glow. . . . And that's a bird-bone flute and also a one-hole bird bone whistler that was used to make a piercing blast during ceremonies. You know—there was trade here that extended from the Pacific Ocean to the Great Plains and deep into Central America. The Apache brought jerked meat, deer skins, and buffalo hide and left with corn, salt, cotton blankets, and pottery."

Nature and Landscapes

Capturing the Magic of the Great Outdoors

I bet you've had this experience: you are absolutely awed by a stunning view, but when you see the photo you shot, you're disappointed that it doesn't look like what you saw. There are reasons: your eye is finer than any man-made lens, and when images are processed through your mind, you automatically add memory and emotion. You can bridge this aesthetic and affective gap through a combination of art and craft. Let's start with art.

Nature photography is about the big and the small: vast deserts, towering mountains, fiery sunsets, and endless starry skies on one hand and the delicate petals of a flower or the myriad details of a busy insect on the other. Your job is to select, compose, and either photograph immediately or exercise patience and wait. Sometimes you have to act quickly to catch a fleeting moment (especially when animals are present), but most of the time, you have to bide your time and anticipate the sun breaking through the clouds or gonzo whitewater rafters exploding into the frame. Sometimes a small detail can express the emotion you feel at a particular place.

After selecting what or who you want to photograph, aspects of craft come into play. For action, burst mode is best as, with a mechanically generated rapid series of images, you've got a better chance of catching a key moment. You probably have burst mode on your mobile phone or camera. Practice before it's needed, and you will know when the moment calls for it.

Be observant about your surroundings. For instance, is there something in the foreground that will either frame or emphasize something in the background? Will the space between the branches of a tree provide a frame for a mountain or a grazing horse? Does your eye follow a series of river rocks that leads to a waterfall?

If you want to capture a wide expanse in nature, opt for a panoramic setting or, when you are editing, use stitching software in an imaging program on your computer.

On our many trips to the Valles Caldera National Preserve, one of the largest

A snowy view of a rustic old cabin in the Valles Caldera National Preserve.

volcanic craters on earth, many techniques and applications were used: wide angle and close-up, burst mode, impulse shooting and patiently waiting, panoramas, portraiture in place and, most definitely, composition. The nearly fourteen mile-wide caldera is home to herds of elk, bears, prairie dogs, and birds, all set against a varied backdrop of volcanic peaks; green, golden, or snow-covered meadows; majestic pine forest; and meandering streams. The look changes constantly with the weather and the seasons. The setting is eternal: the great American Southwest. There are also evocative traces of human habitation from prehistoric indigenous ruins to Old West structures. And the geology is a textbook in itself.

While driving in central New Mexico, I had to be particularly fast on my wheels

With weather as exciting as this, even a parking lot is dramatic.

to spot the sudden and dramatic skies that abruptly appeared as two weather fronts collided. I particularly like the juxtaposition of the sublime clouds above with the mundane gravel RV campground below.

There's no end of subject matter and opportunity for unforgettable outdoor photos in New Mexico. So don't just snap a photo. Be creative—ancient people and Nature were.

Part Five

SOUTHWEST

La Llorona Park on a dry stretch of the Rio Grande in Las Cruces.

Introduction

We spent a few days in a forested spot on the outskirts of Silver City. While in the area, we had the pleasure of climbing to the cliff dwelling where people of the Mogollon culture lived about 700 years ago. For Native Americans, these ruins are places of worship, where the ancestors still reside in the spirit world. We learned more about them by visiting the famous collection of their whimsical, brilliant, black-on-white pottery.

Another time, we decided to go to Las Cruces and base there for a week. Two and a half months later, we bid adieu to the city and headed for home. Every day we had a different adventure either in the city itself or within an easy or relatively short drive.

Every night, I wrote an email home to a group of friends who asked to be included in daily travel updates. "How is it possible that there is so much to see and do and it's only four hours from Santa Fe?" they asked. "I'm stunned myself," I replied.

Las Cruces feels like Old Mexico—no, surprise, because it used to be part of Mexico. People are friendly, they have time to talk and hang, and you don't feel rushed. When asked for walking directions, they often offered to accompany us. They willingly recommended their favorite hikes, restaurants, and sections of the city. They voiced appreciation of the mild winter climate. When we went to the Farmers & Crafts Market on Saturday, several vendors recognized us from the week before. And we were surprised at how affordable things are. Also, every time we looked up, the Organ Mountains—named for their resemblance to church organ pipes—had changed color and seemed to be watching over us. I have never experienced any city with such an intimate connection to a mountain range.

No matter what people's interests are—history, art, archeology, nature, beauty, paleontology, animals, food, music, views, authentic culture, books, western lore, spirituality, sports, agriculture, museums, architecture—they are thrilled with what they uncover and discover. Our only disappointment was that we had to leave at some point and say goodbye to new friends.

Gila Cliff Dwellings National Monument.

Gila Cliff Dwellings and Mimbres Pottery

Where Ancestral Spirits Still Speak to Us

Takeaway: Special words are your personal invitation to adventure.

I have often said, "I love the sound of that word" or "the name of that place sounds intriguing." That's what happens when a word or name sings to me. Of course, it's up to me to decide whether or not I wish to sing along. If I ignore it, life goes on as though nothing happened. But when I choose to join the chorus, it may lead to someone or something surprising or exciting. Friends are mystified about why I would travel based on a few words I hear, but I've never been disappointed.

I was on a supermarket line when I first heard someone mention the Gila Cliff Dwellings. A woman behind me was talking about her upcoming trip there. Several weeks later, we were in Silver City, and over a Continental breakfast our host asked if we were interested in going to the Gila Cliff Dwellings. I dropped my croissant. "Is it close to Silver City?" I asked excitedly. "About 45 miles to the north."

We bought a picnic lunch and headed out . . . still with no idea what to expect. I generally do no advance research because I want to discover things for myself.

After a pleasant drive we turned onto a sinuous, forested mountain road and when we saw a sign saying "Overlook," we figured it would be a great picnic spot. We sat on a low stone wall, our feet dangling over the edge, and beheld a vast scene of green mountains under a cloudless, periwinkle heaven.

About 700 years before our picnic, approximately ten to fifteen extended Mogollon families lived in dwellings they had constructed inside natural caves. A cave consisted of perhaps forty rooms used for sleeping, storage, ceremonies, and clan rooms. The people were hunters, gatherers, and farmers, and they traded with other populations: shells from the Pacific coast, scarlet macaw feathers from distant breeding centers, obsidian and turquoise from mines.

On top of mesas and along the Gila River, they planted the three sisters: corn, beans, and squash. They hunted for deer, elk, waterfowl, turkeys and foraged nuts and berries. They used throwing sticks to catch birds and rabbits and wove sandals from yucca.

In 1907, President Theodore Roosevelt established the Gila Cliff Dwellings National Monument to preserve the precious ruins. To access them, it's a relatively easy ascent of the one-mile loop trail, across several wooden bridges and up dozens of stone steps to arrive at the mouth of a large cave where we marveled at the ingenious construction inside the natural shelter. Dwellings included T-shaped doorways, once-plastered walls, and holes for vigas, or rough-hewn wooden beams that are still used in southwestern-style houses today. Sometimes fallen rocks were incorporated into the architecture.

Most visitors probably complete the trail in the recommended one hour. But we are slow travelers, in no hurry, and so we lingered, took notes and photos, and got rewards.

"Those circular stone shapes may have been used for fires," the woman volunteer who guarded the site said. Blackened smoke could still be seen on stone ceilings. "If you climb those wooden ladders and peer into a room below, you'll see corncobs on the floor and images of a man and a snake that were painted in red," she added.

We saw the corn cobs, and by craning our necks we saw the faint red shapes. "I see you like pictographs and petroglyphs. You should visit the ones near the Scorpion campground, where I'm living. And you must see the short film in the Visitors Center before you go," she offered.

We did exactly as she recommended. The short educational film at the Visitors Center supplied fascinating information about links between the Mogollon and the Pueblo people of New Mexico today. Parrot petroglyphs may indicate the Zuni parrot clan; T-shaped doorways were important to the Hopi and can also be found at Canyon de Chelly, Chaco Canyon, and Mesa Verde; Masao was a spiritual being who walked the earth humbly with a planting stick, a gourd of water, and some seeds, and told the people to leave their footprints where the ruins are today. Between 1276 and 1281, most trees were cut for use in construction. By the early 1300s, the cliffs were silent, and people were gone. There had been a twenty-four-year drought, it became hard to find game, the fields dried up, water became scarce. Some cliff-dwelling refugees trekked 300 miles south to Mexico's Copper Canyon, and many merged with ancient Puebloan people.

For Native Americans, these ruins are places of worship, where the ancestors still reside in the spirit world. They live on in songs and dances of the Zuni, Hopi, and Acoma Pueblos.

The Mimbres people who once lived there as part of the Mogollon culture, produced brilliant, dazzling black-on-white pottery, and the best collection of their prehistoric pottery is in nearby Silver City.

Our spontaneous itinerary was now set: first the Lower Scorpion site trail, and then the Mimbres pottery in Silver City.

The 1/4-mile, wheelchair-accessible trail leads to a small cliff dwelling and a magnificent stone wall of pictographs (paintings on rocks) of humans, animals, and dancing figures rendered in a mixture of water and powdered hematite. Across from it is a huge, dark boulder whose use is a mystery: Was it a place to sharpen tools? A slide for kids?

The next day, we headed for Western New Mexico University to see the famous Mimbres Collection. Hard to find, we finally located it in the Fleming Hall University Museum across from the library. There I saw brilliant examples of my favorite pottery designs in the world, created by Mimbres artists—minimalist, stylized, whimsical, black-on-white animals, human figures, and geometric shapes that adorn brewing vessels, ollas (water jars), bowls. I fell in love with the jackrabbit, the man with a fish on a stick, a butterfly larger than a human with a basket on his head, humpbacked Kokopelli with his crook, a coatimundi, bat, deer, and squirrel. And I was moved that I had visited the habitations of cliff dwellers where such pottery was made.

All of this came from hearing the words "Gila Cliff Dwellings" while standing on a supermarket line. It was a clue from the universe that I heard and followed.

The other clue I followed led me to special people, who somehow stand out from the others around them. They have a je ne sais quoi, a special air about them. And I met one in Las Cruces.

For more information: https://www.nps.gov/articles/gila.htm
https://museum.wnmu.edu/about/collections/

Kristen Worthington delivers gourmet dishes at her pecan farm.

Gourmet Dining in a Pecan Orchard

Takeaway: If you slow down and spend time talking with special people you meet, it will often result in unanticipated adventures.

Whenever I travel, in familiar or unfamiliar places, I'm always on the lookout for interesting people. Often, they have followed an unusual path to discover their passion in life, love talking about it, are not in a hurry when speaking to folks they don't know, and teach me something new. When I met Kristen Worthington at the Saturday Las Cruces Farmers & Crafts Market, I knew she was one of them.

She was selling pecans or, more specifically, *everything* pecan: pecan-based beauty products, pecan oil, sweets, and multi-flavored pecans that came from her farm. Although potential customers were milling about her stand, once we started talking, she smiled at all of them but continued telling me a story about her life in the pecan grove and how she got there. She'd lived in northern California and had no experience in farming, much less nut farming. But she was crafty. Her husband had bought her a spinning wheel, she got some angora rabbits, and created a cottage industry of fibers and yarns. She had also made soaps. And in the five years since she moved to Mesilla Park, she has ramped up production on a ten-acre orchard and has plans for the neighborhood pecan farmers to form a cooperative so they can share resources and expand their market. She is also environmentally responsible, doesn't spray for pests, and says pecans trees are a low footprint crop.

On our first visit to Worthington Farms, she greeted us wearing her "Keep Farmers Farming" T-shirt. Her husband Shawn joined us; he's an electrical engineer with a background in mechanical engineering and was also a chef. Between them, they had all the skills needed to become pecan entrepreneurs.

My first question was, "Why are your trees are painted white on the bottom? I've heard so many reasons for that." "It's to protect young and transplanted trees from sunburn before their foliage comes out." Her voice grew tender when she talked about the little saplings. And it had never occurred to me that young trees could be burned by a pitiless sun.

Kristen does her own pruning with a chainsaw. As she spoke, she picked two nuts off the ground and skillfully cracked them in the palm of her hand. Impressed by her macho display, I tried it. Two pecans. One palm. No results. My hands were made for pens, not pecans.

I asked if there was a difference between freshly harvested pecans and store-bought. "Supermarket shelved pecans can be two to three years old. They are darker in color. The new ones are much lighter," Shawn replied. Kristen first shelled a year-old pecan and gave it to us to taste. Then a lighter, newer one. They were decidedly different. The one-year-old was predictable, a little tough. The new one was peppy, meaty, with a distinctly fresh taste. "In their shell, they keep for months. If frozen, pecans can keep for two years," she explained.

We progressed on to Sex Ed: there are no male or female trees per se. "There are just two different kinds of trees, and no need for bees as they are wind-pollinated," Kristen said. "Some pecan trees shed pollen first and their pistillate flowers are receptive to pollen later in the season. Other pecan trees have pistillate flowers that are receptive to pollen first and then their catkins (flowers) shed pollen later in the season."

"Is pecan oil good for you?"

"Sure is," said our pecan professor. "It's heart healthy and lower in saturated fat than olive oil. It has a smoke point of 470 degrees Fahrenheit, so you can fry with it or barbecue."

Factoid: Pecans are the *only* nut native to the United States. Second factoid: Doña Ana, where Mesilla Park is located, is the largest pecan-producing county in the United States. The roads we drove were lined with miles and miles of pecan trees. And a third: The local pecans have a "paper shell" that makes them easier to crack. But perhaps not in the palm of my hand.

Kristen was obviously busy with the demands of running a farm and a multifaceted business, but she seemed to have all the time in the world as she showed us around. It made me realize how many interactions with people are rushed, and how good it felt to slow down and enjoy the experience. Kirsten walked us behind her house to meet the chickens. They love pecans and came running and clucking when Kristen tossed them the nuts.

And then we saw what Shawn's engineering brought to the farm. He set up a custom assembly line of machines for washing and shelling the pecans. "We didn't have machines, and it was too hard cracking the nuts in our hands," he said. "What's the easiest way to shell them?" I asked. The couple showed us their collection of nut crackers. Eight different ones, but only a few are an efficient match for those paper shells and elusive nut meat. The pecans are an easy nut to crack but hard to extract.

For our second visit, we signed up for Kristen's private gourmet pecan dinner in the orchard. It was the first time she had done it, and we were the beta testers before she offered it to other guests. Our table was adorned with a fancy tablecloth and matching napkins, and a centerpiece she created from flowers and feathers. Completing the bucolic imagery were the distant Organ Mountains, the trees, and a retro red 1950s-vintage tractor.

Kristen handed us designer menus for the chef's tasting table five-course meal she'd created for the day. Her dad was a cook, and Shawn was sous chef at the famous Stein Eriksen Lodge in Park City, so she is doubly inspired in the kitchen.

Our languorous two-hour dinner began with Sour Dough Pecan bread, dipped in pecan oil and balsamic vinaigrette. The second course was what I would call a democratic salad: each ingredient was perfect on its own, and yet blended well with all the other elements. It was a colorful garden of candied pecans nestled among fresh blueberries, strawberries, yellow bell peppers, blue cheese crumbles, cherry tomatoes, and a light pecan oil. The third course? A Creamy Pecan Soup made with roasted pecans, onions, garlic and topped with sour cream and chives. The rich, silky pecan milk base was a counterpoint to the crunch of the nuts. The taste suggested a delicate, flavorful cream of mushroom soup. The fourth was hearty pecan crusted chicken thighs with lemon pepper pecan stuffing and crunchy, sauteed green beans in pecan oil.

"I hope I end the meal with a bang," Kristen confided. She certainly did, thanks to her pecan brownie cheesecake with pecan crust and chocolate pecan ganache topped off with pecan *roca* and coco pecan frosting. That night we had pecan dreams.

Kristen, whom I've dubbed "The Pecan Princess," does tastings, parties, and dinners in her pecan kingdom. It's a place where guests can slow down, ask questions, listen, and learn. And, in this instance, savor. Without hesitation, this beta tester recommends the one-of-a kind gourmet adventure of pecan immersion to foodies everywhere.

I also recommend a singular way to experience a mighty river that is having a rough time.

For more information: https://worthingtonpecanfarm.com; 575-415-3344

Rio Grande foreground, Organ Mountains behind.

Hiking to Honor the Thirsty Rio Grande

Experiencing and Photographing the Unique Point of View of Fish

Takeaway: Even if you go on well-trod paths, you can seek a different point of view for a unique perspective.

I always approach the Rio Grande with reverence. The river starts in the snow-covered Rocky Mountains of Colorado and ends in the Gulf of Mexico 1,900 miles later. It was the lifeblood of early wanderers, ancestral people, and it was a great gift to thirsty wildlife and farmers whose fields ached for irrigation.

As a New Mexican, one of my greatest pleasures is walking and picnicking along the shores of the river, past cottonwood trees and tall grasses.

Although it was always deemed a mighty river, the Rio Grande is struggling through a period of severe drought. In Las Cruces, it is bone dry for much of the year, and there is rejoicing in the souls of fishermen, rafters, swimmers, farmers, ranchers, and aquaphiles when water dammed upstream is released during the summer months.

During the winter, Paul and I went to La Llorona Park, named for the Spanish woman of legend who drowned her children and now, as a ghostly spirit, weeps and searches for her lost little ones. The park is one of the best places in Las Cruces to access the once-mighty Rio Grande or, as it is called in Mexico, the Rio Bravo.

We started walking in the dry riverbed, but a fierce wind arose, and a great cloud of dust blew us out of there. We vowed to come back, and one must never break a vow so, two days later, we returned.

When the river is dry and devoid of aquatic life, it is actually filled with more subtle forms. Twelve-to-fifteen-foot-high grasses, the color of beige wicker, line the banks and are anchored by the sand. When we touched them, the strands were both friable and pliable, and we could break off a piece and hold it in our hands as we walked.

I had never seen the grasses from a river's perspective before. They look quite different from shore. There, they perhaps invite admiration, but inside the dry riverbed, they begged for a touch. Paul turned a piece on its side and said, "Look at the structure. It's made up of hollow tubes."

Our attention was arrested by mystifying tracks in the sand. They crisscrossed the wide riverbed, were about an inch and a half in diameter, and bore evidence of a paw, or some appendage with nails. What was strange about them is that they were in a single, straight line, fairly equidistant. Which animal puts down one paw at a time or perhaps only has one foot? I wondered. I remembered a brilliant tracker-guide I'd met who looked at a print in the dirt and knew instantaneously not only which animal it was but also its age, speed, and how recently it had passed. Without someone like him, we could only make uneducated guesses.

In the middle of the riverbed is an island covered by what looked like giant cattails. The sun played there. It lit up the stalks, paused for a moment, and then was gone behind a cloud. Paul waited patiently, camera poised, for the next illumination.

The sky was light blue on one side of us and dark blue on the other. For the moment they coexisted, perhaps negotiating who would dominate when. The balance of light and dark seemed metaphoric because that is how life is and that is how the human mind is.

As we approached the cattails, we saw that they grew on bamboo-like, segmented, tawny-colored shafts. The stalk was so strong that when I pull it from the sand, I could almost use it as a light walking stick. As an experiment, I actually did that.

Off to the right, in the distance, the shadows on the Organ Mountains looked like large, abstract splotches. This dry riverbed is a visual and physical playground which we could never have experienced it if the river was running.

I picked up a tiny dead plant that looked like screws. Appropriately, it is called screwbean mesquite. Then we stooped to examine shells. The point of view we had is usually reserved for mollusks and fish. And if our amateur tracking had any validity, we saw evidence of javelina, coyote, raccoon, and dogs with their human companions. There was a little sneaker print from a kid who recently gamboled there.

We found a few objects in the sand of the Rio Grande: a skeletal fish head, a snorkeling mask, a cigarette butt, and one black feather. But when we climbed up onto the bank that parallels the river, we were appalled by the filth of human litter: paper masks, bottles, plastic containers. Hey, fellow humans—nature recycles, so why can't we?

Hiking the dry Rio Grande.

We crossed the sand of the river and passed by a concrete bridge as we approached our car. When we looked up, it was the golden hued Magic Hour film people speak about. The sun was like a roving spotlight that focused on and highlighted first an island in the river, then the trees, the mountains, the sand, a couple on the shore, our car.

The dry river is not just the absence of water; it is the river—waiting. It is joyful to appreciate its life-giving flow, and also very moving to walk with it and in it while it's paused in time.

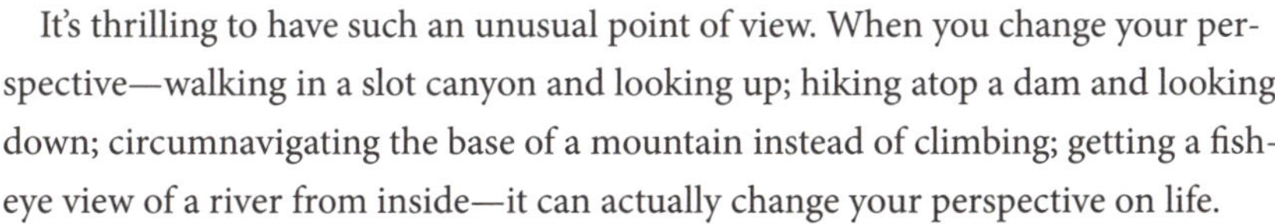

It's thrilling to have such an unusual point of view. When you change your perspective—walking in a slot canyon and looking up; hiking atop a dam and looking down; circumnavigating the base of a mountain instead of climbing; getting a fish-eye view of a river from inside—it can actually change your perspective on life.

It was a short distance from Las Cruces and La Llorona trail that something else changed our perspective: an Indigenous tribe most people, ourselves included, had never heard about. And we were there for their most sacred celebration.

For more information: La Llorona Trail is at 3440 W. Picacho Avenue, Las Cruces

If you're hungry: You can picnic near the river with take-out from Andele's Restaurant. We had their house special *tacos al carbon* (marinated and flame-broiled chicken with grilled onions, cilantro, lime, and beans), chile rellenos, and green pork enchiladas.

Generations continue traditions, Tortugas tribal celebration.

Tortugas Pueblo

Three Days of Sacred Ceremonies That You Can Attend

Takeaway: No matter what your religion, beliefs, or orientation, experiencing a sacred ceremony is a blessing in your life.

While driving in Las Cruces, a new friend pointed out the distant "A" mountain and said the Tortugas Indians climb it during their annual three-day festival—December 10 to 12.

All my senses lit up. *Tortugas* Indians? Three-day festival? I wanted to go.

On the evening of December 10, we drove to the town of Tortugas, south of New Mexico State University and Interstate 10. We were greeted by a procession of dancers called Danzantes in iconic Matachine-like regalia (a blend of North African, Spanish and Native American dress). Traditionally, the religious dances of the Matachines represented the battle between indigenous paganism and Catholicism and the triumph of the latter. The men wore high white headpieces called *cupils*, and two little girls in white symbolized purity.

Don Parra, a friendly Tortugas man who stood next to me, said he danced with a different group, called the Danza Guadalupana Azteca. "You'll recognize us because the leaders wear blue, and the others wear green. We start dancing when we're very young," he explained. "The dancing experience gets deeper as we get older. We dance because it's a vow to the Virgin of Guadalupe. This Guadalupe Festival is our Christmas. Christmas itself is just another day to us. You will see all the groups dance on December 12th."

I was lucky to meet Felipe Chavez, who asked what I knew about the Tortugas. "Nothing," I replied. "Good place to start," he said. "Our name is Los Indigenes de Nuestra Señora de Guadalupe. I married into the Tortugas forty years ago and have been assimilated and granted positions of importance in the corporation."

If anyone thinks "the corporation" refers to a fictional evil empire, they'd do well to think again. Over one hundred years ago, Felipe said, the Tortugas declined to

Los Matachines dancers, Tortugas celebration.

apply for Federal Recognition because they didn't want to be under the thumb of government. Instead, they incorporated and became a non-profit community. "I think we're the oldest and longest surviving non-profit in the state," he added.

Felipe explained that the Tortugas were originally comprised of Piro, Tigua, and other Indians; they didn't share a common language but had to get along for survival. So, they joined together as the Tortugas. They accept outsiders like him "into the pueblo because their numbers are dwindling and they want their heritage and customs to be passed on." I listened intently as he spoke. "You'll see some of our traditions if you climb the mountain tomorrow."

December 11th is a religious pilgrimage day for the Tortugas. They climb 5,000 feet up Tortugas Mountain (known to locals as "A" Mountain for the enormous white letter that honors the Aggies football team at NMSU). We parked at the base

Tortugas annual mountain pilgrimage.

of the mountain and met a woman in hiking shoes who was exiting her car. "Please, can you tell us where the easy path is?" I asked. She laughingly replied, "That's exactly where I'm going. Follow me. I'm Martha." She explained that normally the pilgrimage draws huge crowds of climbers, but the official climb was canceled during the pandemic. Consequently, we had an intimate experience of a non-official pilgrimage.

"There's something called a *quiote*—it's a staff made out of yucca stalk. They're gathered and brought to the mountaintop, where the priest blesses them, and people decorate them with yucca flowers. I'm sorry you won't see them this year," Martha said.

No sooner had she uttered the words when a man passed us on his way down the mountain, carrying a large, decorated quiote staff.

Climbing farther, we passed a man carrying a statue of Guadalupe on his back. Another man wore a Guadalupe image on a large cloth in front of his face and another behind his head. It was clear who the star of the pilgrimage was.

Near the mountaintop, several small groups of people made fires and enjoyed pilgrimage day picnics. At the summit, rock shrines to Guadalupe were painted red; the altars were covered with votive candles and the image of the Virgin surrounded by her golden rays. The view from the top was extraordinary. We could easily see 50 miles in each direction.

One large fire with a lot of smoke called a *humero* was maintained by a Tortugas captain and a group of men. Chris, a Tortugeuño, said this was a special fire. "People write their prayers on little papers and bring them to the fire. The smoke carries them towards heaven." Martha addressed the four directions and tossed her *huami* in the fire.

That night we drove to the Tortugas community again and heard drumming. In the ball field close to the church, the Danzantes from the night before were dancing. With few spectators, we could stand close to them and watch through the fence.

As the sun sank lower, we heard drumming coming from another location and discovered Danza Chichimeca, a dance group whose regalia was bright red, like roses. Images of Guadalupe adorned their clothes, and they carried red gourd rattles, bows, and arrows. One dancer wore bright lights sewn into his clothes and another had little bells, and dust flew up under their pounding feet. We were hypnotized by the rhythm: 1-2-3 tap. 1-2-3 tap. 1-2-3 tap.

Felipe Chavez said the Tortugas are passionate devotees of the Virgin of Guadalupe—the patroness of Mexicans, Latinos, and Native Americans. He tried to explain the relationship of the community to Catholicism. "We are together, but separate." "What practices separate you?" I asked. "Well," he said thoughtfully, "we do things like the feeding of the drum. The drum is the heart of the Pueblo. What you call a drum, we call *tumbé*. We've had one drum for as long as anyone can remember."

December 12 is the day the of the Virgin of Guadalupe, and there was palpable excitement in the air.

In the morning, something hypnotic happened: the four different groups danced their devotion both sequentially and simultaneously in the courtyard of the church and in surrounding areas. Everywhere we looked, walked, or stood, dancing and the pounding beat of drums drowned out our mundane thoughts and forced us to surrender to the experience.

The Indios danced in the courtyard. The men wore brown two-piece regalia fringed in red, and the women wore black Pueblo-style *mantas* (long sheath dresses) that covered one shoulder. They performed their intricate steps to drum music that is complex and changes rhythm frequently. "The dance steps are different for each song and each group," Don Perra explained.

Next, the Danzantes filled the courtyard. Then men's faces were covered by satiny kerchiefs, with only their eyes revealed. Multicolored ribbons flowed down the dancers' backs, and their glittering sequined rattles caught and reflected the sun. A young female fiddler accompanied them.

As they danced, the mass inside the church came through loud outdoor

A dancer rests at annual Virgin of Guadalupe festival.

speakers. The words of the Catholic mass, the singing from inside the church, Indian, Spanish, and Mexican dances and drumming—it all somehow flowed together as each devotee focused on their steps and their group. Intermittently, rifles were fired to dispel evil spirits or express joy. Like several babies in carriages, I jumped every time.

At noon, the dancers paraded down the dirt streets to a drum beat and gathered in front of the *casa de comida*, where free celebratory food is served to all festival participants and attendees. The most anticipated and beloved elements of the meal are the *albondigas* (meatballs) and the *biscochos* (sugar cookies). During the pandemic, alas, the feast was closed to visitors from outside the community.

Later in the afternoon the dancers and community carried the old, sacred, and revered image of the Virgin from the church through the village streets. Afterward, some dancers and community members entered the church to pray the rosary. We stood outside the open door, listening to the singing.

As night fell, we heard drumming again. Across from the church, the Indios' dancing was a swirl of beauty, faith, and prayers manifested in movement. "It's a blessing," said one woman.

No matter what peoples' beliefs are, blessings are always welcome.

In our arid state, water is also a blessing. Most people we know always carry a water bottle with them. In fact, the only creature that is not water dependent is a rat.

For more information: https://www.lascrucescvb.org/the-feast-of-our-lady-of-guadalupe-in-tortugas-is-more-than-a-tradition-its-an-experience-of-a-lifetime/

Chihuahuan Desert Nature Park.

Chihuahuan Desert Nature Park

The Best Kind of Ecological Multitasking for Mind, Body, and Spirit . . . and Why You May Envy the Kangaroo Rat

Takeaway: Take every opportunity to learn no matter what the activity. Every adventure has the potential to teach you something that enriches your knowledge and life.

Chihuahuan Desert Nature Park. I knew nothing about it but liked the name and found out it was only twenty-five minutes from our rental house in Las Cruces. I also discovered that it's not accessible on Apple maps. A pimple on a horse's rump can be found on Apple maps, but not this park. I found it—sort of—courtesy of Google. With a few U-turns, we found the parking lot, and ours was the only car there besides the one belonging to the site manager.

We stepped outside our car and to the east we beheld the San Andres and San Agustin Mountains. They were formed by uplifts from the floor of a shallow ocean 70 million years ago. They made the always-dramatic Organ Mountains, formed volcanically from an eruption from 43 to 33 million years ago, the new kids on the block.

To the west, we saw the Doña Ana Peak and the Checkerboard; the latter is a latticed rock face that fits its name and is beloved by climbers. And a volcanic dike runs down the former. Over time the surrounding soft rock was weathered and washed away, leaving a linear projection of hard rock that looks like the spine of some gigantic prehistoric beast. And after we spotted Vista Hill and Mt. Summerford, we learned that the latter has an unfortunate history. In 1905, Henry Summerford bought a forty-acre track for $110. Three years later, he died from injuries sustained when riding a bronco. Moral of the story: we learned never to buy a house or property if we intend to be rodeo riders. It is now owned by NMSU.

The Chihuahuan Desert Nature Park is a 935-acre outdoor classroom where schoolkids learn about the marvels of the desert. I'm a perpetual student and learned that that the Chihuahuan is the largest desert in North America, spanning between 175,000 and 200,000 miles. It ranks #1 among all deserts of the world for the variety of its mammal, aquatic, animal, and cactus species.

The park is working in conjunction with Jornada Experimental Range to study how decreasing rainfall is affecting plants. I asked the affable park manager, "What are the ramifications of global warming and drought on plants here?" He got very agitated, mentally and physically. "It's very complicated," he said. "Whew. That's a very big question. Whew. It's so big."

Eventually, he said something like, "These are hardy plants, but they are affected by drought. They decrease 50 to 75 percent of their biomass." Then he went on to say that animals use the plants as shelter and for food, and the soil is affected as temperature increases and moisture decreases. "This has implications for the future. Plants won't be able to take up as much carbon, there will be drastic effects of flooding and not enough vegetation to hold the soil. This will raise temperatures with no or less plant cover."

And then the manager was gone, leaving me to ponder our ecological apocalypse and even more appreciative of the surrounding desert beauty.

In order to maximize our visit, we had to be multi-taskers because we were learning, hiking, and inhaling the aroma of fresh air and nature's bounty all around us. The signage is terrific and acquainted us with vinegaroons (forbidding but harmless scorpion-like insects who spray a mist of acetic acid or vinegar when disturbed); honey mesquite or *Prosopis glandulosa* (they look innocent but their thorns can really take a bite out of an innocent human who passes by); claret cup, fish hook, and hedgehog cactus (the latter resembles a barrel on a diet); Christmas cholla and desert zinnia. The clouds floating above in the Wedgewood blue sky looked like headless, long-legged ballerinas in white tutus. In front of us, a long-eared jackrabbit bolted from a bush and then disappeared.

The main hike around the base of the mountain is 1.2 miles, but we also opted for some of the side trails, so our feet covered closer to three.

We took the arroyo loop trail and learned something about the colors we have seen in arroyo walls. The reddish-brown soil is an indicator of a wet environment in the past. A white or light brownish-gray soil suggests a dry climate. And paleosol (love that word!) is an old soil that formed during previous environments. The youngest paleosol is on top of the arroyo wall—it looks thin, and it's mainly sand and gravel; this "baby" layer was formed 8,000 to 15,000 years ago.

We walked forward and turned backward to ogle the gorgeous, dramatic vistas provided by the mountains. Paul spotted the only sign of birds—an empty nest in a mesquite tree.

We said hello to three other visitors who arrived after us and were walking the trail: young newlyweds and the woman's mother. "Don't you just envy the kangaroo rat?" the bride gushed, leaving us to wonder.

We continued on, past banana and sotol cactus and grinned when we saw the latter. Once, on a small press trip to Mexico, Paul was the only journalist who volunteered to drink a potent sotol brew with a rattlesnake at the bottom of the olla (wide jar). The others grimaced and took photos of him.

The trail is easy, with a few altitude changes and some rocky patches. As we headed back to our car, we took another short side path where we learned about the hunter gatherers and early farmers, and how climate change impacted their life. We read that in game drive hunts, groups of hunters swept over an area to harvest many rabbits and pronghorn.

And then, like the bride, when we learned about kangaroo rats, we began to envy them. These little guys can live an entire lifetime without ever taking a sip of water. Their modified kidneys allow them to concentrate urine, and I told my bladder to pay attention because—and this is true—they never pee. They also have special nasal passages that minimize water loss when they breathe.

As I was reading the signage, the bride's mother arrived and inquired, "Would you rather have plastic surgery to look like a wide-eyed fifteen-year-old, or get a kangaroo rat makeover where you never have to drink or pee?" I had never before considered that.

Then we hungrily ate our picnic of fresh green chile cheese tamales from Roberto's Mexican Food in Las Cruces and drank plenty of water because it's the desert and we're not rats.

I think more to our bladders' liking was the remarkable wetlands and the wizard we discovered.

For more information: https://www.newmexico.org/listing/chihuahuan-desert-nature-park/1947/

David Patterson at La Mancha Wetlands.

The Man of La Mancha

The Wizard of the Wetlands

Takeaway: The unexpected happens when you have no expectations.

I wasn't expecting much. I heard that La Mancha was a little three-acre wetlands area, but that was before we met the Man of La Mancha: David Patterson. On the phone, he spoke humbly and told us he was a volunteer who came from Georgia three years ago. I figured oh well, three little acres in Mesilla, a transplant from Georgia, barren land in the winter, we'll do a quick in-and-out visit. After two hours, we were like hungry birds hunting for more and more information seeds at the site.

Patterson suggested we meet at an easy-to-find spot so he could lead us to the out-of-the-way wetlands. When we arrived, we could hardly see him because three snow white, little, bouncy, long-haired chihuahuas filled up the side window of his white Prius. As murders of crows circled overhead, we followed him down a long gravel road and then a dirt one where the nature-animal-plant-pet-people magician emerged from his car. Tall, gray-haired, lanky, and wearing flannel shirt, jeans, hiking boots, and a cap that proclaimed, Trees Are Good.

He introduced us to the first man-made wetlands we had ever visited. Apparently, the land was owned by a developer who donated it in 2005 to the Southwest Environmental Center. Founder Kevin Bixby wasn't told that the developer allowed a construction company to dump broken concrete on the property, and a lot was buried under the surface. It took Bixby ten Kafkaesque, nightmarish years to extract concrete, get water loaned to him so he could dig a pond, obtain a permit for digging, and another from the State Engineer's office. Finally, from a dry expanse of cattails and concrete, a lush man-made wetlands area was born.

Patterson is now the volunteer in charge of La Mancha, and he explained that every time he has to dig and plant, he still hits large chunks of concrete. Undaunted, he uses a pry bar to dislodge the concrete. "It's my gym," he said. He then uses the concrete to make flower beds and berms to hold water. He proudly showed us one site where he planted penstemon to attract hummingbirds.

Patterson explained that the pond is low in the winter, but as soon as the now-arid river runs, it will fill up.

At La Mancha, Patterson oversees the native plans that provide food for birds and pollinators. "There are over 2,000 varieties of ground nesting bees in the southwest, and they don't make honey, but they are pollinators. I have seen them here myself!"

Patterson introduced us to his beloved plants—four wing salt bushes that provide shelter for the bird and whose seeds feed birds, quail, and rabbits; screw bean mesquite trees whose seed pods actually look like screws and that feed skunks, coyotes, rabbits, and rodents and provide a habitat and hiding place for birds; wild asters that turn purple in late fall and are covered by hundreds of butterflies; Arizona rosewood that provides seeds for the birds; and *Sporobolus airoides* (forgive me if I call them "sporos" for short) that offer shelter to wildlife and seeds for the winged ones.

"The Audubon Society comes here more than any group," said Patterson. "Bird lovers appreciate it here." And he went on to tell us excitedly that he planted milkweeds and attracted the first Monarch caterpillar this summer.

I never thought it would happen, but I became excited about the globe mallow that Patterson waters, and it blooms from spring to fall. I was sad when Patterson said "it's like shooting fish in a bowl for the hawks to find birds here. So, we provide cover and food for them."

It's easy to understand why Patterson attracts enthusiastic and loyal volunteers who build birdhouses for kestrels, sparrows, finches, curve-billed thrashers, and cactus wrens, expand and maintain the trail, and create beautiful areas near the pond.

La Mancha needs human help. Feral cats are a problem because they eat birds. Tumbleweeds blow into the water where fish and ducks can't get through them. Beavers have been digging up cattail roots and the willow trees need protective wire around them because the large rodents, who are marvelous ecosystem engineers and a keystone species, can cut down a tree in an hour. They use the branches, trunk, and limbs to build their lodges. "Look," Patterson said. "They eat the cambium layer under the bark."

Tumbleweed and cattails are two invasive species, "but the real invasive species is humans," he said.

At the end of the tour, Patterson told me about a new project. "We're making natural bee motels by taking pruned tree limbs and trunks and drilling different sized holes in them, and placing them strategically around the property. Pretty exciting, eh?" And Bixby has now founded Wildlife for All, an organization dedicated to reforming wildlife management in all fifty states so that it is more ecologically driven and compassionate.

"Just have your readers contact me if they want to visit La Mancha or volunteer," Patterson offered. He inspired me, and I feel confident he will do the same for others. They might volunteer to participate by building a bee motel (there are also bat houses). Surprising things happen when we let go of expectations.

A week later, I practiced having no expectations at a destination where the reward was animals that lived tens of millions of years before the dinosaurs.

For more information: To arrange a visit with David Patterson call 575-993-3997.

You can search for La Mancha Wetlands on your favorite navigation app, but I highly recommend calling Patterson for an intimate and memorable experience.

For more information on wetlands restoration: https://lascruces.com/projects-bring-wildlife-back-to-the-rio-grande/

Actual fossil footprints.

Trackways National Monument

Time Travel Back 280,000,000 Years

Takeaway: Insider information in situ can influence and guide your trip.

I've often longed to go back into the mists of time, and we were transported there as soon as we arrived at Trackways National Monument, in the Robledo Mountains near Las Cruces.. A site little-known outside of the scientific community, it represents the most diverse and abundant Paleozoic terrestrial trace fossils in the world.

The fossils are an astounding 280,000,000 years old—tens of millions of years *before* the dinosaurs. At the time, New Mexico was lying on the equator and had a dry, hot climate like East Africa today. Las Cruces, however, dry as a bone today, was located on the edge of a vast inland Permian Sea. Think: tropical coastal environment. At the end of this period was the greatest obliteration of life the planet had ever known, and some of the tracks are from extinct animals and life forms that existed a quarter of a billion years ago. The best of the 2,500 slabs with fossils can now be seen at the New Mexico Museum of Natural History and Science in Albuquerque.

We decided to go for an easy hike, but it was getting late in the day, so we just followed footprints in the dirt which led us into a wash. Perhaps some would see it as a rock-strewn gully with natural walls on either side made of stones encrusted in old mud. But to me it was a wonderland of geology, about which I know nothing. Water had sculpted the wash and the stones had piled up for eons in successive flooding. I picked up a mustard-yellow rock and I think it had small, fossilized plants in it. Paul picked up a heart-shaped quartz and handed it to me. I can't think of many colors that were not represented in those magical stones. I lifted them from the earth at my feet, held them, turned them over in my hand, and tried to imagine how much time they had seen, as opposed to me and my short life on earth. Then I placed them back on the earth.

As it got closer to sunset, we climbed out of the gully and walked along a road towards where our car was parked in the distance. "Hi!" a male voice called out. "Hello!" we called back to a man who stood at the back of his camper. Turned out he is a field biologist and ecologist and to him, Trackways is a startling site few know about. We talked about his life, his plans, fabulous hikes he and his brother made in the canyons in the area, and the utter magic of this overlooked National Monument. He said some people come here, go "eh," and can't understand its special significance.

"The next time you come here, drive all the way up in your four-wheel vehicle. Park in the sandy lot and you will see several trails. Take the one on your left. It's a bit steep at the beginning and then fairly flat."

It was insider information that made us return to do exactly what we were told. We climbed up a fairly steep hill made of you-can-easily-slip stones, and then followed the trail for magnificent views of the old mine with its tailings piled up atop a mountain, and a panorama of mountain ranges in the distance, topped by white saucer-shaped clouds in a clear sky.

Flat? I wouldn't describe the trail as flat for very long. The ascent wasn't difficult, but the descent required inching down the loose stones while clutching my vulnerable body parts. I did not want a repeat of a fall I took while descending a mountain in Slovakia, the souvenir of which is a metal plate in my wrist.

The trail was less than two miles but it was exhilarating to walk along the upper edge of a canyon and, among rocks of every hue that were hundreds of millions of years old, I was able to feel the insignificance of trivial problems in my own life.

As we were leaving the site, a backpacker with a lemon-yellow shirt and a matching ribbon around her ponytail said, "You'll probably like the Trackways exhibit in the Museum of Nature and Science in Las Cruces. The exhibit has been in the making for almost 300,000,000 years."

We went. It was impossible to just look at the impressions preserved in the ancient mud and go, "Nice. I saw some prints that look like paws and claws. Now let's go have lunch." An appreciation of the exhibit required that we slow down, open our curious minds, and learn about a magical world of paleontology that was only discovered in 1987. For 280,000,000 years no one had seen or touched the tracks. And then along came Jerry MacDonald. He first found five perfect big reptile tracks, and then he discovered hundreds of layers in the solidified mudstone that he said were like the pages of a book. And the slabs with their layers were like an encyclopedia with volumes. Each layer, MacDonald said, covered the surface with something like a plastic-wrap film, and he could peel back the covers and read the volumes underneath, one by one. The earth kept her library, a history of life on the planet.

For more than seven years MacDonald carried the heavy slabs of solidified mud

Cast of a Dimetrodon skeleton.

stone out of the remote site on his back and walked with them for half a mile to his vehicle. Many of them weighed more than one hundred pounds. From the tracks he learned about the animals' behavior—where they stopped, how they moved, when they turned. Maybe those early creatures were only at the spot where their prints were preserved for a few hours. But the footprints of animals big and small were evidence that they moved around the mudflats eating, drinking, resting, hunting, and—if lucky—avoiding predators.

A highlight of the exhibit are screens where you select different subjects and watch MacDonald himself talking about them with his humility, inspiration, and buoyant enthusiasm. And then, of course, there are the tracks, the footprints, the tail prints, models, and paintings that help you visualize these animals, who predated the dinosaurs by many million years. Some looked like giant lizards with sail-like spinal fins and others resembled fat frogs with bulging eyes.

Before leaving the museum, we stopped to look at the live Gila monster. Of course, we also had to look at the live tarantula and the albino axolotl, part of a species that is critically endangered. And who wouldn't want to see the huge skull of T. rex that is covered with injuries? Yes, the big boy was fragile; prone to injuries and disease. Sadly, he may have died of starvation because his injuries prevented him from hunting.

The museum was closing, so we exited through the gift shop and into the present. And it was in the present that we learned how to find and use a product that Indigenous people, Hispanic folks, and early settlers found readily available in nature.

For more information: Prehistoric Trackways National Monument: https://www.blm.gov/visit/ptnm

Las Cruces Museum of Nature & Science: https://www.las-cruces.org/1608/Museum-of-Nature-Science

Soap tree yucca.

Fort Selden and the Secrets of Shampoo

Takeaway: Something you know nothing about can lead to unusual (and hair-raising) adventures.

Sprightly Alexandra McKinney is a historian and educator at Fort Selden in Radium Springs, about fifteen miles north of Las Cruces. Every time we learn something from her, I imagine a class full of rapt students; she has a gift for making things fascinating.

No one speaks much about Fort Selden, and many people who have lived in southern New Mexico all their lives have never thought to stop there. But when McKinney said we'd like it, we had to go.

Outside of the museum and visitor center is a large garden of local flora from the Chihuahuan desert with identifying signs, and I grinned when I saw my favorite yucca: it looks like a tall, pencil-thin cheerleader holding large pompoms. I read the name of the yucca: soap tree. I asked McKinney about it, and she said that Indigenous and Hispanic people once used it as soap because it contains saponin (from the Latin word for "soap").

When I encounter something that I have never heard of before, I have trained myself to stop and find out about it. In my experience, when people hear something unfamiliar, they generally just bypass the unfamiliar and go on with the conversation. It's not inappropriate or embarrassing to ask and I have found that pursuing unusual small details will lead to an adventure.

"Do you know anyone who has tried using yucca?"

"As a matter of fact, I used it for dish soap. And a guy I worked with tried it as shampoo for his buzz cut."

I never thought I would be intrigued by a yucca plant, but suddenly there I was. "Can we learn to make soap with you?" I asked. McKinney nodded yes. But first she wanted to show us the rest of the historic site.

I've mentioned before that I have zero interest in military history, weapons, and forts, but in New Mexico the forts are conduits into history. They were built to defend the settlers and traders against Indian attacks, which were to be expected because Indigenous people were defending their land. When trains came to the area, the soldiers protected people building the railroads from bandits and outlaws. The fort was also intertwined with Spanish commerce along the Camino Real de Tierra Adentro. It started in Mexico City and covered 1,500 miles to Ohkay Owingeh Pueblo north of Santa Fe. Long before that, Indigenous people had used the trail as one of their trade routes.

Anyone who thinks that life on the frontier was thrilling will be rapidly disabused of that idea. At this two-company fort (cavalry and infantry) we checked out the food rations: pork or bacon and corn meal. And for every 100 rations, they added in some beans and peas, rice or hominy, coffee and tea, sugar, vinegar, soap, salt, pepper, potatoes when practicable, molasses, and star candles. It couldn't get more boring than that. No Chinese food, wraps, sushi, pasta, pizzas, or hummus.

Okay, so the food was monotonous, but surely there were other forms of excitement, right? Sure. They got drunk, fought, and went to Leasburg for gambling, saloons, and brothels. It seems like wherever there was a fort, the entertainment was a nearby wild west town with liquor, ladies, and lawlessness.

The barracks, officers' residences, and other structures were built out of adobe, but when we asked McKinney why the jail was made out of stone she replied, "You could dig your way out of an adobe prison." Then she pointed out one of the mysteries of Fort Selden incised in the stone walls of the jail—mostly vertical lines and scratches. Were the inmates counting days? Attempting escape? Bored? We'll never know.

Another thing we don't know is if there will be a Fort Selden site in thirty-five years. That's the estimate of how long it will take for the total delamination and disintegration of the structures without further preservation.

The most famous resident at Fort Selden was Douglas MacArthur, the head of the American forces in the Pacific theater in WWII. His father was the post commander, and little Douggie (there is a photo of him as a child with blond curls) lived there from 1883 to 1886. There's a story of him disappearing and getting lost, and they couldn't find him. They located him when the searchers heard him scream because he encountered a camel. The army had tried to create a Camel Corps for desert warfare against the Indians in the Southwest. When that didn't work out, the animals escaped or were turned loose, and there were supposedly camel sightings until the 1940s.

At one spot among the ruins I felt palpable sadness. Alexandra postulated that it was because two officers shot and killed each other there when it was discovered that the wife of one was having an affair with the other. Besides a free audio tour of the Fort, McKinney has set up stations where kids (or kid-like adults) can make a souvenir adobe brick to take home, or paint a potsherd, in tribute to the Jornada Mogollon who lived there from the fourth century CE until the 1300s. They lived in pit houses and were foragers but also depended on farming beans and squash.

We stopped at the museum (fascinating nineteenth-century photography) and were about to leave the site when I remembered the soap tree yucca. So back we went, and McKinney showed me how to cut three or four long, sharp leaves, scrape off the waxy coating with a knife, mix that with warm water, shake it up, and voila, foamy soap. I took some extra leaves with me when we departed.

That night, I grabbed a steak knife and scraped a few long, thin, pointy, potentially weaponous leaves of the soap tree yucca plant. I added them to warm water, strained out the pieces of green waxy stuff from the plant, and poured the warm water into an empty bottle. I shook it up, ran into the shower, and poured the foamy liquid onto my head. It didn't feel like shampoo. It didn't feel like soap. It didn't foam on my head. And yet, when I washed it off, my hair was squeaky clean and shiny.

That was the beginning of our ongoing soap tree shampoo experiment. For the next few weeks, we only used homemade yucca shampoo. And when we went to a hairdresser, she said our hair was clean and had real body. As I write these words, we have used nothing other than soap tree shampoo for ten months.

After I learned to become a shampoo maker at Fort Selden, I began asking Indigenous and Hispanic friends if soap tree shampoo was used by their families. Our new friend Liz, who grew up on the Navajo reservation, said she learned to make the shampoo as an eight-year-old child—from the Girl Scouts. She told me about a series of YouTube videos about soap tree shampoo-making with a Navajo grandma. Rick Quezada, director of the Cultural Center at Ysidro del Sur Pueblo in El Paso, told me his grandmother used to make it from the yucca root. But no one knew of anyone making it today.

If people call her in advance, McKinney will be their fort guide and shampoo coach, and they just might end up with lustrous, full-bodied, and squeaky-clean hair . . . thanks to the Native Americans who used the natural resources of the land. It's a welcome sign of changed times that a fort which was built to fight Indians and destroy their culture is a place where today Native people are honored for their culture and ingenuity.

After our visit, it was an easy twenty-five-minute drive to Hatch, which bills itself as the chile capital of the world, to eat at tourists' funky fave, Sparky's Burgers and BBQ. It's a cross between a diner and a BBQ joint, and is the locus of tacky Americana, like outrageously oversized statues of Bob's Big Boy, Colonel Sanders, KFC, the Tin Man, and Uncle Sam. Since burgers aren't our thing, we opted for chicken and pulled pork. Then we headed home for a shampoo.

And the next morning, with full-bodied, clean hair, we headed for a place that everyone we met said had nothing of interest. That was a good enough recommendation for us.

For more information: To reserve a tour with McKinney: alexandra.mckinney@state.nm.us; 575-202-1638.

To visit Fort Selden: https://nmhistoricsites.org/fort-selden

To watch a Navajo grandma making shampoo from the soap tree yucca and teaching about her culture: https://www.youtube.com/watch?v=KCxLSUTR3cY

Sparky's in Hatch: https://sparkysburgers.com

San Miguel church.

You've Probably Never Heard of It, Which Is Why You Might Want to Go

Takeaway: There is no place that has nothing of interest.

Why in the world would we go someplace of no interest? When people say "There's nothing there," my hackles go up. There is something interesting everywhere. All you have to do it look for it.

We first heard of the village from a San Miguel-based grower at the Las Cruces Farmer's Market. "What's interesting there?" I asked. "I can assure you—nothing," she replied cheerfully. We got the same answer from everyone we asked at the market.

Spurred on by the challenge of *nada*, we set out. It took about twenty minutes to get from Las Cruces to where our GPS said San Miguel was located. About a mile before our destination, our attention was arrested by the unusual architecture of a neighborhood church that was located to our left, along the main road. The outside was like a patchwork quilt of black lava stone and gray cement. Perhaps many local hands worked on the outside wall, imbuing it with prayers and devotion. We found it very humble and appealing.

We parked, and it turned out that, contrary to what the British woman on our GPS said, we were in San Miguel already. As we walked towards the San Miguel Catholic Church, a small red car pulled up in front of us. The driver rolled down his window and asked if we needed help, presuming that the only reason strangers would stop was because they were lost.

That was Bob. He arrived in San Miguel twenty-five years ago and, coincidentally, both he and Paul went to school in Boston, so they bonded over that. Bob is a short, pudgy fellow who is all heart. "When I arrived here, I realized how hard everything was back in Boston. It was hard getting to work in traffic. Hard getting the right job. Hard keeping up with rising rents. I came here, and it was easy, and beautiful. It was also warm. I fell in love with the mountains, the open spaces, and the local gal who became my wife. I go to church here in San Miguel, and but not as often as I should," he confessed sheepishly.

The church was locked, but he offered to show us around the outside. He heard that part of the church had burned down and been rebuilt in 1984. Then he called his wife and another church member who verified that the original church dated to the 1800s.

As we followed him to the side of the church, Bob described to us in detail where the altar and choir loft were located and who sang in the choir. It was an unusual tour of a church, which we never entered.

As we were talking, a young couple arrived. The man addressed Bob. "Is it okay if I pray here?" "Sure," said Bob, "but the church is locked." "That's okay," said the man. And as we stood there, he dropped to his knees and started to pray in front of the church. His prayers were so urgent he couldn't wait. We tiptoed past him to the yard with a faded folk-art mural of a church and red flowers beside it, and piles of lava rock that were like those embedded in the exterior church walls. Beyond it, acequias with banks looked perfect for walking.

Paul asked Bob if, as both an easterner and outsider, it was hard for him to be accepted there. He said that he felt comfortable from the get-go. "I'm Italian and I was used to grandma cooking and large family gatherings around food. The Hispanic culture felt very familiar. But I really got accepted when I needed heart surgery. Everyone came out to help me. After that, I really belonged."

To the left of the church was a long line of adobe row houses with protruding vigas. It was certainly not built within the last hundred years. Maybe it was used for storage or animals because it had six doorways and no windows. Next to it was another stretch of an adobe row house with windows and doors; this was likely where people lived. And across the street, the old brick dance hall. We could almost hear the salsa music and dancing feet stepping against a forgiving wooden floor.

Close to the church we spotted a large yard with a plastic calf and metal barrels. It was a training area for rodeos where locals could practice their roping and barrel racing skills.

We passed streets lined with pecan trees and long acequias thirsty for the water they would get later in the year. Behind us, a wrought iron gate beckoned as the entry to the Panteon San Miguel. The cemetery was a blaze of plastic flowers and ribbons: red, blue, pink, yellow, orange, rose. Off to the side was a large pit where people deposited flowers that were old and faded from sunlight. When it filled, they would be covered over with earth, buried, perhaps for future generations to excavate.

Four stone steps led up to the oldest part of the cemetery. Many of the graves were marked with weathered wood in the shape of a person, a cross, or just a board that stood vertically. The names of the departed were hand-written and painted in black. On many of the wooden pieces, the names had disappeared, erased by wind, rain, and sun. A few had pillows of black lava rock or were composed of a horizontal slab of cement covered with small white stones. One sepulcher was sculpted out of cement and shaped like a church. Sometimes two crosses hugged each other, one behind the other, like lovers. Some of the names seemed like they could be sung to a long-gone melody: Enedina Maya, Jesusita Valles.

The setting of the stones was one of the most moody and evocative I have seen in any cemetery. Large green cacti grew in clumps and had bright yellow buds that drooped downward, as though they were crying. And they cried the most at the section for young children who had died. Many bore the inscription: *Recuerdo de sus padres*. Remembered by their parents, who were probably bent over with grief for the loss. One had a little snowman in the soil, another a toy car, a third an angel, a fourth a toy truck.

We learn so much about the living from cemeteries. Plastic flowers lined both sides of the road that led around the burial site. They honored their dead. They visited them often. They kept the *panteon* clean and the plastic flowers and ribbons looking crisp, bright, and new.

We felt as though we had been lifted out of time, and in a few short hours we were immersed in a different reality: a tiny rural village, stories about how outsiders got accepted, what it's like to be an Italian from Boston who finds it all familiar, where locals train for rodeo, the piety of residents, and how people stay connected to their ancestors.

Our foray confirmed our conviction that anyone who goes to a supposed place of no interest, if they slow down and use their five senses, will have the pleasure of discovery and uncover someone or something that they will long remember.

I got to use my five senses plus an extrasensory one a few days later when we went to a ghost town, and I was greeted by a spectral resident.

For more information: San Miguel Catholic Church: 19217 NM-28, La Mesa; 575-233-3191.

As of this writing, there is no website for the town of San Miguel.

Lake Valley Ghost Town.

Lake Valley Ghost Town and a Strange Appearance

Takeaway: Just Say Yes!

One of the most important things I learned from traveling is to always say yes. If someone asks if I want to find out how praying mantises mate, I say yes. Would I like to visit a site with discarded dental tools? Sure. A Mexican bar that serves a drink formerly given to sacrificial victims so they wouldn't feel the pain? *Si, si, señor.* I've often been surprised and have never left without learning something new.

If you say yes to everything (that's not harmful to you or anyone else), it opens wide the door of possibility. Something obscure could be boring but, at best, it's a portal to adventure, and you'll end up with fond memories and a good story to tell.

But say no and there is no potential for magic to happen. Yes pulls you out of the humdrum of daily life and nudges you onto an explorer's path.

A recent example of this happened a few months ago in the southwestern part of the state when a woman I met on a hike asked, "Do you believe in ghosts?" I smiled and shrugged noncommittally. "Would you like to go to a ghost town—where I saw one?"

I could have said no, and the story would have ended there, right at the beginning. But Paul and I headed for Lake Valley Historic Site. It's along the Lake Valley backcountry byway, about thirty miles west of Hatch and seventeen miles south of Hillsboro.

A strange thing happened when we arrived and parked across from the church. We were looking out over the Black Range mountains and the wind- and rain-blown ramshackle houses, adobe, stucco, and stone ruins that dot the landscape. I saw a man about fifteen feet from the car, wearing brown trousers tucked into dusty boots. His hat, jauntily perched on his head, sported a little feather. I instantly knew that he was a first-rate raconteur and an optimist-dreamer whose charisma drew people to him. They invited him for meals and bought him drinks. He came to the town or stayed in the town because of his young daughter, who he loved very much. He told me this wordlessly . . . and then he was gone.

In the small museum that used to be the Lake Valley schoolhouse, old photos are displayed in the center of the main room. In one of the photos, I saw a stagecoach and a lineup of working men. One of them is wearing dark pants tucked into his boots, a hat with a small feather on his head, and a young girl off to the left of the line. Her standing position, the position of her feet, is exactly the same as that of the man with a small feather in his hat. I think he was her father.

When we met the caretaker of the site, I told him about the man I had seen. "Doesn't surprise me a bit," he said. "It's a ghost town. You saw a ghost. Happens to a lot of people."

He smiled as he saw me trying to absorb the information and after a long pause asked, "Did you happen to see the guest book in the museum? Lots of folks just pass it by."

I had seen it, and besides the photo of the man I affectionately and somewhat possessively call "my ghost," it was the most evocative item in the museum's collection. The book is reserved exclusively for former residents and their kin. Almost every post is about the dances in the schoolhouse that were run the first Saturday of every month. They were much-anticipated and sought-after family affairs, and entries bring to life the dancers who were "cold, happy, and dancing on the old, echoing floor," and the dust that rose from the old wood floor I was standing on. As I read further, ghosts were probably leaning over my shoulder, enjoying the stories.

One of the entries tells a tale about someone's grandma and grandpa who eloped in 1916 and paid a preacher with a gallon of moonshine to perform the marriage ceremony. Other memories are from folks who camped out on mattresses in the trunk of their car after the dances. One ancestor worked in the manganese mine. Another came and homesteaded. Someone's great grandfather was a miner who died when a basket load of ore fell on him. "Have you ever heard of a "Paul Jones dance" where people changed partners at pre-arranged signals?" I asked *my* Paul. Paul, who I lovingly call "Mr. Nerd Head" because he is like a

Historic photo of a ghost?

Jeopardy contestant, drew a blank. But the guest book has memories from dancers who participated in them.

On one of the walkable paths in Lake Valley, we were surprised to find a cemetery for rusted tin cans. The tumble extends out across the valley like a rivulet of cylinders. In another part of town, its counterpart is brown and clear glass bottles; they shimmer and sparkle in the afternoon sunlight. When I asked the caretaker about the can and bottle cemeteries, all he said was, "Yup. There are cans and bottles."

A little farther on and all by itself, in the middle of weed field, is an old, rusted safe, clearly once part of a local business. On top of it, people leave sherds of pottery (one says "Made in England"), clear and purple glass, and other artifacts that they have found as they walked around.

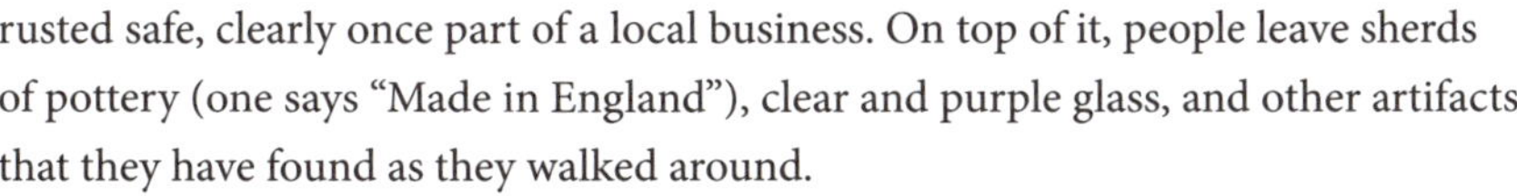

If visitors use their imagination, they can visualize what the architecture of the silver mining boom town once was. Like many western towns, it had false-front façades, covered boardwalks, and wood sidings on the adobe walls. Adobe was the basic building material, but "Anglos" added pitched roofs, wood floors, and other protective and design elements.

"Lake Valley has quite the mining history. Am I correct in assuming you want to know about it?" the caretaker asked.

Of course, I answered yes. I've never been particularly interested in ore and mineral extraction operations, but since we were in an old mining town, why not find out? My yes led us back to the museum, where the caretaker pointed to information posted on one of the walls that we had missed. It told a fascinating story that started with the "Bridal Chamber" in 1881. It got its name because of sparkling lights that reflected from an untold number of crystals of cerargyrite and calcite on the roof of a cavernous excavation. Contained in that space was one of the richest silver deposits ever found. A newspaper of the day said the concentration was so dense that ore could be melted from the ceiling of the deposit with only the flame from a burning candle. It was so pure that it shipped unsmelted to the US Mint.

The news spread fast. The word was that the region held other bonanzas like Bridal Chamber, and it would be heaven in earth for prospectors and mine owners. Fortune-seekers came from all over the United States and Europe. From the 1880s to the 1890s, there was a boomtown population of more than 4,000. The town had newspapers, a dozen saloons, hotels, general stores, churches, a school, and a brothel—with transportation to and from other towns provided by horse, mule, or stagecoach. The local Madame, Sadie Orchard, even ran a stage coach line in addition to her booming brothel business. It was a hardscrabble life, and it's easy to conjure images of saloon fights, stage coach robberies, guns, alcohol and the other entertainments and vices of a western town. Apache raids could be pretty frightening, but the Bridal Chamber had a seemingly endless supply of wannabe grooms who came courting it. Reportedly, that one mine yielded millions of ounces of silver.

Alas, reality couldn't sustain the bright sheen of dreams. The Bridal Chamber was one of a kind, the railroad came and spelled doom for the stagecoach era, and in 1893 the price of silver plummeted, and mine closures forced people to leave. In 1895, the wooden buildings burned, and the entire business district of Lake Valley was gone in half an hour. An arsonist was put in prison, but that didn't rebuild the once prosperous enclave. By 1900 there were only a few hundred souls left, and the flu swept through in 1918.

But Lake Valley was the little town that could. There's a story that a man named Lucius Fisher reportedly won most of the mining property in a poker game in Denver and started large scale mining operations which lasted only a few years until the Depression hit. During WWII, some mines were reopened to produce manganese used in the manufacture of high-grade steel. By the 1950s, the population was reduced to a few dozen. It had returned to being a town that couldn't and, in 1994, the last living resident left.

Once again, I experienced that answering in the affirmative leads to expanding one's horizon and deepening travel. The more we dig, the higher chance we have of finding—so to speak—our own Bridal Chamber. And it may even come with a ghost.

We had a different kind of experience when we arrived at another nearby town with zero expectations. In fact, all we knew about it was its name.

For more information: https://www.blm.gov/visit/lake-valley-historic-townsite; 575-525-4300

To see a Paul Jones dance: https://www.youtube.com/watch?v=bUwQ7Wz8Abg

Evocative Old West architecture, Hillsboro.

Follow the Artists

Takeaway: Artists often choose to live in interesting, off-the-radar places.

Sometimes little-to-unknown locations offer an opportunity to cut loose from expectations and set out to explore without an agenda. We often challenge ourselves to land in an unfamiliar place and find something that resonates with one or both of us. It doesn't matter if no one else would be interested in it; travel is a personal engagement with the world, a private itinerary of connecting and having unique experiences. A traveler may find these destinations by chance, or maybe someone suggests they go there or they overhear a conversation that piques their curiosity. The information can come from anywhere. What matters is that they go there.

One way I have discovered gems is to follow artists. Many of them seem to have a sniffer for cool places to live that are rich in atmosphere, nestled in beauty, affordable, and not well known. The newcomers bring their sense of color and design and find innovative ways to make a living because of the vagaries of the art world.

Hillsboro is such a place. It's a charming town about thirty miles from Truth or Consequences and seventeen miles from Lake Valley Historic Site. Founded in the 1870s, it's tucked into the graceful, rolling hills of the Black Range. The population is small, and artists are attracted to the quiet, peaceful life it offers with ranchers and miners as neighbors. The few streets are made of dirt, and a bumper sticker on a car gives you an idea of the pace. It reads: Hillsboro, NM, *carpe mañana.*

Restoration has brought some of the Victorian-era homes back to life, and a free map available on Main Street tells the background of each historic house. Locals are friendly, and if the map is hard to follow, they are happy to point out the evocative ruins of the old courthouse and stone jail or homes on the

A classic restored home, HIllsboro.

National Register of Historic Places. My fave is the Geo. T. & Ninette Stocker-Miller House on Eleanora Street, which is built from the town's smelted slag (the left afters of processed ore) cast into brick. On the side of the house is a mural done by artist Glenda Jackson; it portrays two proper Victorian women dressed in black.

But Hillsboro was not always placid. Buried underneath the quaint and charming veneer is a whole lot of blood, whoring, drinking, money, and fighting. In short, it was a Wild West mining town situated smack in the middle of Apache territory. And the Apache were not happy about it. As miners' land claims extended to outlying areas, and deep into traditional Apache territory, Indigenous people fought back with ferocity. There was both bad and real blood between the two, and deaths on both sides.

In 1879, the Apache attacks intensified under the leadership of the legendary Victorio. Ten Hillsboro citizens were killed. The US military was effective at protecting settlers and in campaigns against Indians, and periodically soldiers were stationed in Hillsboro. When Victorio died, he was succeeded by Nana. Bolstered by reinforcement from the Mescalero Apache, he spearheaded vengeance raids. Homes were burned, ranches were ransacked, and people were killed.

In spite of the hostilities, the soldiers were enough of a deterrent that the population grew. Hillsboro became the Sierra County seat, with a beautiful brick

Ruins of the old courthouse, Hillsboro.

courthouse. It stayed that way until the 1930s when the county seat was relocated to Hot Springs (now Truth or Consequences), and the residents of Hillsboro sued the county commissioners for election fraud. Certainly, those words—election fraud—are no strangers to modern ears.

Well, the folks in Hillsboro did not fade peacefully into the night. Records kept disappearing from the courthouse in Hot Springs and ending up back in the courthouse in Hillsboro. And don't think the county commissioners backed off either. They sold the Victorian courthouse in Hillsboro for salvage. Today, only the arch and a few sections of wall remain to tell the tale.

Paul calls the area around Hillsboro "barren beauty." The landscape is peppered with hills, snowcapped peaks appear in the distance, and a chain of mountains surrounds you as you navigate the winding roads. Although we were practically the only visitors in town on a wintery day, the Tradin' Post, bar, eateries, Hillsboro General Store, and Black Range Museum are attractive to tourists during the warm months. It's also easy to imagine the hustle and bustle of the past, which allegedly includes the last operating stage line in the United States.

It was also frequented by one of my favorite New Mexico women, whom I've mentioned before: Sadie Jane Creech Orchard. Her life spanned the years of 1860 to 1943, and legends about her abound. The local museum has a room full of artifacts attributed to her. Sadie came to the booming mining area and achieved both fame and notoriety. She was a sex worker and an excellent businesswoman. She opened brothels, built and ran hotels and restaurants, and not only co-owned but was reputedly also a driver for a regional stagecoach line. Was it true? Who knows? Many stories circulated about Sadie, and some of them she invented herself. But Sadie was not just a colorful woman and successful capitalist. During World War I, she, according to a historical marker, "tended the less fortunate, and during the 1918 flu pandemic, she nursed children and cared for the sick and dying." In the words of New Mexico writer Erna Ferguson, "for a bad woman she was one of the best."

Local artist Nolan Winkler has lived in Hillsboro for twenty-nine years. Her work is on display at Rio Bravo Fine Art in Truth or Consequences, and her heart is in Hillsboro. She said, "What we love and hate about Hillsboro is that everything is slow. But that's what keeps it as quaint as it is. My friends here are writers and artists. I am a competitive cyclist and Hillsboro has the best training roads in the world. And it's great that young people are moving in now, so you can do things like get a massage, and meet people like Jessica Wertz in her open ceramic studio."

I had no idea we'd find so many Victorian homes. I didn't know I was in Apache country. Paul had no idea it would be so photographically promising. Hillsboro is a great place to slow down, walk around, stop and sip at the Black Range Vineyards, shop for art and décor, spot wildlife, and have an experience that is all your own.

Back in Las Cruces, we stopped briefly at an antique store and saw a small, brightly colored ceramic figurine from Mexico. It was the impetus for our next trip.

For more information: https://townofhillsboronm.com
https://sierracountynewmexico.info/attractions/hillsboro-new-mexico/

Pancho Villa: bandit or folk hero?

Finding Out Who Pancho Villa Was and Walking to a Foreign Country

Takeaway: Curiosity about famous historical figures may lead to discovering other sides of a story.

I hadn't lived in the state for long when I first heard about the invasion of the United States in 1916 and wondered why the last hostile action by foreign troops happened in the tiny village of Columbus. I had forgotten about it until a historian in Las Cruces said, "it's bigger than a New Mexico event; it's an American history story."

It took about an hour and a half to drive there from Las Cruces. One of the gaudy delights of the road through flatlands dotted with desert scrub were the huge billboards promoting a place where tourists could see *The Thing* and also buy moccasins and slurp a Blizzard. As a child, I loved those roadside billboards; they fired my imagination and I, like most other kids, nagged my parents to stop so we could see *The Thing* or its equivalent.

We passed a few nut orchards, a large dairy farm, a field of cotton, and then miles of miles. The most striking feature of the landscape was the sudden appearance of three tent-shaped mountain peaks that were surely an ancient hotbed of volcanic activity.

Our destination turned out to be a two-story, beige and brown 1902 building that used to be a train depot and is now the Columbus Historical Society Rail Road Depot Museum. A large sign outside introduced us to the first of several women who were unknown heroes of the resistance to the invasion. Susan Parks was a switchboard operator at the time. When the troops of Francisco "Pancho" Villa attacked the town in the early morning hours of March 9, 1916, she braved gunfire and calmly summoned the National Guard in Deming from her switchboard. She and her infant daughter were wounded but survived.

Inside the gem of a museum, we began to question the image we had of Pancho Villa as a ruthless, violent, scruffy Mexican bandit who wore a broad-brimmed hat pushed back to reveal his face, and two crisscrossed bandoliers of bullets over his chest. Even though he hated the United States—and the feeling was mutual—we were surprised to learn that President Woodrow Wilson first supported Villa when he seemed to be leading a successful revolution in Mexico. In Columbus, which is three miles from the Mexican border, Sam Ravel, who owned the mercantile store, made most of his income by selling arms and ammo to Villa and Mexican revolutionary factions. But when Villa started losing battles in Mexico his popularity waned, Wilson turned away from him and supported Mexican president Carranza, Villa's enemy. Wilson allowed Carranza to transport troops on US soil and banned the sale of weapons to Mexico. Villa was outraged. He felt that he had been protecting American interests, and he was betrayed. He gave the order to kill every American in sight. He was determined to convince the United States of his powerful position in Mexico and exact revenge. It is also possible that he had paid Ravel thousands of dollars for weapons and after the ban took effect, the money was not returned.

A wonderfully intelligent video in the museum recreates the raid from beginning to end. First Villa's ragtag soldiers killed Americans in Mexico, and after they had widowed a woman, they tied her to her horse and forced her to ride with them and watch the attack on Columbus. She was half-starved and fully horrified. And then she was taken before Villa himself, and she expected to be murdered. Instead, he set her free, unharmed. Another heroine who lived to tell the tale.

At the time of the raid, the military Camp Furlong was located in Columbus. The attack was so unexpected that Lieutenant John P. Lucas, who was sleeping, never had time to put on his boots. He dove out of bed and led a significant part of the battle against the Villistas unshod. The raiding, looting, and fighting were fierce. Eighteen Americans died and more than two hundred Villistas met their end. And Villa's reputation was burnished in Mexico.

Was he a terrorist or a hero? He caused tragic loss of innocent lives and destroyed Columbus. But as a charismatic guerrilla and revolutionary, he inspired his countrymen.

There are many versions of what happened in Columbus that fateful day in 1916 and many theories about why Villa did what he did. It is not even clear that Villa himself was present for the attack. And after the unexpected invasion across the border, ten thousand US troops were sent to little Columbus, as well as the entire air fleet of the US military at that time: all eight planes. That's how important Columbus was.

After visiting the museum, we needed time to process what we had learned. We got takeout from one of the local restaurants and ate at Pancho Villa State Park, where we pondered the irony of such a tragedy providing little Columbus with visitors and much-needed income.

We walked around the little town, seeing the only building left from the time of the raid—the Hoover Hotel. Eighteen-year-old Bessie James was on her way there, seeking refuge, when she was killed by a gunshot to her chest. She was the only woman who died in the attack. As we walked around reading the historical panels, we learned about people like Charles Chase Miller, who resided at the hotel. A true hero, he braved gunfire and dashed to his drugstore across the street to get guns and ammo for people in the hotel to defend themselves. He was shot a few feet from the hotel, with his store keys still in his hand. Another character in the drama was Mr. Frost. It was his thirty-fifth birthday, and he was shot while driving his car, with his mail-order bride beside him. She had never driven a car, but she took over the wheel and saved them.

Fascinated by the story and curious about how it was perceived south of the border, we drove three miles, parked our car, and walked over the border to Palomas, Mexico. No one looked at our passport or asked us a single question as we continued on foot to one of our favorite countries. We were the only people crossing.

In the center of town, near a huge bronze statue of Pancho Villa heroically galloping on horseback with a gun drawn and pointed in front of him, live musicians played to a growing audience of locals. "Do you know who that is?" a mustached man standing next to me asked. Before I could answer, he continued proudly, "He's a hero of the Mexican Revolution."

Wow, I thought. Latitude determines attitude when it comes to Pancho Villa. He is considered a terrorist three miles away from a country where he is honored as a hero.

We walked back to the US border crossing and this time we were required to show our passports and asked five times what we were doing in Mexico and where we lived in New Mexico. Finally, a female agent said she liked my green hat, we passed muster, walked to our car, and headed back towards our temporary home in Las Cruces.

Both of us were uncharacteristically quiet on the ride. We had a feeling that something sad was soon to happen.

For more information about the Historical Society Museum:
575-531-2620

Desert Peaks National Monument.

Desert Peaks National Monument

When You Leave a Place You Love, Always Say Goodbye

Takeaway: Thanking a place for letting you visit is payback for what you have been offered.

I had never realized that a hike can be a sacred activity in the temple of nature until the last day we were in Las Cruces after a two-and-a-half-month stay. We had grandiose plans of driving to remote destinations, but the more we thought about it, the less we wanted to spend our time in the car.

Paul suggested we drive to Organ Mountains Desert Peaks National Monument, which was accessible, and where we hadn't gone before. He also thought it would be a good place to say goodbye to our beloved Organ Mountains—the majestic, spikey peaks that change color throughout the day and have such an intimate relation with the city. They are a reminder that life is glorious, that there is hope, that beauty is everywhere, and that the sun and moon are the directors of drama on the stage of existence. They have secrets, those Organs. But they also are comforters, friends, guardians.

It was mid-afternoon in the middle of the winter when we arrived at the National Monument. That turned out to be the perfect time on the perfect day in the perfect season for meeting the mountains on their own terms. At the start of the Bar Canyon Trail, we were greeted by a panorama of different peaks—gray, purple, brown, and black, in full sunshine adornment. There were traces of snow on the north side and spring-like greenery towards the south. The golden grasses were almost my height, and they swayed gently in the breeze. It was the kind of place where you ask Nature's permission to enter her temple because the beauty was so sacred.

The hike wasn't difficult, but it kept going upward towards the mother mountains, over dirt and then rocks. At one point we came face-to-face with a two-toned monolith boulder; it was darker brown on top and beige on the lower half.

In front of it was a large volcanic heap, and over the ancient, black, explosive stone nature had created a covering that resembled rust-colored bricks.

We kept climbing. To our right was a yawning tree; it had a gaping, mouth-like hole in the middle, and its right limb was extended, like a human arm when doing a full-body stretch. Behind it, a mountain peak and above that, an afternoon moon.

The trail ended at a waterfall, but it was no Dripping Springs (another famous hike in the area). It was more like a dripping water faucet, and art-designed ice trickles had formed below it, frozen in time. On the hike back to the car, the light had changed, the sun was lower in the sky, and the multicolored, light-drenched hills were in subdued evening attire—soft browns, mostly.

We realized that we had fallen in love with Las Cruces, and that it was not unrequited love. It kissed us goodbye with a hike laced with holiness and we will forever be grateful. We said thank you for all we had been given.

For more information: https://www.blm.gov/programs/national-conservation-lands/new-mexico/organ-mountains-desert-peaks-national-monument

Meet the People

At the Masonic Cemetery in Las Cruces, we asked another visitor named Adelina if she knew where Pat Garrett (the lawman who killed Billy the Kid) was buried. She showed us the way, and then added:

"There's another famous man buried here who you never heard about. Fabian Garcia was the father of New Mexico agriculture who developed all the chile varieties we eat today. In a blatantly racist omission, Garcia was the first Hispanic person inducted into the agriculture Hall of Fame—and it only happened two years ago. You would walk right by his grave and never know the king of chile lies there."

The owner of the apartment we rented introduced us to his grandma Nellie Morales, who lived next door to us. We loved listening to her stories of growing up in the old days in Las Cruces.

"My mother used to crawl on her knees three blocks to the church dedicated to the Virgin. And I said to my mother, 'mama you don't need to make that sacrifice because Jesus already made the sacrifice for us.' But she wouldn't listen and kept on crawling. When I was a child, I got pneumonia and my mother made me dance to the Virgin and I was healed."

An employee at the Old Train Depot and Museum in Las Cruces was a history buff, and I asked her if there had been segregation at the depot.

"There sure was. The men and women were separated into different rooms. Ladies of the time did not want tobacco spit on their pretty dresses."

When I asked if there was segregation between Black and white passengers the director jumped in to answer:

"I heard one sad story that when the train arrived in Texas, they made the passengers dismount so they could separate the Blacks from the whites. I know there were Black porters on the trains and that provided a work opportunity."

I inquired of a young woman from Tortugas Pueblo if she participated in the Native American dances on December 12 each year to honor the Virgin of Guadalupe.

"They dance in rain or snow. They dance no matter what. They rehearse for months. It's a very big commitment. It's a promise to the Virgin. It is very serious. They keep going, tired or not. I couldn't make that commitment."

We were ambling along a path alongside the bone-dry arroyo (irrigation canal) in Mesilla, past plowed fields ready for planting, with the majestic and jagged Organ mountains in the distance. A woman dressed from head to toe in turquoise blue was standing with her walking cane on the other side of the arroyo. We exchanged hellos and she said she had come there thirty years before on a pilgrimage. "It was a personal pilgrimage," she explained, "and when it was over, I had found my little *querencita*. My beloved place. People search and find their beloved place and they move there."

While we were waiting for take-out food in Mesilla, we met Alex Mares. He has worked in protection, preservation, conservation, and interpretation of Natural and Cultural resources in both Texas and New Mexico for more than thirty years. He explained that he is of "Diné and Mexican American descent," and he said that this is his personal opinion and does not represent any of the entities he has worked for:

"Non-Indians sometimes talk about what and how Indians think, believe, worship, fight, etc. But there is no single block of people in the "Indian" category. We are separate tribes, different groups. We had and continue to have unique languages, cultures, and practices. In the past, there were tribes that were allies, antagonists, and somewhere in between. Some collaborated with the Spanish and the Americans and the Mexicans because it was a matter of survival, or it was a way to thrive. Some were like Crypto Jews who adopted a religion on the outside but had another identity inside. Others sincerely adopted the religion of the invaders and settlers. Some were forced to relocate and live together with other Native groups with other ancestral homelands, but they wanted their own place, they wanted to be with their own group. Sometimes they united for survival. Sometimes not. Sometimes they were attacked by the same tribes that attacked the Spanish and the Americans, and they joined with the latter for mutual protection and perhaps revenge. There were power shifts, and they were sensitive to who was in control, and to when and where their bread was buttered. Native people have different geopolitical and political and economic and linguistic realities and skills. They were manipulated by occupying, invading people, in order to pacify them and take their land and resources. And sometimes, they were able to manipulate some situations and remain under the radar."

On the grounds of New Mexico State University, we encountered some members of the Society for Creative Anachronism, an international organization that embraces and recreates practices and lifestyles of Medieval Europe. Lord John, the group's leader, suggested we ask two young warriors—Lana and Kelly—how they met. The duo wore helmets and armor, carried bared swords, and were breathing heavily from the effort of hefting weapons, wearing armor, and vying in combat. When they stopped briefly, Lana explained:

"We were sparring here six years ago. I stabbed him in the face. I was fighting with a glaive with a butt spike." Kelly added, "It was love at first stab. I am definitely not intimidated by strong women. Nor is there any shame in a woman 'killing' me."

Let's Get Emotional

How Your Photos Can Convey Feeling

When you have an over-the-top travel adventure, the best way to corroborate that it really happened is via photos. Yes, you made the difficult climb to the top of a mountain. Yes, you were the only one of your friends who could eat a restaurant's hot chile special. Yup, you zip-lined over a high-altitude lake. But did you convey the pride and excitement you felt? Close-ups that show you and your reaction are only part of the experience. Did you also capture the reactions of others? Who was with you? What was your point of view? The answer to those questions is the *emotional content of your photographs.*

What did you feel when you were with other people? Did an artist smile when she held out a paintbrush to you? Did a chef make you laugh? Capture those moments and let us see what the experience was like for you. It makes for more interesting portraits than static, posed photos. Which of these brought you more pleasure: your kids standing with lasso in hand, or them gleefully throwing the rope under the guidance of ole Gus, the ranch hand? Sometimes you can photograph others for a surprising or humorous effect. Start with a standard road trip photo of a happy driver behind the wheel of a car. Then show the bigger picture: the vehicle is stalled and completely entrapped by a herd of sheep. A happy driver in a car is a portrait; the situation makes it into a surprising story. The emotion conveyed can be yours, or the feelings of the people you are recording.

At the weekly farmer's market in Las Cruces, we were threading the gauntlet of arts, crafts, and food vendors when we met pecan entrepreneur Kristen Worthington. She hadn't been farming that long but was already well on her way to creating a mini empire of inventive pecan products which ranged from cosmetics to flavored nuts to a delicious, and healthy oil (I bought a lot of it). Not long afterward, we became taste-testers for her latest venture: a pecan-centric, multi-course dinner that she created, cooked, and served in her orchard. I was impressed with her culinary and farming prowess, but how would I show that? I chose the chocolate

Kristen Worthington and her chocolate pecan cheesecake.

dessert and placed the cook in the setting of her pecan farm. Who wouldn't love the unique dining experience?

Fort Selden was a different plunge into emotional storytelling. The former frontier garrison is now in evocative ruin but filled with fascinating information about its history and relics from its past. The indoor/outdoor museum includes a small garden of native plants and, thanks to historian and educator Alexandra McKinney, hands-on opportunities to experience the technologies of those who once lived on the land—like the playing-in-the-mud fun of crafting your own souvenir adobe bricks. McKinney told us that Native Americans made shampoo from soap tree yucca (*yucca elata*). Readily accessible in the surrounding desert, the plant was used by everybody who later arrived in the area from Spanish conquerors to American soldiers, traders, and settlers. McKinney agreed to show us how to make the shampoo. I watched her with fascination as she performed the first step: she *very carefully* reached in to cut some of the sharp spiney leaves, before scraping off their waxy coating and mixing it with hot water. McKinney's lesson, backdropped by desert, mountains, and the fort, told itself.

Once you're aware of what you and the subjects of your photos are feeling, it

Historian Alexandrea McKinney, Fort Selden.

will change and expand the way you take photos that tell a story. The next time you're tempted to shoot a picture of a particularly good meal or exotic drink, let us know how special it was for you by using what's around to make it look appealing. Move it to a place in the restaurant where the light is good. Include some of the background (even out of focus, for a feeling of depth). Involve the staff: bartenders, servers, and chefs love showing off the food and being stars. You're guaranteed to have fun in the creative process and to make your viewers ooh, aah, and perhaps want to go there to taste it themselves.

Part Six

SOUTHEAST

A small herd of feral horses.

Introduction

What we discovered in southeastern New Mexico can be summed up in two words: thrilling peace. You're probably thinking that's an oxymoron, but the area is singular because it is exciting, vibrant, alive, and it is also a place to chill in nature and hit the pause button from the hectic or stressful pace of daily life.

We booked two different cabins in the woods in Ruidoso and fanned out from there. We'd wake up to a view from our bedroom of elk munching on tree leaves, pull our car over during the day to watch feral horses grazing by the roadside, have happy hour back on the cabin porch, and sleep with forest air wafting in through the windows. That was the peaceful part.

Our adventures ranged from experiencing an ancient traditional ceremony on the Mescalero Apache Reservation to the sport of axe throwing, walking in the footsteps of Billy the Kid, marveling at the panoramic beauty from a mountaintop lookout for forest fires, hiking, going on a shamanic journey, visiting the state's largest photo gallery, walking on an ancient lava field, relishing the vegetarian version of the green chile cheeseburger voted the best in the state, to discovering a forgotten World War II story that we still can't believe.

The best part is that you can experience all of it too.

Outside a cabin in Ruidoso.

A Cabin in the Forest

A Once-in-a-Lifetime Thrill

Takeaway: Wildlife may call to you in your urban life.

I'm a city girl. My turf was concrete. In the summer, my family went to the country, and most of the details of those trips are vague and impressionistic. I hazily remember tadpoles and frogs, wading in streams, and swimming in lakes. I got dirtier than I did in the city, and no one complained about it. It was expected in "the country." My usual encounters with wildlife were in parks and zoos, and with animals that ran freely like squirrels, mice, and the occasional raccoon.

After several decades in New Mexico, I had spotted larger animals. I saw deer in the forests and heard the eerie whistle of male elks during the mating season. But I had never traveled expressly to meet wildlife face to snout.

Ruidoso changed all of that. In the spring, we reserved five nights at Story Book Cabins in the woods, and the owner said we were in the "celebrity cabin" where sports stars often stayed because it had a private hot tub. He volunteered that we could probably see some elk that meandered by to feed on leaves on a hill across from us. On the second evening, when we peered through our binoculars, we saw two female elk casually enjoying their evening meal. The cabin was comfy, the owner was responsive to all our needs, and when it came time to check out, we decided to extend our stay. All the cabins were booked, so we moved to more rustic, older cabins at Dan Dee Cabins next door. And that was when we hit wildlife gold.

I awoke the first morning, opened the cabin door, and gasped when I saw two female and one male elk eating the foliage twenty feet away. As they ambled off to the next dish on their arboreal smorgasbord, a deer approached me, and was so close I could see the texture of the hair on his back. Those animals had no fear of humans.

It was out of the question for us to leave. So, we stayed for another week. The first thing I saw in the mornings through the cabin window was an elk face, and the last thing I saw before the sun went down was an elk butt as it sauntered away. No matter how many times the animals were visible from our patio, I never got over the delight and privilege of being so close to them. A young girl in a nearby cabin was feeding a deer some lettuce until her mother reminded her that it was prohibited to feed wild animals. The girl walked over to me, and we admired the fauna together. I felt like we were in a fairytale where humans and animals were kin and had a natural and close relationship. I was close to bursting into song. I couldn't remember a time when I had felt so carefree and connected to the four-footed ones. I wished that everyone could experience—at least once in their lives—the thrill of being so intimate with the natural world and its inhabitants.

The cabin with elk and deer would have been enough until we were driving along a country road north of Ruidoso and saw a herd of feral horses. I had only seen them once in my life, in the Camargue of southern France. But there they were, placidly grazing in New Mexico. They were magnificent—brown, roan, and white. They are federally protected and free to roam in Lincoln County. We got out of the car, kept a respectful distance, and watched them for half an hour. They were unselfconscious. Over the next week, we saw the feral horses along other roads, and even in town near a school. Once the beautiful beasts caused a traffic delay as they crossed a road, but no one seemed to mind. Passengers in a few cars got out to snap photos.

I wondered where they came from and learned that Spanish colonizers and settlers first brought horses to New Mexico in the 1500s. There's speculation that these feral horses came from the Mescalero Apache Reservation, which is near Ruidoso. They have been roaming freely for decades, and locals have deep affection for them. They are outraged when horses are killed by speeding motorists and advocate for more stop signs, speed limits, and posted warnings. It is hard to imagine the horror of a car striking one of the magnificent creatures or even speeding by or harassing them when there is a chance to admire them. According to park ranger Laura McRee from Oregon with whom we shared a long moment gazing in wonder at a small herd, "The Forest Service does have a Code of Federal Regulations violations in place for the protection of wild horses, which law enforcement will enforce if they witness the public harassing them."

There is a great peace to sharing the land with wild creatures. The problems of the urban world vanish because they have nothing to do with the present in nature, and the incomparable honor of watching animals breathe, eat, play, and stare back at us.

After being happy observers, we became players, quite literally.

For more information: https://www.discoverruidoso.com/cabins-condos-and-vacation-rental-homes

https://www.discoverruidoso.com

Axe throwing, Ruidoso.

What Your Axe-Throwing Style Reveals about Your Personality

Takeaway: Try something new and you may learn about yourself in unexpected ways.

One of the strongest lures of travel is that it offers the possibility of learning about nature, history, culture, customs, food, and beliefs. It also provides opportunities to learn about yourself, and often in unanticipated ways and in unexpected places.

In Ruidoso, we were invited to try a trendy sports experience at the Win Place and Show Bar on Sudderth Drive, the main street. I almost always say "yes" to new experiences—as long as they don't harm me or anyone else. But axe throwing? I agreed reluctantly.

Mike Cheney, the owner, wearing a fluorescent chartreuse shirt, blue neckerchief, and denim baseball cap, handed us legal forms to sign. He seemed like a sane, sober, trustworthy guy, but I thought about backing out. I pictured a Paul Bunyan-size axe that could lop off my foot, ear, or any of the other body parts listed in the release. I wasn't disposed to part with any of them. I shuddered when I read that the sport could result in death. Why had I agreed? I used to have nightmares about an axe murderer, and now I was going to wield the lethal weapon?

As with most things, imagination is often worse than reality, and the small, two-pound axe was the length of my forearm. Cheney demonstrated the right technique, explained to us that all we had to do was stand behind a line, lift the axe with two hands behind our heads, extend one foot forward, aim for the wooden target, throw, and get the axe to stick in it. Easy peasy, right?

Wrong. We were signed up for one hour, and no matter what I did and how much strength I mustered, I couldn't get that axe to stick. I tried throwing overhand, underhand—it was like bowling in mid-air with a sharp weapon instead of a ball. I did it with one hand, two hands, but the axe flew, bounced, and then clattered to the ground. Cheney observed that I was twisting my wrist. I consider myself a pretty straight shooter, so to speak, but apparently not with an axe.

Five minutes before the end of the session, and just when I was ready to give up, that puppy stuck in the middle of the target. Cheney gave me a big thumbs up. Bullseye. That was it. Finished. I accomplished my goal. I was William Tell and the target was my apple.

For Paul, it was a different story. He figured out how to get his axe to stick in the target after about forty minutes. But then he kept going. Sometimes he missed and sometimes he scored, but he was undeterred. When the hour was up, he kept analyzing his throws and went for the target again and again. By the time he finished, he was hitting the bullseye almost every time.

"Wow," I thought. "We are so different. I was happy to achieve one goal, and that was good enough. Paul, who is more perfectionistic, kept analyzing and refining his throwing style until our time was up."

Next to us, two men started hitting the target as soon as they began. I figured they were regulars, but they said they had never tried the sport before. Their success secret was that they were team ropers in rodeos . . . who had spent most of their lives aiming for a moving target. They took pleasure in trying to do their personal best, without competing with each other.

I reflected that some of the other axe-tossers—adults and kids—were either jokingly or seriously competitive with each other, but competition was never an issue between Paul and me.

I decided to talk to Cheney about what behavioral traits he noticed from watching many, many people throw an axe. He framed it as a series of questions axe-throwers could ask themselves, and I think it applies as well to other sports:

1. Do you focus so hard on the competition that you lose sight of the fun?
2. Do you accept the rules and try to succeed, or do you look for excuses?
3. Are you a good loser?
4. Do you congratulate the winner?
5. Do you contribute to the overall enjoyment or detract from it?
6. Do you put down someone who doesn't succeed?

Axe-throwing venues have popped up in many places in New Mexico and, in fact, all over the world. The experience provides an opportunity to find out more about oneself and get the thrill of success or notice how we deal with frustration and failure. The experience is likely to be both sharp and edgy.

After flexing our axe muscle in Ruidoso and working up an appetite, we realized we were a few doors away from Hall of Flame, which is highly recommended by locals. We discussed our axe-tossing style over crisp fries and chile-laced burgers. Since we are not beef eaters, we opted for plant-based burgers and weren't disappointed. I thought I was hallucinating when I lifted my bun to my mouth and out of the corner of my eye saw an elk crossing the street. He took his sweet time and then disappeared behind one of the shops. "It's a wild life in Ruidoso," punned one of the servers with a smile.

After sports and wildlife, it was time to pay attention to our inner lives, and we found the perfect place to do it.

For more information: https://www.winplaceandshowbar.com/events

Axe-throwing is considered a safe sport, but be vigilant when it is at a bar and combined with alcohol.

Well-being experience at Rare Bird Workshop.

Rare Bird

Spirituality and Inner Peace

Takeaway: When it comes to adventure, exploring inner life can be as exciting as experiencing life outside of you.

The word has been spreading slowly in Ruidoso, and that's okay with Stacy Tatum, the owner of the recently opened The Rare Bird Workshop. From the moment we walked into her downtown space, we realized that she is all about retreating from the frenzied, achievement-oriented pace of life and exploring fun, joy, creativity, inspiration, meditation, and movement in a safe environment.

Tatum herself is the rare bird. She's a performance artist who has delighted corporate and general audiences as a member of The Three Painters and Artrageous, whose shows last anywhere from two to sixty minutes. Two minutes? Yup. Tatum is a speed painter who can produce a work of art instantaneously in front of your eyes. And, for the last two decades, she has studied various forms of meditation and movement. At Rare Bird, she pulls it all together with a singular vision for adults and children: a creative space surrounded by art where guests can create art, dance, make music, meditate, explore movement in space, and enjoy themselves.

I'm not a big fan of the word "spirituality," and when people introduce themselves as being spiritual, I tend to put on my best running shoes and sprint off in the opposite direction. Too often the word is used to extract large sums of money from or exert power over others. To me, spirituality is about how you behave with other people on a minute-to-minute basis. How do people feel after they have contact with you? Do you make them feel comfortable, empowered, excited, appreciated? Tatum scores in all of those categories. She offers some classes by donation only, and others—that she or others helm—are admirably affordable. "I don't want to exclude people because they have very limited means," she says. "Self-expression, liberation, fun, and opportunities for creativity should be available to everyone."

Paul and I took two workshops with Tatum: Healing Meditation and Conscious Dreaming. The first one was accompanied by soothing music that slowly replaced the noise and agita that fill our minds. Then Tatum invited us to focus inwardly and send ourselves physical, emotional, and mental health. A delicious calm set in, and we were guided to send healing light to those we love, then to our community, and finally to our planet. It was a chance to focus on a few people I knew who were ailing. Only two others were in the class, and we felt connected at the end of the workshop, even though we hadn't spoken. We had shared a sweet space in time.

The second workshop involved Tatum drumming as induction into a shamanic voyage. It was unexpectedly difficult for me, as I chose to take a trip into a fear I was experiencing. The drumming got faster, I began to feel anxious and then I had a vision of a lizard who appeared and seemed to watch over me. Together we watched the fear, rather than getting sucked into it. I emerged relieved and grateful that Tatum holds such a safe place for people to explore their inner environments. I welcomed the opportunity to face down something that was bothering me. Paul had a thoroughly pleasant experience and emerged relaxed and happy.

Rare Bird offers experiences that resonate with both locals and visitors. A Latin belly dancing class? Creative arts and theatre for kids? Full moon drum and dancing? Ecstatic dance? Meditation for children? Juggling and Polynesian poi balls? Line dancing? They drop in for a single workshop or have an ongoing experience if they live in Ruidoso or are there for extended time.

Travel affords a perfect opportunity to step back from the stresses of daily life, and dive into some memorable mind, body, and spirit experiences. At Rare Bird, it's easy, accessible, and something visitors can take back with them when they go home.

On the way back to our cabin, Paul and I talked about our experiences and, in the process, brought emotions to the surface that surprised us at the next destination.

Monjeau Peak recovering from a devastating fire.

Monjeau Lookout

Drama and Beauty in the Wake of Ecological Disaster

Takeaway: If you are receptive, a place may give you something important to think about long after you leave.

While we were in Ruidoso, Paul and I were concerned about the disastrous forest fires raging across New Mexico at that time and how many people had lost homes, land, and livestock because of them. One day, a local friend mentioned, in passing, a lesser-known site that was built as a fire lookout in the Lincoln National Forest. It was an unanticipated indication of where we needed to go.

The drive up into the mountains from Ruidoso was very dramatic. The road twisted and turned, and all around us were ghost trees that past fires had burned to black char or stripped to a deathly white pallor. Off in a grassy area, away from decimated forests, feral horses munched serenely on grass, hardly looking up as our car passed. They were a visual relief, but the higher we went, the fewer signs of life we saw; we were surrounded by devastation. We became acutely aware of how frightening wildfires are for all animals. What did the elk eat when the leaves were gone? What did the bear consume when she came out of hibernation? What happened to the horses' grasslands? Where could birds nest? Even fish were choked out of ash-laden streams.

Higher and higher we drove until we arrived at Monjeau Lookout. We were not expecting such magnificence. It was late afternoon and no one else was there. We could see the White Mountain Wilderness area . . . about one hundred miles in the distance. And so many of the mountains were denuded by prior fires.

Huge gray-brown boulders were piled around the site as though they had dropped from the heavens and tumbled over each other. Overhead, vultures were circling. Signs to the right of the parking area indicated footpaths that led to expansive vistas.

To the left, perched above us, accessible by a steep dirt path and stone steps, and

at an altitude just shy of 10,000 feet, was the Monjeau lookout tower—a three-level rectangular stone and wood tower that gets progressively smaller towards the highest part, which is called the cab. The tower offers a panoramic view of the surrounding mountains but, more important, it provides the forest service with a lookout for wildfires. The style of the tower is referred to as "rustic architecture," and it was built by the Civilian Conservation Corps in the 1940s. It was added to the National Register of Historic Places in 1988. In 2012, the Little Bear Fire spread rapidly through 44,330 acres, overtook Monjeau Lookout, and damaged the cab. A year later, the structure was rebuilt back to its pre-fire state.

As we stood there inhaling the clean air, distant parts of New Mexico were burning with two of the largest fires in the state's history. Both had tragically resulted from human causes and devoured hundreds of thousands of acres. Farms and ranches were destroyed. People and livestock were being evacuated.

The drive up to the tower had been an emotional journey into the reality of fires where wilderness homes are consumed quickly and disappear. Lifetimes of memories, photos, and artifacts are gone forever. The echoes of shock and fear were still audible.

When we descended from the tower and followed one of the footpaths, we saw a picnic table and regretted that we hadn't brought lunch with us. It was one of the most dramatic picnic spots I had ever seen.

Monjeau Lookout is a place to marvel, contemplate, experience the vastness of nature in New Mexico and feel empathy for all who have been affected by wildfires. A little lizard without a tail slithered by and somehow it seemed apt—an animal that is vibrant and fast, but who has suffered an injury like the mountains and forests, and like many of us too, but has survived. It is a site that gives you something important to think about.

On our way down the mountain, we spotted several feral horses. We got out to watch and admire them. I decided to get more information about how they are protected and subsequently called the Public Affairs Office of the Lincoln National Forest. I was fortunate to get connected to Laura Rabon who explained, "Horses are not a native species to North America; they were brought from Europe by the Spanish as livestock. Some of the feral horses around the Lincoln National Forest were intentionally released and others escaped. In some cases, Congress has

(*opposite page*) Monjeau Peak Lookout.

designated some protections for certain herds of horses, but ours are not included in that—at least not yet. Technically, the state of New Mexico owns all large game in the state; but feral horses are not classified as game. In 2018, a judge ruled that the New Mexico Livestock Board did not have jurisdiction over the horses either, so jurisdictionally they are in a gray area, and it's complex. Horses are beloved in our culture and people feel a strong connection to them. But, on the other hand, the feral horses are relatively new to the ecosystem. There has been a proliferation in the last twenty-five years; the herds are growing larger, and they have no natural enemies. They use the same resources—namely, grasses—in the forest as native species, and the land can only support a certain number of animals. The village of Ruidoso has some ordinances governing the interaction of humans and horses." She explained that it is illegal to feed them there. They haven't been owned and exposed to human contact, and they can be easily spooked and become dangerous. The ordinances are to protect both horses and people.

I was surprised that our simple drive to a lookout turned out to be such a powerful learning experience. After leaving our perfect spot for viewing the horses, we drove for what seemed like forever on Ski Run Road. There was a steep drop enroute to Ski Apache. Night was coming soon, and all the animals were out. The roads were tortuous and the views spectacular. We saw that in 2012 and again in 2021, fire came to the edge of the ski lift area and was mercifully stopped by heroic wildland firefighters. We were above the tree line looking down on burned trees and out into the distant mountains. We carefully took the hairpin drives with views around every bend. Evening shadows were falling over the green, yellow, and brown mountains. Deer darted in front of us. We looked out at some tree-covered mountains in the distance and wondered about the seemingly arbitrary lines where the fires had stopped. Now the deer were bounding like rabbits, and horses bolted across the road. We had to be very careful and vigilant as we drove.

All was beauty. All was quiet. It was the antithesis of our urban lives. We had discovered drama and elegance in the wake of ecological disaster. The ghost trees seemed sculptural and mysterious, as though they held secrets of things seen and experienced. Even the charred stumps had their own stark artistry. New generations of animals had appeared on the landscape.

As Rabon eloquently told me, "We are dealing with a lot of the issues—drought, fire, changing ecosystems, flooding—that people have been dealing with since the beginning of time. As humans, we are here for a short amount of time from a geological perspective. When we experience nature, we think this mountain or that stream has always been here. But it's not necessarily permanent. We live and exist in a world that is in a constant state of change."

Fires have changed the landscape and destroyed everything in their path. But I realized that there is an enduring beauty in nature that morphs, modifies, and transforms, but that nothing can destroy.

And I was filled with gratitude to wildfire fighters, who risk great danger to preserve our homes, animals, and the beauty of the land. I soon learned a lot more about them.

For more information: https://www.fs.usda.gov/recarea/lincoln/recarea/?recid=80034

Smokey Bear Historical Park.

He Was Real!

Smokey Bear Historical Park

Takeaway: When you put a face on heroes and ecologists, your connection becomes personal and more meaningful.

When I was growing up, I took his words to heart: "Only YOU can prevent forest fires." They were spoken in a deep, soft, bass voice by a gentle, lovable, animated bear named Smokey. He personified and personalized the message for generations of children and made me feel that I played an important role in keeping the forests safe from blazes. I heard his voice echoing in my head and was watchful around campfires, matches, and people smoking.

But the fire prevention bruin was not just legend; there was a living Smokey. In 1950, a tiny bear cub was found after his home was burned by a wildfire in the Capitan Mountains of Lincoln National Forest. The story was enough to rip your heart out: the badly burned and orphaned baby bear was clinging to a blackened tree. He was airlifted to Washington, DC, and became the national symbol for fire prevention. He remained the First Bear for twenty-five years, when he was replaced by another orphaned black bear from the Lincoln National Forest.

The original Smokey died but was not forgotten. Today he is buried in Smokey Bear Historical Park, within sight of the mountain where he was found.

When I think back, I begin to wonder how and why city kids like me cared about a bear and felt responsible for forest fires? The answer may lie with Walt Disney: *Snow White and the Seven Dwarfs* featured animated forest animals who befriended and protected Snow White after she fled from her cruel and envious stepmother. She cared about the forest fauna and asked a baby bird, "Are you a little orphan?" The forest in *Sleeping Beauty* is alive with chipmunks, birds, rabbits, deer, squirrels, and an owl to whom Princess Aurora, AKA Sleeping Beauty, confides that she has met her prince charming in her dreams. And who could ever forget Disney's wide-eyed deer Bambi, whose mother was killed by a hunter and

Firefighters are honored at Smokey Bear Historical Park.

who, like the other animals, fled a campfire-caused forest fire? Or Mowgli, who was raised by anthropomorphic wolves in *The Jungle Book*? We were sensitized to the relationship between human beings and animals. And Smokey taught us about our connection to nature itself and how we are its protectors.

Children and adults from all over the country were also moved by Smokey's story and come to pay their respects to the original bear at his graveside in the park. They buy cuddly, plush toy Smokey bears that personify the updated message to include fires in grasslands: Only You Can Prevent Wildfires.

In 2019, an important element was added to the historical park: a memorial to fallen wildland firefighters and their support personnel who perished in the line of duty. I stood for a long time in front of the bronze statue of a firefighter who kneels next to the boots of a fallen comrade. He looks sad and exhausted, but soon he will be back to the face the flames.

I generally avoid the word "hero," because it is used for sports figures and other celebrities who may be luminaries but are not my definition of hero. To me, firefighters are the real deal. In New Mexico, where fires have scorched vast slashes of charred forests and grasslands, destroyed homes, resulted in the evacuation of tens of thousands of people, killed and displaced wildlife, spread choking smoke to towns and cities, we owe a great debt to the folks who courageously leave behind the comforts of their daily lives and battle roaring blazes fires to protect us, our homes, and our precious land. What impels them to do it?

I got an answer from Angel Montoya, a Forest Service Engine Captain, whose ancestors have been here, in his words, "since Billy the Kid." He grew up in an agricultural environment, learned how to drive a tractor when he was five or six years old, and reminisced that "every time a fire truck went by and I saw the lights and sirens, I wanted to be one of those firefighters." At 16 he became a junior firefighter. "It was a personal calling. I was the only one at my school who became a volunteer. My uncle was in the Forest Service, and he was almost like a father figure to me. That took me away from being a structure firefighter in the big red engines. In wildland firefighting, the trucks are green," he explained.

After twenty years as a firefighter, Montoya is a supervisor, and his pay is a little over $28 an hour. That seems very low for someone who risks his life, but, with overtime, it's almost a living wage compared to seasonal wildland firefighters who get $13.78 an hour. "If we're on a large incident, we can have sixteen-hour days. I watch the firefighters closely, tell them to take a break; 16 hours is a lot. If you work sixteen hours, you're entitled to eight hours of rest. On an initial attack—if we're trying to catch a small fire—I've worked forty hours straight with no sleep."

Montoya says he's living his childhood dream, and really enjoying it. "How can you 'enjoy' such hard, dangerous work?" I asked him. "I never really thought about it. It's the people I'm around. We're a tight group. When I started out, I liked being out there, helping the community. I didn't want houses and the landscape to burn. I guess you can say it's like the military. But instead of bombs going off, the enemy is the fire." When I inquired about women firefighters, he said "When I started, there were one or two women. Now there are a lot more."

He was forthcoming when I asked about fear. "There's always that fear in the back of your mind—something could happen to myself or my guys—getting burned up or a tree falls on them. The last few days we had a lot of lightning—and you wonder if that's going to start a fire. I do get anxiety, especially if it's dry and windy. When I get home I kind of relax, but I'm still waiting—are they going to call me?"

He spoke about the 2012 Little Bear fire, "that was right in our backyard. The pressure was a lot higher. People we knew were losing houses. It was in our community. We did our best to save houses, but sometimes Mother Nature said, 'no, not today.' And later on, with phones, everyone calls to see if their house is okay. You don't want them to panic. I guess you kind of get used to it. I've been doing it for so long. But in the back of your mind the fear is still there."

I thought about the firefighters sleeping in a tent, sometimes for two weeks at a time, in a sleeping bag on top of a space blanket on the ground. I pondered what the food must be like, and learned that they are required to eat 6,000 calories a day. The joke among them is that for each meal, there's always an Uncrustable—a peanut butter and jelly sandwich without a crust made by Smuckers.

My ultimate question was this: in a society where selfies rule and selfishness abounds, where people are looking for fame and glory, why are firefighters content to work behind the scenes, not thinking of themselves as anything special, not seeking the limelight? "It's my job," Montoya explained. "It's what I signed up for. The community comes up to us when we're in uniform. They say, 'Thank you for what you do.' We say 'thank you' back to them for their respect and support. You're not a hero. In all my years, I never heard a firefighter bragging. You do it because it's your job."

I hope we all agree that they are true heroes.

And the polar opposite of heroes is villains. There's no consensus when it comes to one of the most famous in the west. Was Billy the Kid really one of them?

For more information: https://www.emnrd.nm.gov/sfd/smokey-bear-historical-park/

If You're Hungry: The Oso Grill, across the street from Smokey Bear Historical Park, is burger bliss for anyone who wants to bite into what was voted the best green chile cheeseburger three times at the New Mexico State Fair. It comes on a large, puffy, soft roll that is branded with the Zia sun symbol and stuffed with juicy burger, fresh salad fixings, tasty dressing, and fried green chile strips; the crunchy latter may be the secret to the burger's success.

Montoya works in Capitan; I hope when people see a green fire truck, they wave hello.

Historian Tim Roberts at the site of Billy the Kid's escape.

Billy the Kid

A Man in Love with the True Story and a Woman in Love with the Kid

Takeaway: It's exciting to go to the place where events really happened.

The most famous kid in New Mexico, hands down, was Billy. He went by different names—William or Billy Bonney, Henry McCarty, Henry Antrim—but it was the moniker "Billy the Kid" or simply "The Kid" that stuck. He also had many iterations in his short life: thug outlaw, rebellious teen, leader of the nineteenth-century Brat Pack, icon of the Wild West, scapegoat, serial escape artist and fugitive, cattle rustler, outlier seeking justice, and participant in the Lincoln County War (1876–1879), which was a violent feud over dueling interests in land, cattle, money, and power.

Like any legend, The Kid had a colorful life embellished by input from those who knew him, those who knew about him, and storytellers of every stripe who made him up as they went along. In the morass of myths, there are quite a few facts, like the date May 13, 1881, when Billy was scheduled to hang from a noose in the town of Lincoln and made a daring escape. Since that time, Lincoln itself has become a player in the Billy saga.

We figured the best place to leap into the legend was to head to the town and check in at the Bonito Valley Brewing Company, where owner Tim Roberts—a historian, historic preservationist, and former director of the Lincoln Historic Site—leads a new, free, once-a-month, one-hour tour of Billy's local life from 1877 to 1881. On the day we followed Roberts as he traced The Kid's footsteps, cowboys, would-be cowboys, Billy fans and fanatics, accidental and intentional tourists downed their beers and joined us to hear the tale.

According to Roberts, Billy was employed by John Henry Tunstall, a local mercantile (dry goods store) and cattle owner who was murdered. The justice of the peace issued a warrant to the Regulators, a group who roamed the countryside to capture those who were responsible for the killing. The Kid was one of the members.

The burning question was: who had a motive for killing Tunstall? Apparently, Tunstall was competition for James Dolan and Lawrence Murphy, who had a lock on the cattle and mercantile businesses in Lincoln and resorted to violence to defend it. The Regulators staged an ambush during which Billy shot and killed Lincoln County Sheriff William Brady who was possibly complicit in Tunstall's murder. The plot quickly thickened. Dolan and Murphy used their influence to have the justice of the peace removed, and Billy and the Regulators were retroactively made outlaws. Billy was indicted for the murder.

In 1879, Governor of the New Mexico Territory (and author of *Ben Hur*) Lew Wallace stayed in Lincoln and heard people serenading The Kid and saw them bringing him food every day in jail. "Billy was kind to those he didn't shoot," Roberts said, as we stood next to Tunstall's actual store "and he was charismatic. He testified against the Murphy Dolan clan. There were so many murders here, and only Billy was accused and indicted. Why were the others set free? There were no white hats and black hats. No good and bad parties. All had dirt on them."

The gripping tour of the historic structures and places where it all happened finishes where The Kid's story in Lincoln ended. It was the two-story clapboard building that had formerly been the headquarters of Murphy and Dolan. Murphy had died. The company was bankrupt and had to sell their assets. Their offices became the town's first purpose-built courthouse and jail, and it was ripe for the incarceration of The Kid.

Billy had escaped from his prior jailing in Lincoln and was arrested by lawman Pat Garrett in Fort Sumner. According to Roberts, "Billy had been transferred to Lincoln to be executed. He was held in Murphy's old bedroom. Pat Garrett and two men watched him day and night. Pat Garrett had to leave to attend to business. On April 28, 1881, the other prisoners who hadn't been indicted yet were escorted across the street, one by one, to the Wortley Hotel by one of the guards. Just one guard named Bell was left watching Billy. Billy later said he convinced Bell to let him go downstairs, and that he had starved himself so he could slip out of the manacles. He grabbed Bell's gun and tried without success to get him to surrender. He refused, so Billy shot and Bell died."

The shots were heard by Bob Ollinger, the other guard at the Wortley Hotel, and an unsavory lawmaker who Billy despised. Ollinger came running to the courthouse, and Billy called down from upstairs. When Ollinger looked up, The Kid shot and killed him. Supposedly he then jumped on a horse and rode off humming or singing a song. Seventy-seven days later, Garrett tracked twenty-one-year-old Billy to Fort Sumner where he shot him dead.

Our tour group was transfixed as Roberts stood at the base of the staircase of the old courthouse building, telling us the details of Billy's two murders and escape. He made the legend breathe. Before our guide left, he gave a shout out to someone important among the tour participants—Lori Goodloe, who is president of the Billy the Kid Outlaw Gang. She waved to our tour group before they disbanded and headed back to the brewery where they drank craft beer and listened to live country music. I stayed to talk to Goodloe, who said, "Our group has been in existence since 1987. Our mission is to promote the story of Billy the Kid. I started researching him in college for an assignment and was hooked. I'm biased but I think Billy was the good guy. He was the only one indicted for any of the murders. Billy loved performing and acting in plays in elementary school. No one knows who his father was or exactly where he was born—in Indiana? Missouri? Ireland? He was good to women, a very good dancer, and always took off his hat, was polite, and not a monster."

Goodloe continued talking about her favorite subject. She said Billy told Bell to run because he didn't want to kill him. He just did it to escape. Billy hated Ollinger and they were on opposing sides. He killed Ollinger with the latter's own shotgun, and then threw the shotgun on his body. "Billy had a lot of girlfriends. He gave candy hearts to one named Sally and had a sweetheart in Fort Sumner named Paulita Maxwell. She denied it till the day she died, but Billy was supposed to escape to Mexico, and many think he went to Fort Sumner to get Paulita to flee with him. She was from a wealthy family, but she didn't care about money. He only killed four people. I love him. I have a tattoo of Billy's signature." And she proceeded to show us her leg tat to prove it.

Our experience in Lincoln once again reminded me why I love traveling to places where history and events actually transpired. It's one thing to read or hear about them, and it's another to smell the air, walk the land and streets, peer into the buildings, perhaps go with a local or a guide, and let your imagination take you back in time so you are there. I believe that our memories are capable of storing facts, but our hearts, souls, and minds thrive by hearing and remembering

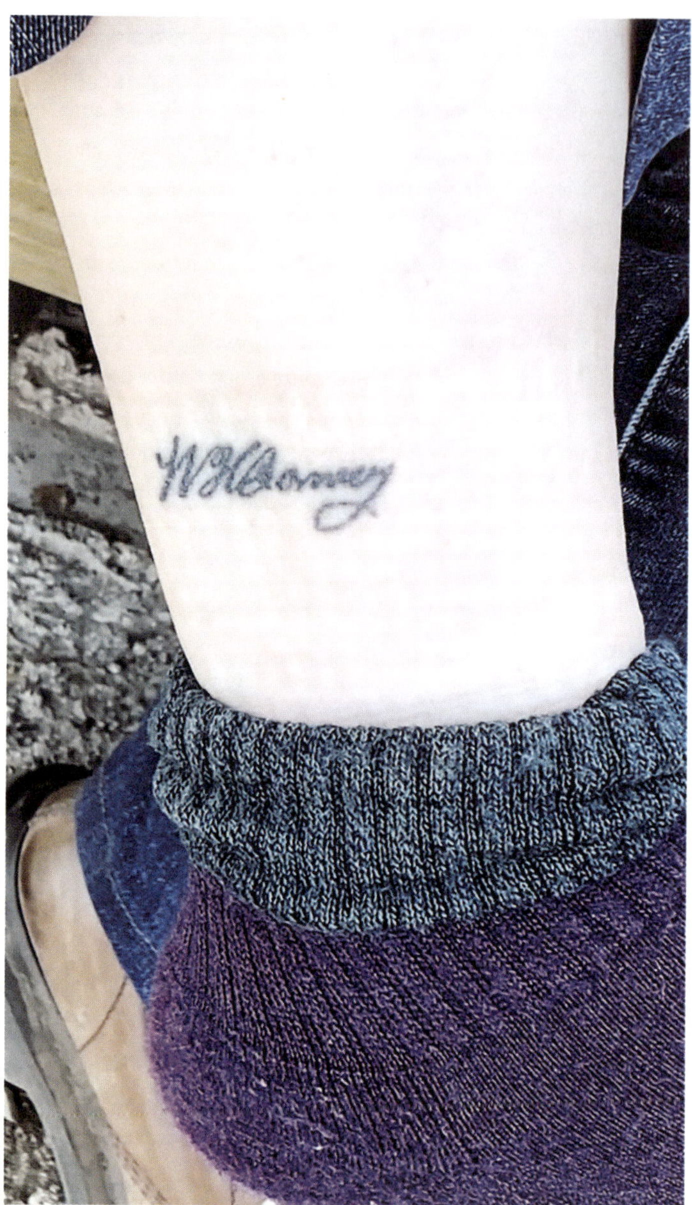

A fan's tattoo of Billy the Kid's signature.

stories. I will certainly recall the story of Billy in Lincoln any time I hear or see The Kid's name.

When I studied history in school, it was all I could do to stay awake. But in New Mexico, it's history that wakes me up, and that includes prehistory. We had an unexpected awakening when we changed our plans and found ourselves confronting mysteries from ancient times.

For more information: Lincoln is about thirty-five minutes from Ruidoso.

For Billy the Kid tours and events and other historical tours, check out Bad Hoss History on Facebook, or call the Bonito Valley Brewing Company: 575-653-4810.

Three Rivers Petroglyph Site.

Thoughts at the Three Rivers Petroglyph Site

Takeaway: Change your plans, Change Your Life.

It was a mild mid-winter day, and we were heading towards another destination. Then a small road sign and the majestic, snow-covered Sierra Blanca peaks beckoned us to revisit the Three Rivers Petroglyph Site, seventeen miles north of Tularosa. "Do you want to stop?" Paul asked me. "I know we've got other plans, and we're making good time on the road." "I'm not sure," I replied. "We haven't been to Three Rivers in twenty-five years, and I'm afraid we'll never recapture the feeling of awe we had then." Paul sighed. I sighed. We continued on our way, but the pull was so strong, we turned around.

"Return to the route!" our GPS demanded.

We looked at each other and shut her down.

I had seen ancient petroglyphs—images carved into rock—all over the southwest, but nothing rivaled the 21,000 images and mysterious symbols left at Three Rivers by members of the Jornada Mogollon culture between 600 and 1,000 years ago. They left us enticing clues in stone about their lives and connection to the natural and supernatural worlds. The current, well-maintained, one-mile trail that winds up and down the hill with the petroglyphs hadn't been there twenty-five years ago and walking the volcanic ridge was rougher back then—but I smiled to see that there were numerous turnouts and alternate paths where we could still experience a sense of discovery.

Three Rivers is such a mysterious and sacred place that I felt it was important to ask for permission to enter it. Many of us who live in New Mexico have learned to do that. I put my hands out, palms up, as though waiting to catch rain. I received the blessings of acceptance and permission and proceeded with the visit.

We climbed slowly through and past enigmatic symbols. Usually, petroglyphs are above eye level or inaccessibly incised in high cliff walls. But at Three Rivers, they surround you—on black-faced, igneous rocks next to your feet, at knee level, waist level, eye level, and sometimes calling out to you to look up. They are your guides and companions, simultaneously unknowable and approachable.

Only four other visitors were there. They hurried by. I was surprised that they were just using the site as background for speedy exercise hikes and selfies. I waved hello to them, and then slowly entered into dreamtime or timelessness, where magic happens. Images emerged that were evocative and elusive. Some were one of a kind, and others appeared in multiple places. Each begged to be experienced, emotionally felt, but not really understood; their true meaning swallowed up by time.

To the right, I saw a pecked-out drawing of a man positioned like a frog with arms outstretched and extended legs bent at the knee into a right angle. Nearby was a bird etched vertically, as though suspended in mid-air; a zigzag pattern; a shield bearing the four cardinal directions, surrounded by dots; spirals; a deer looking back over its shoulder; a ceremonial dancer; a two-headed figure, masks—records of a cosmological worldview held by people who had stood where we were standing and walked where we were walking.

My mind and heart swirled through possibilities. Was this a sacred space or temple in nature? A school? A place of initiation? A pilgrimage site? A high place close to Spirit? A story to be entered . . . without knowing the outcome?

We kept climbing up the hill in the lap of the Sierra Blanca on the right, and on the left we looked down over a vast river valley. The images were fewer as we went higher, and some were on huge boulders out of reach—an eagle head, a human face, a large hand print. Was this higher place restricted to certain people? The answers were known to ancients who lived in a nearby village, but today all that is left of their lives are silent stones.

The petroglyph trail is clearly a place to connect to ancestors who recorded and passed on their knowledge. But maybe this isn't rock *art*, I thought. Maybe it's an ancient communication system that different tribes with different languages understood—like many of the symbols we use that are internationally recognized: the sun or moon; a stop sign; railroad crossings; stairs; or an adult holding a child's hand. Maybe these mysterious signs are like Mayan glyphs and Egyptian hieroglyphs. Perhaps they, too, are a language. Unless the petroglyphs themselves wish to be revealed to descendants or epigraphers, we may never know.

I sighed deeply, recognizing this experience as the reward for having made the change to our original plans and listening when something else called out to us. If we had been in an RV, we would have spent the night and seen a private, celestial show. But, in daylight, we were content to picnic in silence—our hearts filled with unscheduled and timeless gratitude and joy.

It was a reminder that sometimes plans are a suggestion and they are not—like petroglyphs—set in stone.

If the petroglyphs were not really "art," clearly the photography at our next destination belonged in that category.

For more information: https://www.blm.gov/visit/three-rivers-petroglyph-site

A rock and roll museum and photography gallery, Carrizozo.

The Biggest Photo Gallery and Most Personal Rock and Roll Museum in New Mexico in a Little Town with a Population of 942

Takeaway: Big surprises may be found in small places.

It was a hot Saturday in Carrizozo. A street fair was in progress, but only a singer and a few spectators braved the mid-afternoon sun. We ducked into the Tularosa Basin Gallery of Photography, hoping for air conditioning. The gallery is located in the Lutz Building, which was originally a mercantile built in 1917.

Roy Dose, the sales manager on duty, welcomed us with a bottle of cold water and some surprising information: "We have about 80 photographers represented here. It's the largest photo gallery in the state."

"In Carrizozo?" I asked incredulously. "It's the middle of nowhere."

"Actually," Dose said, "it's the middle of everywhere. People come here who are going from somewhere to somewhere else. We're at the intersection of 380 and 54, and we're the county seat of Lincoln County."

"How did this gallery get started?" I inquired.

"It opened in 2014, and it was very small. Now we're at 7,500 square feet, and we have about 900 photos for sale. All were taken in New Mexico," he said proudly.

As I began to stroll around the vast space, I was struck by the quality of the art. "These are winners," I commented, and Dose immediately replied. "That's literally true. These are the current *New Mexico Magazine* photo contest winners. It changes every year, about January, when we show the new winners. We have 35 of them right now."

The photos range from portraits to landscapes, from barren desert to pine forest. They are peopled with sun baked cowboys, lowriders, and local beauties. They pay homage to tame and wild horses, and loyal hounds. They portray great expanses of open land and sky, and small details that are visual synecdoches; they represent the larger lives and events of which they are a part.

"Would you like to have a look downstairs?" Dose inquired.

Our surprise at finding the gallery on the ground level was matched by our wonder at Carrizozo Rock and Roll Hall of Fame below. It's the love offering of local resident James Lane and features his lifetime collection of memorabilia. "He did laser shows for Earth, Wind & Fire and Pink Floyd," Dose explained.

Just as the photographers above documented their love for New Mexico, Lane recorded his admiration for rock luminaries that began when he was eleven years old. He was the son of a preacher who took over the Pasadena, California, church from Sherly Cooper's father; Sherly is a dancer and the wife of Alice Cooper, and the Coopers used to sit in the back of the church.

Lane moved to Portland, Oregon, and was a regular at clubs where Nirvana, Sound Garden, Stone Temple Pilots, and others performed. He traveled to catch Hendrix, Joplin, Mercury, and Bowie shows. He got a degree in Electrical Optical Engineering and became a roadie who worked on sound and lighting for many bands. Along the way, he collected guitar picks, photos, posters, backstage passes, ticket stubs and signed guitars for fifty years. In his spare time, he also made jewelry—most notably a necklace for Steven Tyler of Aerosmith.

In the basement permanent exhibit of Lane's love affair with rock and roll, we lingered as we looked at the Gibson guitar signed by Ace Frehley, who was lead guitarist and co-founder of Kiss, and the Cat Stevens album cover that the singer signed with "Peace, Yusuf." We smiled at the Van Halen unshredded guitar picks, the AC/DC concert ticket, the autographed photo of Fleetwood Mac, the guitar signed by Crosby, Stills & Nash.

Across the street from the photos and rockabilia, the Honey Girls serve up a sweet assortment of coffee, pastry, tamales, turkey melts, sandwiches, and friendliness in their little shop. It was the perfect choice for late lunch.

The Carrizozo visit reminded me of the treasures and pleasures we always find in little towns. You can drive by them or through them, or you can park, linger, walk, talk, and have the joy of discovering big surprises of your own.

Big or small, outdoors or indoors, every place we visited had singular, fascinating stories of their own. And at one site, we found one that verged on unbelievable.

Fort Stanton is remembered in a souvenir coloring book by a historical reenactor.

Fort Stanton

An Incredible German Story and What the Coins Mean at Military Cemeteries

Takeaway: Turn on your inner Sherlock Holmes and go after the little-known and unusual stories.

I asked Brittany Porter, curator at historic Fort Stanton, what surprised her most about the site. "The German story," she replied without hesitation. She was right. Some visitors may recoil when they learn that the fort encroached on Apache hunting grounds and was built as a base of military operations against Indigenous people. It was part of the rapacious hunger for westward expansion. Others may be fascinated by the exhibits about how the fort was selected by the Marine Hospital Service to be the first federally run tuberculosis hospital in 1891. TB was called "the white plague," and by the late nineteenth century, it infected between 70 and 90 percent of urban dwellers in our country. By the 1920s, health seekers made up almost 10 percent of New Mexico's population. The hospital kept patients busy and raised morale by offering photography, ceramics, painting, bingo, croquet, baseball, golf, hiking, camping, and tennis.

All of this is of great interest, but I have to agree with Porter: the most surprising thing is the exhibit about the period from 1941 to 1945 when the fort was an internment camp that held 411 German crew members from the *SS Columbus*—a luxury German cruise ship that featured a shipboard swimming pool, large dance platforms, and spacious dining halls. When Germany invaded Poland in 1939 and World War II broke out, it was not safe to be sailing in a German ship. The bewildered passengers were offloaded for safety in Havana. The ship and its crew sailed to Vera Cruz, which was a neutral port. They were intercepted by a British destroyer. The German sailors scuttled their ship, and the Brits lowered their flag to half mast, in honor of the sinking vessel. The German crew escaped the sinking shop, and they were ultimately transported by the US Navy to New York, where they were held at Ellis Island.

Anti-German sentiment in the United States was strong, and it created a problem about where to hold the 411 German civilian crew members. The US Border Patrol was tasked with confining them, along with seventeen Japanese Americans, and Fort Stanton became an internment camp. Wilhelm Daehne, commander of the *SS Columbus*, was urbane, educated, spoke five languages, and was very popular with the crew. The management of most internment camp affairs was turned over to him and his staff. By that time, Fort Stanton had served as a Depression-era CCC (Civilian Conservation Corps) public works camp for civilians who were gainfully employed by the US government. That camp was closed in 1940.

Under the expert leadership of Captain Daehne, the camp was converted, refurbished, and rebuilt into barracks, a galley (kitchen), a laundry, and washrooms. He maintained a high level of shipboard discipline for four years, and carpenters, blacksmiths, mechanics, and cooks exercised their skills and trained apprentices. In their free time, the internees could enjoy boxing, swimming, concerts, tennis, and movies. The astonishing captain also purchased two Model-T cars so his charges could learn to drive. They were allowed to hike, with the stipulation that they had to be back by 5 p.m.

In 1941, when the United States declared war on Japan and Germany, the internees were no longer considered "distressed seamen" and were reclassified as Enemy Aliens. A fence was added to surround the camp, and movement outside of it was monitored. There were clearly more restrictions imposed, but generally life under the captain continued much as it had before.

Germany surrendered, the war ended, and the last German sailor left the camp at the end of August 1945. But it remained open for two months for the Japanese Americans. They were accused of being dissidents, and all but one of them were deported to Japan, in another disturbing chapter of our history.

People still find artifacts on the grounds of Fort Stanton, but it is illegal to take them. One visitor returned a rusty lock and enclosed a note that said the lock had brought nothing but bad luck. "I'd rather just send it back and be done with it," the note read.

It's a short drive to the Fort Stanton State Veterans Cemetery, where most of the grave markers are white wooden crosses—some bearing names and some that are blank. They are mostly the resting places for veterans who died during and after World War II, but some are from the First World War. A few standing stones are more than one hundred years old.

It was in that cemetery that I encountered something else fascinating that I had never heard about before. A volunteer at Fort Stanton heard me ask about what was most surprising, and suggested I visit the cemetery and learn the story of the coins.

A piece of history returned for good reason.

Coins had been left on some of the headstones, and apparently there is a lot of meaning behind them. A coin is a message to a deceased soldier's family that someone has come to pay respects. If you leave a penny, it simply indicates that you have visited. A nickel communicates that you and the deceased trained at boot camp together. Leaving a dime means you served together in some capacity. A quarter conveys that you were with the soldier when he was killed. The money left at the graves in veterans' cemeteries is eventually collected and used to cover cemetery expenses or help indigent veterans.

The practice became common during the Vietnam War, when the country was politically polarized over the war. Leaving behind a coin was more practical than contacting a soldier's family, which could devolve into political argument. In some cases, when a veteran visited the grave of a fallen comrade and left a coin, it was considered a "down payment" on a beer or a game of cards when they were finally reunited.

Often, when we visit a site, I ask folks who work there what surprised them the most when they learned about it. I take their answers as suggestions and go off to find out why they were surprised. In situ signage, photos, and artifacts are a big help as we learn about something new to add to our memory bank that we can later share with those who might be interested. When someone asks us about a trip, it allows us to have a response that is more engaging than, "It was great."

At another site, the name itself was so surprising that even though a storm was raging, we darted out of our car and had to run inside.

For more information: https://www.fortstanton.org

Museum of the Shroud (of Turin), Alamogordo.

Where Faith Meets Science

The Shroud (of Turin) Exhibit and Museum

Takeaway: Saying "maybe" has more potential than saying "no."

In 1978, I happened to be in Turin, Italy, and walked by a seemingly endless line of people waiting to see what a small sign indicated was the shroud of Turin. I knew what a shroud was, as my ancestors were buried in them. But I figured that if that many people were patiently waiting in line to see a particular burial cloth, I should do the same.

What I saw was startling: on a long, rectangular piece of linen was the negative image of a naked man, his hands crossed over his groin area, with shoulder length hair, blood stains from crucifixion nail holes, and a crown of thorns. The material was a revered relic, as the lifeless man it once contained was thought to be Jesus. I went reeling out of the viewing room. Was it possible?

Over the years, I occasionally came across an article that debunked the authenticity of the shroud and claimed it was a medieval forgery. Soon after, a rebuttal would appear. The Catholic Church did not come down on one side or another. In 2013, Pope Francis referred to the shroud as an "icon of a man scourged and crucified."

I forgot about the shroud until recently, in a thunderstorm, when we were driving through downtown Alamogordo and parked until the obscuring deluge passed. Through the fogged-up window, Paul saw the Shroud Exhibit and Museum that was located on New York Avenue. Intrigued, we ducked in. A friendly woman named Connie Garcia welcomed us, and when she heard I had seen the actual shroud and had questions, she called Deacon Pete Schumacher, the founder of the museum. Despite the downpour, he hurried over to meet us. Schumacher arrived and put down his rain drenched umbrella. An unassuming, balding man in rimless glasses, with a prominent cross suspended from his neck and a phone holster on his belt, greeted us warmly. From that moment on, we were in a world of science, faith, mystery, information, and interactivity.

Schumacher first got involved with the shroud story in 1972, when he was at a low point in his life. An electrical engineer, he worked on image processing and remote sensing when those fields were in their infancy. He was also an amateur radio operator and knew about wavelengths. He developed a 3D machine (on display at the museum) and a way to make a 3D image of the shroud from an exact, full size replica photo (the photo is the central attraction in the museum). He established connections with the folks who were doing scientific evaluation of the famous linen image. Some of the experts were from New Mexico, and, according to Schumacher, "They were part of the world's largest expedition launched to study a single artifact."

Schumacher frequently gives talks about the shroud, and he shared with us his information about why the 1988 study that threw shade on the authenticity was done incorrectly and unscientifically with insufficient samples and no blind study. He told us the fascinating history of the linen and all of the theories—from chemicals to radioactivity to paint to bursts of energy that structurally altered the linen—of how the negative image was produced. None was a satisfactory explanation or would hold up to scientific inquiry.

He showed us miniatures, photos, documentation, and interactive exhibits in the one-room museum, and then he prompted us to use our mobile phone cameras and invert the image on the shroud, turning a positive into a negative and somewhat magically revealing a 3D image on our phones.

Garcia excitedly told us that many people come to the museum from all over the world, and some ask for prayers for healing and well-being. In fact, there is a notebook where anyone can request such prayers. It is at this point that faith and science converge.

If I had dismissed the possibility of the shroud being authentic, I would never have had the experience of the museum. By saying "maybe," I was led into a world that is fascinating, informative, and a bit of a brain twister.

When the thunderstorm finally subsided, and as we were leaving, Garcia said she or Schumacher would be happy to show curious visitors around.

I guess that's why we always say yes, or maybe—invariably, doors of possibility fly open.

It certainly happened on the Mescalero Apache Reservation.

For more information: www.shroudnm.com, and if the museum is closed, you can call Garcia directly and arrange for a visit: 575-805-6405.

St. Joseph's Apache Mission Church, Mescalero.

Geronimo, Jesus as a Medicine Man, an Homage to Apache Warriors, and a Magoosh Who Took Care of Women

Takeaway: Focusing on the details will lead you to the bigger picture.

One morning, I asked Paul if he wanted to visit the Mescalero Apache reservation about thirty minutes from Ruidoso. I didn't have to ask, as he always says yes to travel and adventure, and off we went. I had heard about St. Joseph Apache Mission Church, which is dramatically located on a hill inside the reservation. It was constructed on the floor of a prehistoric Jornada-Mogollon culture ruin and is on the National Register of Historic Places.

After we climbed the stone staircase and entered the church, I was agog, and walked around slowly, noticing one surprising detail after another. We have been in many Mission churches and sometimes there's a nod to the Native Americans who built them by including some Indian art or, during a guided tour, mentioning that the Indigenous builders had incorporated small details of their culture in the construction. But the St. Joseph Apache Mission Church was very different: the Native story was woven into the very fabric of the church.

After World War I, a priest name Father Albert Braun wanted to honor the bravery of the Apache warriors on the battlefields of Europe where he'd served as a chaplain. With a dream and $100 of Army pay in his pocket, he recruited volunteers to work with him in constructing a church that is an homage to both the Apache warriors and their rich, deep culture and spirituality.

The most startling element in the church is a huge image behind the main altar: it's an Apache Christ. He wears the regalia of a traditional Apache medicine man—a warrior shirt, breech cloth and moccasins. He carries a deer rattle, and a medicine bundle of sacred items spreads out from an Apache basket at his feet.

Around the periphery of the sanctuary, each stained glass-window has an Apache element—Mary, for example, is depicted as holding a baby Jesus in a

Jesus depicted as a traditional Mescalero Apache medicine man.

Mary with the baby Jesus in a cradleboard.

cradle board, and St. Cecilia has a flute and drums. Along the rear wall, above the door, are portraits of four Apache heroes who defended the Apache from the Mexicans, Spaniards, and the US government: Geronimo, Cochise, Mangas Coloradas, and Victorio. An image of a tipi and feathers adorns the wooden cover of the baptismal font. Kateri Tekakwitha, the seventeenth-century Native American saint and patron of ecology, the environment, exiles, and Indians, is venerated at her own altar. She took a vow of chastity and married Jesus. She was sickly, died at the age of twenty-four, lost her family in a smallpox epidemic, and reputedly practiced self-mortification by fasting and sleeping on a mat with thorns. She lived a life of devotion, abnegation, and worship.

Because we are interested in voluminous church architecture, Native American culture, Apaches, and devotional art, we loved the church. I should also mention that Father Al is buried on the altar, and Brother Salesius, a Franciscan friar who assisted him in building the church and died when he was crushed by stone in the process, is buried right outside the entrance.

I longed to find a local expert to learn more about the singular house of prayer. I was directed to knock on the priest's office door and ask if I could speak to him. Father Dave Mercer opened the door and said he was in the middle of teaching a Bible class. I quickly asked if we could visit the church with an Apache expert, and he gave me his phone number and said we should come back in three hours. We complied and when we returned, his office door was locked, he wasn't in the church, and my phone calls went unanswered.

A little disheartened, we were driving back to Ruidoso when my cell phone rang, and it was Mercer, very chatty and friendly. He explained that he had been ministering to a young man and would be happy to give us a tour of the church the next day. I wondered whether he would be accompanied by a member of the Mescalero tribe, but I didn't ask, and he didn't offer the information. An hour later I received his text informing me that Donna, one of his Mescalero Apache teachers, would call me that afternoon. As promised, she did, and we arranged to meet the following day at 10 a.m.

I can't tell you how it happened, but Father Dave, Donna, Paul and I were standing in front of a painting of the sacred Gan dancers who were dancing at night in a shaft of white light. I asked if the light came from the moon, and Donna replied, "The white is the reflection from the deity down on the Ga hé [Gan in English] dancers. He protects them and gives them their strength. They are the healers." I smiled at her, and she smiled at me and that was the beginning of our friendship. We became inseparable. Over enchiladas at a nearby Mexican eatery called Old Road Restaurant, located on one of the only non-tribally owned parcels of land on the reservation, Donna told me that her father was Jewish, and I laughed out loud and said my grandmother thought *everyone* was Jewish.

We learned more about Donna during the afternoon. Her current job is grant administrator for the tribe, but she is also an anthropologist, a cultural expert, a designer, and her résumé is about as long as Rapunzel's hair. She spent most of her youth in Tucson after living in Gallup and San Francisco, her first language was Apache, and she has big vision. She is a traditional Apache with nontraditional ideas about how to generate success, growth, and income for the tribe.

She took us into the tribe's museum to meet Joey Padilla, the director, and I spent about an hour looking through a notebook with his art that is designed to teach traditions and ceremonies to young tribal members. His images derive from his dreams. Joey is also a medicine man. Paul and I bought two of his drawings of traditional dancers—one was done with black pen and ink, and the other with a combination of colored pens and watercolors.

In the small but fascinating museum of Apache outfits, artifacts, photographs, and information about the Mescalero, Chiricahua, and Lipan Apaches who live on the reservation, I was struck by a 1930s photo on the wall of a man surrounded by women. Joey said he was a Magoosh who took it upon himself to take care of Apache women who were on their own because of widowhood, divorce, or other unfortunate circumstances.

And then I had a Marcel Proust madeleine moment. In an early scene in Proust's brilliant and famous twentieth century, seven-volume novel *A La Recherche du Temps Perdu*, the French author bites into a little madeleine cake and is transported back to a buried memory of eating crumbs of madeleine as a child. Today a madeleine moment refers to a taste, sight, or smell that takes someone back to a forgotten memory.

About twenty-eight years ago Paul and I went to Carlsbad to experience the first public cooking in the earth and eating of the mezcal cactus that had happened for the Mescalero community in many years. The Spanish called the tribe "Mescaleros" because they traditionally used the cactus-like mescal plant for food, drink, and fiber. When the slow-roasted mezcal came out of the ground in Carlsbad, a Mescalero man explained to us that they used to eat it all the time and travel with it because it contains so many nutrients. They gave us a sample and I never forgot that it tasted like burnt pineapple. It was sweet but not overly so.

In the museum, Joey said he had a gift for Paul and me. He opened a small bag and said his son had just done a mezcal roasting the night before and the bag contained freshly cooked mezcal. It still tasted like burnt pineapple and I was flooded with memories of our experience almost three decades before.

When we left, Donna told us, "Tomorrow morning, at seven o'clock, I'll meet you at the ceremonial grounds for a Mescalero puberty ceremony. I'll be waiting for you in the bleachers." We were bleary-eyed and still half asleep, but we met Donna, and she introduced us to her thirteen-year-old granddaughter Diandra. "I wanted her to see this coming-of-age ritual because in a few months I'll be making the ceremony for her. It is a very expensive undertaking, and preparations begin when the girl is very small," Donna explained. "There are so many items that must be bought, and people have to be hired, and a dress must be made for the girl and gifts must be given to the Crown Dancers (another name for Gan dancers), the singers, and the medicine man and medicine woman. I must take my granddaughter into the woods where she will cut down a tree to make one of the tipi poles. She must butcher an animal for the feast. She begins the four-day ceremony as a girl and by the end she is a woman. She has learned all these skills an Apache girl needs to survive womanhood. The Apache boys still have ceremonies before they go to war and after they get back. But it's the girls who will become the mothers who will birth the future of the tribe and run the family and household."

We were thrilled when Donna invited us to the four-day ceremony for a girl who reaches puberty. We felt that going to the age-old rites as guests would be a once-in-a-lifetime experience.

All of this began when I noticed the details of the Mission church and followed them into adventure. And what an adventure it turned out to be.

For more information: Mescalero Culture Center and Museum: https://mescaleroapachetribe.com or 575-464-4494

To visit the church: 626 Mission Trail in Mescalero; 575-464-4473. They are currently working on a self-guided tour and app.

A coming-of-age ceremony on the Mescalero Apache land.

A Coming-of-Age Ceremony

The Making of an Apache Woman

Takeaway: Sometimes just bearing witness to a spiritual ritual can have a lasting effect on your own life.

When I was thirteen, I stood on the elevated *bimah* of the synagogue and faced an audience of family, friends, and community.

When Diandra turned thirteen, she stood on a deerskin hide in the Big Tipi while friends, relatives, and tribe members watched from outside.

I was flanked on either side by the rabbi (spiritual leader) and cantor (vocalist who leads the community in song and prayer).

Diandra's medicine woman Cassie sat beside her, and her medicine man Bo Kaydahzinne (a direct descendent of famed warrior and leader Cochise) and three members of the medicine society faced her, singing songs and prayers accompanied by their deer hoof rattles.

My tribe is Jewish, and stretches back to Creation, Adam and Eve. Moses gave the laws and sacred Torah to the Israelites.

Diandra's tribe is Mescalero Apache that originated at the Big Tipi, when all cultures, traditions, and religions of the world were formed. White Painted Woman gave language, beliefs, and practices to the Apache. The first puberty ceremony was done for her.

Although our tribes are different, both are at risk of losing language, tradition, and spiritual connection. Preparing and initiating the young through ceremony is a way to maintain and promote cultural continuity and ensure the tribes' future.

For both Diandra and me, the coming-of-age ceremony was an event where we left girlhood behind and became women.

Paul and I were fascinated by the Apache rites and stayed at the Inn of the Mountain Gods resort in Mescalero, where we walked on lakeside trails, met fishermen, boaters, families, Apache staff, watched zipliners and water fowl, and processed the power of ceremonies we were witnessing over four and a half days.

Our friend Donna, Diandra's grandmother, was the sponsor of the rites, and she said that preparation begins "shortly after a girl is born. We have to save up because it is very expensive—it can cost up to $20,000. The biggest expense is food because we feed three meals a day to hundreds of people. We have to provide tipis, cooking pots, grills, tables, tarps, tools, plates, plastic utensils, aprons, kitchen towels, and gifts for the medicine people, cooks, and dancers. We hired three groups of Crown Dancers. Women are the backbone of the Apache people, and how we do the ceremony will determine the way Diandra will be for the rest of her life. If the feast givers aren't generous with food and gifts, the girl will be stingy. If she doesn't help with food preparation, she'll always expect others to take care of her. If she isn't taught to dance hard for long hours in the Big Tipi, she'll be lazy. A girl's feast is her public dedication to Apache ways."

Every aspect of the rituals Diandra had to learn—including collecting and cooking food; butchering a cow; cutting a tree for a tipi pole; ceremonial running—is accompanied by prayers. It is a profoundly sacred ritual.

We attended two sunrise rites at 6 a.m., in a clearing in the woods where all events took place. At the cooking arbor, as sunlight streamed in, women were patting and shaping dough, tossing it into huge bubbling vats on an open fire, and removing it as golden fry bread. Outside, trimmed tree trunks were arranged in a huge circle, and a group of men raised them while Diandra's uncle rapidly ran a rope around them, binding them at the top to become the poles for the Big Tipi. Women who'd had their own puberty ceremonies blessed the first four poles by holding them while the tipi was constructed. The men placed tree branches horizontally across the vertical poles, binding them with green yucca leaves to form the sides of the Big Tipi. Finally, two men climbed the tipi poles—without a ladder—to cover the upper layer with white canvas.

Diandra (and her younger cousin Saige, who was also being initiated) appeared in her magnificent white buckskin dress. It was adorned with fringes, metal jingles, and shaped from about ten deer hides. It was accompanied by traditional beaded jewelry and a reed straw through which she had to sip liquid as she was not allowed to directly touch water. Her regalia weighed about thirty-five pounds. Coached by their respective medicine women, the girls stood on a special white hide, and were then placed face-down and massaged before their first run. An Apache woven basket was placed on the earth at a distance from them, and, wearing their heavy dresses, they had to run as fast as they could to the basket and back. Then young tribe members stood at the back of a truck for a "throw"—they tossed out gifts like candy and toys to the guests, who reached up to catch them.

Breakfast food on the first morning was laid out in plates set on the earth, in ceremonial order, starting from east to west. First, some traditional foods were served—like mescal, mesquite beans, and sumac berries—and then others like fry bread, liver, shredded beef, organ meats, posole (corn stew), beans, potato salad, and fresh melon. After eating, we entered a small tipi where the girls were housed, and they showed us how to bless them, and then they blessed us in return with yellow cattail pollen.

That night, and every subsequent night during the ceremonial period, the girls sat towards the back of the Big Tipi, next to their medicine women, with their legs stretched out straight in front of them. Cassie coached Diandra about sexuality, health, being a wife and mother, and led her through the events. The two medicine women told the girls when to stand and begin their ritual dance, moving side to side, over and over, with their arms bent at the elbow and extended upward. Every night, the girls danced longer, until they danced all night on the final day. In front of the girls in the Big Tipi was a fire pit, and on the other side of the fire the medicine men shook their rattles and sang them verses about trees, mountains, animals, and birds.

In the center of the ceremonial area, men carried logs to make a huge bonfire, and the Crown Dancers (also called Gan dancers or Mountain Gods) executed their sacred and mysterious dance, making the shuddering sound of "hoooo, hooooo." A chorus of drumming singers set the pounding rhythm. The women, wearing colorful shawls, danced around the Gan in a circle. The repetitive sounds and movements were mesmerizing, and we sat for three, four, or five hours watching the dancers, the sparks rising from the fire, the sliver of moon in the black sky, and the circling women. I longed to dance with them, to be so close to the Gan, but I didn't dare.

The last night, I sat beside twenty-year-old Miss Mescalero (Hailey Bigmouth) who said it was okay for me to participate. I wrapped a shawl around me and joined the other women in what looked like a simple two-step. Donna, her mother, and Bigmouth's mother corrected me on how to wear the shawl and

The ceremony continues at night.

execute the steps. As I danced, I felt that the Gan really were spirits. Their prayers, meditations, intense inner focus, years of preparation, and hours-long trance-like state elevated them above the mundane human condition.

At sunrise the last morning, and after dancing in the Big Tipi all night, the girls' faces were ceremonially painted white by medicine man Bo, and they became White Painted Lady, the goddess. I joined a long line of guests as we waited to be individually blessed by Bo. Using a mixture of clay, red earth, and cattail pollen, he painted circular marks on my cheek, palms, and shoes. I felt exalted, lighter, and at peace.

Then the girls did their last run; they ran as fast and long as they could while the tribe cheered them on and encouraged them to go farther and faster. Diandra headed out into the countryside and returned after about fifteen minutes; her cousin Saige was gone for almost an hour. They later told me that the former was a sprinter at her school, and the latter a long-distance runner.

Diandra has a reflective moment.

The run was the final test of endurance and strength that would serve the girls at difficult times in their future lives as women. "Our ceremony started at the time of the Flood," Bo told me, "when Creator taught us how to survive. With what we have done to the earth, and even if we go back to the Stone Age, the girls will know how to survive."

Bo's last act was to give the girls their Indian names.

By the time we left, I felt that what we had experienced was a role model for what we should do for young people. Inviting guests and having a party for them is not enough, nor is it the point. We must guide them, teach them, empower, and celebrate them, and we need to do it through ritual and ceremony.

About two weeks later, I asked Diandra how she felt about her ceremony. "It was hard, but I kept pushing because I wanted to become a woman in my culture," she replied.

For more information: You can attend parts or the whole puberty ceremony which take place almost every week in summertime. Inquire at the Mescalero Culture Center and Museum about when and where the rituals are taking place. See contact information in the previous story.

Meet the People

We've found it to be axiomatic in our travels that locals enjoy meeting travelers, especially if the latter express interest in the former. Here's what happened when we asked folks questions about themselves, their expertise, where they live, recommendations, and random things we were curious about.

We pulled over to the side of a country road when we saw a big, beautiful, black-haired beast and asked a few Central-Casting-looking cowboys who were leaning against a pickup truck and sipping brews, to please tell us about him. Matthew Connell, one of the cowboys and the owner of the ranch, replied.

"That's our yak. His owner got tired of feeding him, so we took him at the ranch. We just call him 'Yak.' I've never paid attention to it, but I think it's male. We just love him. He's part of us."

We inquired of a volunteer at the gift shop in Smokey Bear Historical Park if kids still know who Smokey is.

"I guess it depends on where they live. Adults come here too. They remember him from their childhoods. And lots of them buy stuffed Smokeys. He reminds them they can do something to prevent devastating wildfires."

We spoke with Meredith, a fellow participant in the Billy the Kid tour who was dressed in a cowboy hat and a fringed leather vest, and asked her "What attracts you to Billy?"

"I'm not a fangirl—no way—but I have a fatal attraction to bad boys like Billy. I'll be in Lincoln the first weekend in August for the annual pageant and reenactment of his escape. It's the quintessential story of the Old West, and it's true."

We were talking with a tall, lanky fisherman at Alto Lake who wasn't getting any bites. Somehow the subject of The Kid came up.

"Pat Garret was the famous lawman who killed The Kid, but maybe his daughter Elizabeth was more interesting than he was. I learned about her a while back from a road sign. She was born near here and wrote the official New Mexico state song. She was blind and she rode horses and taught music. I read that sign to my son. He lost his mother, and her name was Elizabeth too."

Laura Jeffcoat, an off-duty forest ranger, was walking her dogs near a trailhead in the mountain town of Cloudcroft. One of her pooches leapt at me, and she pulled him back and chided him.

"I tell my dogs not to jump on people. I raise my dogs like I raise my kids . . . and they damn well better be respectful."

We were very curious to know more about the St. Joseph Apache Mission Church on the Mescalero Apache reservation, and asked Father Dave Mercer about his predecessor who founded the Mission.

"Father Al, who built the Mission, defended the Apache against those who thought they were pagan. In the cornerstone of the Mission, they included some traditional Apache items. They are physically part of the church."

Tori Marden, the young, exuberant assistant manager at the Mescalero Tribal Fish Hatchery, told us something important about the fish and her reaction to them.

"The fish are so sensitive. They can die from overstress. They get sick easily. After the hard work of rearing them, I can't eat trout anymore."

We overheard a Ruidoso resident talking to visiting friends at Valley of Fire Recreation Area.

"Everywhere you look there are fields of black lava. And over there you can see White Sands and the Trinity Site where they detonated the first atomic bomb. It makes me think that destruction comes from nature and from human nature."

Mike Bilbo, a volunteer at Fort Stanton, was costumed in nineteenth-century military garb, and he answered our queries about the uniform.

"I'm wearing Civil War glasses. I bought them and they are almost the correct prescription for me. And this is a sack jacket, used in 1870 in the Franco-Prussian War. They went from the French cut to the Prussian cut, but they couldn't lift their arms in the latter."

Britany Porter, the affable curator at Fort Stanton, was greeting visitors and told us this about the site:

"We honor our collective identity here and who we truly are. When it was a tuberculosis hospital here, the treatment was 4,000 calories a day, sunshine, and fresh air. New Mexico was a territory. One of the reasons it took so long to become a state is because it was considered to be 'too Mexican' and too dangerous. They didn't like the lawlessness. With the TB hospital, a lot of white people came here and by 1912 there were enough white people to become a state. So, without the TB hospital, we might not have become a state, or it would have taken much longer."

Joey Padilla, an artist, medicine man, and director of the museum on the Mescalero Apache Reservation, shared with us what his job really entails.

"I take care of 6,000 Indians—in prayer, in healing, in the things I have to do for them, teaching them traditions. It just takes a handful of people to keep our culture alive. This is the last job I'm ever going to have."

We were talking Donna, who is a cultural expert of the Mescalero Apache reservation, about what all of us see as our purpose in life.

"Teaching my grandkids so future generations will know the culture and traditions that were taught to me by my mother and grandmother . . . that is my purpose. Apache are matrilineal and matrilocal."

How to Tell a Story

What We Can Learn from the Movies

A great way to tell a story is by using a sequence of images, like filmmakers do in a storyboard. Just as with every other art, photography is at its best when telling a story. If one image moves people, a series can do more. It's how movies and video work, as they're actually just sequences of still images. And you can use the same techniques as traditional cinema to tell your story.

Let's start with this example: the story of a traditional celebration of womanhood when a young Mescalero Apache girl comes of age. Here are the basic elements you're dealing with: the event (celebration), the participant (the girl), and the spectators (family and friends). Of course, each has facets and how you approach, record, select, and order your images determines what story you are telling, how you feel about it, and what you'd like others to feel.

I'll use standard motion picture terminology and then define it with a particular illustration.

Establishing Shot

Here we are outside, in the forest, at the ceremonial site—the setting for the story.

A long shot establishes both setting and participants.

Medium Shot

Your "star" in this case is Diandra, the young girl.

You have a choice of how many photos you want or need. These should be candid, not stiffly posed, in order to convey the greatest amount of emotion and action.

(Reminder: Never photograph children without previous parental consent. And, if you intend to publish the children's images anywhere—including on social media—get permission. In this case, I asked Diandra's grandmother Donna, who sponsored the ceremony, as well as Diandra herself.)

Moving in for a medium view directs the viewer's attention to the main action or person being featured.

Close-Up

Use the close-up to capture a significant moment, like joy, intense concentration, or pride as expressed on Diandra's face, or perhaps hers alongside the face of someone with her. Your focus will be on the details of the proceedings: intricate beading on the dress, flames and sparks of the fire, a dish of traditional food, etc.

At a traditional or religious ceremony, ask in advance if there is anything you should *not* photograph. In this case, no photography was allowed inside the Big Tipi during the ritual. In general, when photographing people that you don't know, always ask permission. I've found that most are happy to be the center of attention. In fact, we've made friends this way.

A close-up image delivers an emotional climax and completes the story.

The cinematic technique described above can be applied to almost any setting. In nature, your first image could be a scenic landscape, like mountains, desert, or the beach. Then you introduce your who: family or friends camping or playing in the water. The emotionally concluding close-up could be as simple as a smiling face or as surprising as a deer who just wandered in to your photo.

Have fun, experiment, and, if shooting video, you can have at your disposal the full range of post-production tools to play with (titles, dissolves, and music). You might surprise yourself.

Conclusion

Dear Amigos,

We've come to the end of this part of our journey together. I hope your eyes grow wide as I tell you that these experiences are pieces in the diverse jigsaw puzzle of New Mexico's culture, history, wildlife, hiking adventures, comestibles, art, music, mysticism, beauty, paleontology, ecology, and cultural encounters. You now have the skills to explore everything I've described, and you know how to make each experience special and unique to you. Hopefully, I've encouraged you to let curiosity be your guide, and your choices be made by an imagination overflowing with ideas, possibilities, and wonder. And whether you travel or not, you can start saying "yes" to opportunities, ask questions, be observant, expand your areas of interest, try new things, give up expectations, connect to others, and be truly open and present no matter what you are doing any time and any place in the world.

As I said in a previous book, "Life is a Trip." I still believe that.

New Mexico is called "the Land of Enchantment" and I wish for you all the enchantment I have found here.

May your days be filled with adventures that call to you and your nights be enriched by sweet dreams of all you have heard, seen, and learned.

Hasta pronto,
Judie

Acknowledgments

Thanks go out to everyone who helped us on our journey:

Northwest

Archie Baca, Jr.
Rose Eason
Raina, Meredith, Sunnye, and Silver Marianito
Jerry Brown
Zuni Visitors Center
Kenny Bowekaty
Jimmy Yawakia
Shelley Morningsong
Fabian Fontenelle
Brittany McDonald
Jennifer Lazarz
Elena Barry

Central and North Central

Prajedes Morales
Darlene McElroy
Linda and Gary Storm
Chris Harrell
Harriet Levine
Barbara King
Julie Bastine
James Jereb
Emily Trujillo
Carlyn Stewart
Karen Butts
Isabelle Sandoval
Orlie Martinez

Northeast

Ray Renfroe
David Powell
Anna Weyers
Mary Feitz
Benito C' de Baca
Louise Moreno
Claudia Floyd
The staff at Vermejo—Ted Turner Reserves

Southeast

Mike Cheney
Stacy Tatum
Tim Roberts
Connie Garcia
Deacon Pete Schumacher
Donna Stern
Diandra Stern
Father Dave Mercer
Kelly Johnson
Inn of the Mountain Gods

Southwest

Kristen Worthington
Bill Acosta
Don Parra
Felipe Chavez
Nellie Morales
Alex Mares
David Patterson
Alexandra McKinney
Nolan Winkler
Garland Bills
Dan Trujillo
Kathi Barit

A special shout-out to the following chefs and restaurants for their generosity:

Jerry's Café (Gallup)
Raina Marianito (Gallup)
Shelley Morningsong and Fabian Fontenelle (Zuni)
Doctor Field Good (Santa Fe)
Jambo Café (Santa Fe)
Arable Restaurant (Santa Fe)
Martín Rios; Restaurant Martín (Santa Fe)
Fernando Olea; Sazón Restaurant (Santa Fe)
Tesuque Villa Market (Santa Fe)
The Ranch House (Santa Fe)
Capitol Grill (Santa Fe)
Adolfo's Food Truck (Las Vegas)
Kristen Worthington (Mesilla Park)
Donna Stern (Mescalero Apache Reservation)
Father Dave Mercer (Mescalero Apache Reservation)
House of Flame (Ruidoso)

Thanks to Nicole Barker and Ellen Barone for paving the way with introductions, to Louise Rubin, our first reader, to Ashley Biggers for the much-appreciated initial connection, to Bridget Manzella for copyediting handholding, and to anyone whose names we have inadvertently forgotten.

Thank you, Stephen Hull, who always has the last word, for being our Wizard of Oz. Your belief in the book and in us is deeply appreciated.

About the Authors

Travel journalist **Judith Fein** lives to leave. She blogs for *Psychology Today* about transformative travel and has contributed travel content to 130 publications, given a TEDx talk about deep travel, and is the author of three award-winning travel-related books including the travel classic *Life Is A Trip: The Transformative Magic of Travel*. Judith ran and wrote plays for a theatre company in Europe for nine years, was a Hollywood screenwriter for thirteen years, and is an award-winning playwright. She is also an opera librettist. She is an inspirational and acclaimed keynote speaker, storyteller, and workshop leader, and she delights in awakening the creativity of readers and audiences and loves to disrupt conventional ways of thinking. To Judith, travel is life and life is travel, and slow travel is the way to add fun, adventure, meaningful experiences, and perpetual learning to your life.

Photojournalist **Paul J. Ross** has won awards for his travel writing and photography and has contributed to more than ninety publications. He is a two-time winner of the prestigious Travel Classics awards for travel journalists. He has taught travel photography to travel journalists and industry professionals, where he emphasizes the photographer's eye and imagination rather than equipment. He is lauded for his use of natural lighting and incorporating humor and fun into his work. Paul has done voiceovers for major studios in Hollywood, and he currently writes and performs surprising and humorous cowboy poetry. He does all the photography for Judith Fein's books and articles and is writing a murder mystery.

Southwest Adventure Series

Ashley M. Biggers, *Series Editor*

The Southwest Adventure Series provides practical how-to guidebooks for readers seeking authentic outdoor and cultural excursions that highlight the unique landscapes of the American Southwest. Books in the series feature the best ecotourism adventures, world-class outdoor-recreation sites, back-road points of interest, and culturally significant archeological sites, as well as lead readers to the best sustainable accommodations and farm-to-table restaurants in Arizona, Colorado, Nevada, New Mexico, Utah, and Southern California.

Also available in the Southwest Adventure Series:

Arizona Family Outdoor Adventure: An All-Ages Guide to Hiking, Camping, and Getting Outside by Chels Knorr

Colorado Family Outdoor Adventure: An All-Ages Guide to Hiking, Camping, and Getting Outside by Heather Mundt

New Mexico Family Outdoor Adventure: An All-Ages Guide to Hiking, Camping, and Getting Outside by Christina M. Selby

South Mountain Park and Preserve: A Guide to the Trails, Plants, and Animals in Phoenix's Most Popular City Park by Andrew Lenartz

New Mexico Food Trails: A Road Tripper's Guide to Hot Chile, Cold Brews, and Classic Dishes from the Land of Enchantment by Carolyn Graham

Arizona's Scenic Roads and Hikes: Unforgettable Journeys in the Grand Canyon State by Roger Naylor

Arizona State Parks: A Guide to Amazing Places in the Grand Canyon State by Roger Naylor

Eco-Travel New Mexico: 86 Natural Destinations, Green Hotels, and Sustainable Adventures by Ashley M. Biggers

Skiing New Mexico: A Guide to Snow Sports in the Land of Enchantment by Daniel Gibson